R. Buckminster Fuller

Ideas and Integrities

A Spontaneous Autobiographical Disclosure

R. Buckminster Fuller

Ideas and Integrities

A Spontaneous Autobiographical Disclosure

Series Editor Jaime Snyder

LARS MÜLLER PUBLISHERS

With full faith in love, in the convergence of whose universal light of truth, the assurance of individualism may cast no shadow, either of doubt or egotism, is this stated to be the working sketch for the greatest of living dramatic compositions. The cast for it shall be the whole of humanity; the settings—the future ages of temporality.

R. BUCKMINSTER FULLER

May 21, 1928

Contents

Introduction

We now have aboard our Spaceship Earth more than ample capability to take care of all humanity for all generations to come and to do so at higher standards of living and individual freedom than any humans have thus far experienced or even dreamed of, while in no way endangering the ecological integrity of our planet.... It is also incontrovertibly demonstrable that it is feasible to accomplish this ... within ten years while concurrently phasing out all further human use of fossil fuels and atomic energy. We can live handsomely on our annual energy income from the sun and the many modes of its impoundment.... It can only be accomplished by a design revolution which produces so much higher technical performance per each unit of resource invested as to take care of all human needs.

R. Buckminster Fuller, *Education Automation* [1977], pp. 172–73.[1]

I think we have a very brief window of opportunity to deal with climate change ... no longer than a decade, at the most.

James Hansen, Director, NASA Goddard Institute for Space Studies; and Adjunct Professor, Earth and Environmental Sciences, Columbia University, in September 2006.

---

1 As Bucky's work often germinated for many years before finding its way into a bound volume, the years given in brackets refer to the year in which the quoted material was originally drafted and/or published rather than the book's publication date; page numbers reference the Lars Müller reprint editions of 2008/10.

In 1961, my grandfather Buckminster Fuller made a presentation to the biennial World Congress of the International Union of Architects (Union Internationale des Architectes, or UIA) in London to call for the launch of a "World Design Science Decade" that would engage architects, architectural schools, and students in a ten-year program to re-design key elements of the world life-support systems, thereby increasing their operating efficiency from 4 to 12 percent, and thus lifting the "high" standard of living enjoyed by 44 percent of humanity to 100 percent using known world resources.[2] His talk sounded a call that reverberated amongst the new generation of students and architects present there, showing up in the architectural journals, interviews, and letters between Bucky and many who would become his associates and partners in the burgeoning movement for a *comprehensive design* revolution.

And it echoed in the subsequent 1963 session of the UIA in Cuba. Bucky was precluded from going to Cuba for the meeting due to Cold War tensions—though he attempted to persuade an acquaintance of his, Undersecretary of State McGeorge Bundy, later National Security Advisor to Presidents Kennedy and Johnson, to allow him to attend by stressing the import of the initiative, it was to no avail. He ultimately presented his further proposal at an international symposium immediately following in Mexico City.

With students and architectural schools inspired around the world, he attempted to coordinate the implementation of a comprehensive game plan from his then recently established headquarters: the World Resources Inventory at Southern Illinois University. Together with young artist and sociologist John McHale, who had just arrived from London to be his point person, they published a series of *World*

---

2 Bucky's calculation of "standard of living" derives from a 1952 analysis he made of world consumption of energy per capita and its relationship to "standard of living" in "developed" and "undeveloped" regions of the world. See R. Buckminster Fuller and John McHale, *World Design Science Decade Document 1* (Carbondale, Ill., 1963), p. 27.

Design Science Decade Documents which included essays and extensive visual mapping of world data, trends, and needs, touching on the "big picture" of every component of the planet's infrastructure.

> Revolution by design and invention is the only revolution tolerable to all men, all societies, and all political systems anywhere. Every nation welcomed the invention of the airplane, and refrigeration. Every nation welcomed and employed the transistor.... All the world, properly informed of the significance of the ... design and invention revolution, will applaud and support the initiative.
>
> *Utopia or Oblivion* [1965], p. 259.

While the impact of these events clearly inspired a new generation of "design revolutionaries," and while the essays from the project showed up in many of Bucky's books of the period, the ten-year project did not spawn the global movement aspired to. Though today we have at our fingertips the kind of computer capability and information technology that we have witnessed facilitate the transformation of powerful ideas into global movements, in 1963 students and architects, spread over the planet, were unable to connect except by traveling to other universities, by preparing work for presentation at periodic meetings, or by correspondence and postal submissions of research. And while Bucky and his team worked diligently to garner state funding for dedicated use of institutional mainframe computers to compile growing bodies of data on global resources, trends, and needs, it was never to materialize.

What makes the "World Design Science Decade" as proposed in 1963 so relevant today is that it may be one of the first "drafts" of a *comprehensive plan* for addressing the "world's problems" and "making the world work for 100% of humanity." With the portfolio of global crises getting bigger each year—nuclear weapons (seemingly ever less secure), systematic environmental destruction, climate change, chronic extreme poverty, failed states, and now this past year the "global financial meltdown"—it becomes starkly evident that what is needed are solutions that are bold, innovative, and, more than anything else, *comprehensive.* They must be comprehensive in addressing both short-term and long-term needs, both immediate symptoms as well as root causes, and, most fundamentally, recognizing the interconnectedness of this web of systemic planetary problems. Solutions that attempt to "solve" certain problems without addressing the others will simply continue to fall short, for they are merely palliatives appearing to move things forward by sweeping messes under the rug that turn out to be someone else's blanket—like sending the waste downstream only to have it foul nearby beaches.

It becomes more and more obvious that we need an immediate and radical re-design of our planet's life-support systems and infrastructure. And yet as powerful as all the networking tools now are, and as broad as the grassroots participation emerging around the planet is, it is clear that the actual implementation of the necessary changes will take many years—a difficult cup of tea to swallow within the quick-fix cultural zeitgeist.

At the same time, the urgency of the matters challenging us is inspiring people, networks, and organizations to action at every level of our society. And there are currently emerging new drafts of *comprehensive plans* for holistically solving the planetary predicament—Lester Brown and the Earth Policy Institute's remarkable *PLAN B 3.0: Mobilizing to Save Civilization* is an outstanding example of one that could not be more comprehensive and do-able with known technology and resources. Another example is Amory Lovins and the Rocky Mountain Institute's *Winning the Oil Endgame: Innovation for Profits, Jobs, and Security.* It is an in-depth, peer-reviewed, Pentagon co-funded, globally-applicable plan for getting the U.S. off of oil within twenty years in a way that revitalizes the very core of the economic engine that is failing. And Rob Hopkins' *The Transition Handbook: From Oil Dependency to Local Resilience* has moved communities, now in the hundreds, around the world to bring comprehensive grassroots self-organized planning to the re-design of local communities. Undoubtedly there are many other fine examples, but, nevertheless, in the proliferation of new solutions to the vexing challenges facing society, comprehensive thinking and design are still all too rare.

How can we nurture this kind of thinking and these kinds of approaches at all levels of our society, on the front lines of our everyday lives? For it is not the comprehensive plans that give rise to comprehensive thinking, it is comprehensive problem-solving approaches that give rise to such brilliant strategies for addressing the urgent global challenges. So, what is the educational curriculum, what is the course of study? What are the fundamental principles that comprise, inform, and give rise to that kind of thinking? Where are the case studies, what are the rigorous practices of such generalized problem solving and where do we go to learn? Generalized because nature can serve up a wicked curveball and the challenges emerging all around us range from local to regional to national to global, from environment, to health, to food, to energy systems. What is the skill set that prepares someone to grapple with the matter of "re-designing" our global system to serve 100 percent of humanity? What are the new paradigms that foster skillful means in this arena?

Bucky saw the answer to this need in the elevation of *design* to a disciplined science founded in awareness of the principles of nature's design. He called this approach "comprehensive anticipatory design science":

"comprehensive" because the critical global challenges are systemic;

"anticipatory" because it is much more efficient to prevent heart disease than to cure it; because it is much more cost effective to use water more efficiently than to dig new wells;

"design" because it is much easier to "reform the environment" by inventing and introducing new solutions, like building a bridge, than it is to reform other human beings' behaviors, such as urging them to swim the rapids;
"science" because we need to apply the best practices for establishing facts, gathering information, and identifying principles through experimentation.

So it was with this in mind that I embarked upon what has become a winter ritual, intensively reading Bucky's books to select and prepare the next installment for re-publication. Mid-winter in full throttle I am in the middle of reading five of his books simultaneously. Almost like a horse race, I move back and forth between the volumes to see which one connects most deeply with me, and the concerns of our day. Buoyed along with the sense of possibility in the emergence of a new U.S. president, by the arrival on front and center stage of the notion of a "green economy," by the broad public consensus to get off the use of fossil fuels, and by the dawning recognition that the problems facing our society are an integrated complex which will only be solved boldly and, with a new word seeming to be in vogue, *comprehensively.*

I keep coming back to Bucky's vision of mobilizing young students—now networked globally, now easily accessing the global database of information provided by the Internet, now able to ultra-coordinate with other such students via laptops or smartphones. I think of the great need, as much as any other, to educate and train this next generation of problem-solvers, who are coming up to speed and already joining the implementation. I keep thinking about the young people, or the young in sprit, who are saying, "I want to be a *sustainer* or a *greener,*" who see a career in creating a green economy, who want to develop in themselves the capacity to *solve* the challenging problems facing humanity. I keep sensing an explosion of people thinking "I want to be an Amory Lovins, I want to be a Lester Brown, I want to be a Bucky Fuller—when I grow up." Where can they go? I think too of the "grown-ups" being required to re-invent their careers and lifestyles, not to mention all the semi-retired individuals with the luxury of being able to re-invest more and more free time to engage in the pressing problems of our times.

It was the need to advance the field of comprehensive anticipatory design science and comprehensive design education in general that brought me to select *Ideas and Integrities: A Spontaneous Autobiographical Disclosure* and *Education Automation: Comprehensive Learning for Emergent Humanity* for this year's publications.

As I re-read *Ideas and Integrities,* I found myself continuing to feel it was perhaps the first textbook of "design science"—providing the curriculum that must proliferate and be offered for undergraduate and graduate level programs in design science. It hit me as an under-the-hood immersion in the mechanics of the "Bucky Fuller-mobile" for those who want to know exactly how it works: the principles, the design strategies, the engineering, and its development.

> The specialist in comprehensive design is an emerging synthesis of artist, inventor, mechanic, objective economist and evolutionary strategist.
>
> *Ideas and Integrities* [1950], pp. 232–33.

Though *Ideas and Integrities: A Spontaneous Autobiographical Disclosure* is chock full of raw, hardcore, mind-stretching context and language, rather than being a technical book it may be one of Bucky's most intimate. The subtitle sets the stage, underscored in his background note for chapter 5, "I Figure," calling the volume a "biography of my thought development." The three opening essays include some of his most elegant and accessible self-reflections: "Influences on My Work," "Later Development of My Work," and "Margaret Fuller's Prophecy," an excerpt of the writing of his great aunt Margaret Fuller who had moved him deeply upon his "discovery" of her in the early years of his re-thinking. The other sixteen essays reveal his own evolution, spanning the period from 1942, as he came into his own as a teacher at design schools during the late forties, and his own great explosion onto the world stage in the fifties and early sixties after the invention of the geodesic domes.

Education Automation picks up where *Ideas and Integrities* leaves off. The opening essay "Education Automation: Freeing the Scholar to Return to His Studies," originally published in 1962, derives from a talk Bucky gave on April 22, 1961 in East St. Louis, to the Edwardsville Campus Planning Committee of Southern Illinois University, which was addressing the design of a new campus. SIU in Carbondale, Illinois, was where, only two years earlier, Bucky had become a professor, and he and my grandmother Anne had taken up residence. In the essay he paints a broad canvas, *anticipating* the future of education in one of the early and truly prophetic descriptions of what, almost three decades later, became the information technology revolution via the "two-way TV"—*we* call it the Internet:

> I would say, then, that you are faced with a future in which education is going to be number one amongst the great world industries, within which will flourish an educational machine technology that will provide tools such as the individually selected and articulated two-way TV and an intercontinentally networked, documentaries call-up system, operative over any home two-way TV set.
>
> *Education Automation* [1962], pp. 72–73.

> Children will be able to call up any kind of information they want about any subject and get the latest authoritative TV documentary.... The answers to their questions and probings will be *the best information* that is available up to that minute in history.
>
> *Education Automation* [1962], p. 68.

And yet much more than his description of the coming technology of education, the book answers the question, "education for what?"—a theme broadly expanded upon in numerous essays by Bucky from 1961 to 1976 and added to "Education Automation" in the 1979 book entitled *Buckminster Fuller On Education,* skillfully complied by Peter H. Wagschal and Robert D. Kahn, and upon which this new edition is based. These further essays explore the great need for a truly *comprehensive orientation* in education which never loses sight of the epochal changes unfolding on our planet and the unique role of the individual in steering those evolutionary changes.

Ideas and Integrities and *Education Automation* powerfully intersect at the epicenter of design revolution with their inclusion of material from the original "World Design Science Decade" talks Bucky gave to the International Union of Architects in 1961. Both books exude the paradigm of comprehensive design education. Both books continue to reference the need for a decade-long planetary design initiative. *Education Automation* had been in the editing process for nearly a month and half just before Bucky's July 1961 trip to London to make his presentation to the UIA meeting. Subsequently, at the key "climax" juncture in the manuscript, the beginning of the final thrust, he weaves in a page of his opening UIA presentation there:

> What I now propose is that all the universities around the world be encouraged to invest the next ten years in a continuing problem of *how to make the total world's resources, which now serve only 43 percent, serve 100 percent of humanity through competent complex design science.*
>
> *Education Automation* [1962], p. 100.

For its part, *Ideas and Integrities,* edited by Robert W. Marks and published in 1963, includes two entire chapters (chapter 14, "The Architect as World Planner" and chapter 15, "World Planning") that derive directly from Bucky's presentation on the "World Design Science Decade" at the original July 1961 presentation, and the subsequent follow-up presentation he prepared for the UIA biennial in 1963. In addition, the opening piece, "Influences on My Work" was initially a 1955 letter to John McHale in reply to questions about the genesis of Bucky's work, published in the July 1961 edition of *Architectural Design* at the time of the London UIA congress.

These two new books, in representing the span of Bucky's career from 1942 to 1976, also importantly reflect the evolution of his work as a teacher and educator. As Allegra Fuller Snyder, my mother and Bucky's daughter, pointed out at a lecture this past spring at the Museum of Contemporary Art in Chicago, "In 1949 Bucky took on his first full visiting teacher assignment at the Institute of Design [in Chicago]. The environment was right. It revealed Bucky as an important teacher because he was challenging himself while challenging his students. They challenged each other."

Much of the material in these two books, as would be the case for much of Bucky's later published work, derive from transcripts of his talks. *Ideas and Integrities* comprises the period from those early days in Chicago when the nature of his teaching was characterized by visiting teaching assignments at design, architecture, and art schools, where small groups of students would work with him for a semester with the central focus of "tackling a design problem"—an "autonomous living package," a "failed" prototype for a new kind of structure he would call later a geodesic dome, or subsequently the countless variants of geodesic dome prototypes, testing every kind of geometry, material, and size. Legends abound of his marathon sessions stretching into double-digit hours. *Education Automation* picks up as his work virtually exploded, with geodesic domes cast around the world propelling him onto the world stage; together with an acceleration of published books and press coverage, the audiences grew more frequent and ever larger.

And so it seemed like some kind of confirmation of the readiness, spunk, and appetite of today's student generation that this past spring I learned that the second annual Buckminster Fuller Challenge, a $100,000 prize to the winner of a juried competition for innovative solutions to critical global problems, was awarded to an interdisciplinary team of international students from MIT. Their "Sustainable Personal Mobility and Mobility-on-Demand Systems" project is a breathtaking strategy for urban mobility systems and only underscores the need to engage the next generation in a new *decade* of design revolution. The Buckminster Fuller Challenge jurors published the following statement about their decision: "The winning project is a perfect example of the kind of radical, transformative change that is possible when we reconceive the old ways of doing things and take a systems-based approach to design.... SPM/MoD isn't just about the design of these lightweight, highly efficient, electric vehicles, it is about inserting that technological innovation into the social and cultural environment and designing an intuitive system within which they function."

In 1973, I took a year-and-a-half leave of absence after my first year at college to journey with Bucky on his very heavy pace of traveling the world. By that point he was delivering a major keynote address almost every three days—usually just a couple of hours—to college and "general" audiences commonly in the thousands. Only rarely did we visit a design school, or stay for more than twenty-four hours in a community.

Bucky called his approach to lecturing "thinking out loud" and he disciplined himself "not to think about what he was going to say in advance." As such, all his life's experiences were his reference, including insights gleaned from his design experiments. And while his idiosyncratic engineering-like language could often sound unfamiliar, his message struck a deep chord with audiences of people generally hearing him for the first time—he always elicited a standing ovation.

Having been so "reoriented" by the experience of journeying around the world with him, observing and participating in the kind of work he was engaged in everywhere he went, after it was over it took me a while to digest what it had all been about. What was that chord that resonated? Clearly it was not just designing new inventions, and certainly most in the audience did not aspire to be design scientists. More than anything, more than his specific inventions or his particular ideas, I concluded it was the universal questions he was asking of himself, and everyone else, such as: What can the little individual do that the great institutions of society cannot?

> I am sure I am but one of several millions who wonder how much the individual can actually affect the evolutionary processes of his day, while starting only upon his self-accrediting of his own initiative, enterprise and effective transformation capabilities.
>
> *Ideas and Integrities* [1958], p. 57.

How can a little individual make an impact?

> So it could also be true that if your experience actually discerned an industrial gap-closing task that needed your particular experienced attention, and no patron of the task could be discovered who was inherently concerned with such tasks, you might then assume you were being directly challenged by natural evolutionary process with doing something about that gap, which challenge and response were no more mystical than the spontaneous dodging from under a falling tree.
>
> *Ideas and Integrities* [1958], p. 86.

What are the principles of being effective as an individual? How do I carry on as an individual? What do I do about earning a living if my priority is addressing the "problems" of the world?

> The minute you were not concerned with earning a living and really tackled problem after problem that the other fellow was not tackling, there proved to be a wealth of solvable problems. In fact the whole mass of problems that are worth tackling is so great that any average individual who goes into that kind of a paradise wilderness garden ought to make very good progress. If I have made progress that is mildly notable it is only because I walked into a vast, unattended, potential harvest.
>
> *Ideas and Integrities* [1958], p. 87.

Before it became impractical to do so, after almost every talk crowds of people would find their way backstage and surround Bucky—to have a moment with him, get a book signed, express an idea, or ask him a question. Undoubtedly the most frequently asked question was, "Well Mr. Fuller, I am this or that and a concerned citizen, and what I want to know is, 'What can *I* do to make the world work?'" And he had *one* answer, "You must ask yourself that question; that is what I had to do—that is what the individual is all about; it is not about following some prescription or formula that I can give out."

So what was Bucky's own answer to the question: What can individuals do that the great political, religious, and economic institutions cannot? What was the conclusion for what he often called his life's "experiment" in the efficacy of "individual initiative"? Perhaps the most concise answer is what he asked that we put on his gravestone: "call me *trimtab.*" What exactly is "trimtab" and why would he want to be called that?

> Something hit me very hard once, thinking about what one little man could do. Think of the *Queen Mary*—the whole ship goes by and then comes the rudder. And there's a tiny thing on the edge of the rudder called a trim-tab. It's a miniature rudder. Just moving that little trim-tab builds a low pressure

> that pulls the rudder around. Takes almost no effort at all. So I said that the little individual can be a trim-tab. Society thinks it's going right by you, that it's left you altogether. But if you're doing dynamic things mentally, the fact is that you can just put your foot out like that and the whole big ship of state is going to go. So I said, "Call me Trimtab."[3]

The beauty of that little trim tab is that it elegantly *demonstrates* the answer to the question: *What can individuals do* to change the world? And it is precisely that Bucky had found a tested and well-utilized invention, derived from the principles of nature, that can bring confidence in its objective confirmation of what is possible for individuals.

But perhaps more importantly, in these times when we are faced with gargantuan problems and unfathomably large forces invested in their persistence, the trim tab gives us a clue as to *how* little individuals can be effective in the face of such odds. Not only does it demonstrate that a little device *can* steer a very large system, it shows us that the absolutely highest leverage spot in steering the system of that ship is perhaps where one would least expect it, at the very trailing edge of the rudder, at the very back (i.e., stern) of the ship.

Trim tabs also remind us that the front lines of the design revolution are not necessarily in Washington, DC, or in any other global capital; regardless of the merits of a given politician, we are being completely imprudent to act as if we can leave "the mess" to them. The trim tabs of "individual initiative" that drive the necessary changes can turn in the day-to-day actions of each and every one of us.

Think of what we are up against in addressing just one component of one major global challenge: coal's impact on climate change. *Plan*

---

3 R. Buckminster Fuller, page 46 of the transcript of an interview with Barry Farrell for *Playboy*, February 1972.

B 3.0 echoes what many have concluded: we *must* rapidly phase out all coal-fired power plants and replace them with renewable energy! Now that's a big ship to turn—over seven thousand coal plants in the world today, and all the jobs they represent. And when one watches how this is playing out in the U.S., where the political and financial forces fight vigorously any action in that direction, or in China, which at present is building one new coal-fired plant every day, it is very easy to get discouraged without the possibility of proliferating trim tabs.

But, if you look a little closer you find, for example, a dramatic trend toward stopping new coal plant construction; with pressure mounting from all sides against them, and new investment ever more reluctant, there are a growing number of states that are banning or restricting new coal-fired plants. And sitting here writing I look on the Internet for current developments and I find that just weeks ago, it was reported that as a result of a decision by the City of Los Angeles:

> The Intermountain Power Agency (IPA) announced Thursday it has given up plans to build an additional coal-fired unit. Its biggest customer–the city of Los Angeles–signaled its intent July 2 to phase out use of all coal-based electricity by 2020. IPA's expansion project had effectively died in its original iteration when the Los Angeles Department of Water and Power pulled out of the deal in 2007, Reuters reported.[4]

Nations change the world, states change nations, cities and counties changes states, communities change cities and counties, and, all the way at the very tail end of the ship, trim tabs change communities!

---

4 Tilde Herrera, "L.A.'s Coal Ban Leads to Another Abandoned Power Plant," *Greenbiz.com*, July 13, 2009, http://www.greenbiz.com/blog/2009/07/13/las-coal-ban-leads-another-abandoned-power-plant (accessed August 20, 2009).

> This young world is about to take over, to help us design ourselves to make man a success on earth.... We must design our way to positive effectiveness, and not just be negative about politicians and what they are doing.
>
> *Ideas and Integrities* [1962], p. 398.

There have been many revolutions in history. The American Revolution famously began with "the shot heard round the world." There was Mahatma Gandhi's profoundly powerful *non-violent revolution* that turned India into a democracy and captured the imagination of the world community. Perhaps the *design revolution* begins with the flutter of *trim tabs flapping*—or maybe it is an altogether silent one, for few in the world would recognize it by that name. Maybe the announcement by Bucky of his "World Design Science Decade" project in 1961 was not the epicenter of an earthquake, but a gust of wind carrying countless airborne seedpods to float off into the landscape on a gentle summer breeze.

> Making the world's totally available resources serve one hundred percent of an exploding population may only be accomplished by a *boldly accelerated design evolution* which adequately increases the present over-all performance per units of invested resources. This is a task of radical technical innovation rather than political rationalization.
>
> *Ideas and Integrities* [1963], p. 339.

When I think of Bucky's advocacy for re-tooling the planet to live off of our "energy income" rather than our "savings account" of fossil fuels and nuclear energy, which, while in his mind from his earliest writings, really blossomed in the sixties; or when I recall the "advanced generation" windmill he prototyped with young aeronautical engineer Hans Meyer on an island off the coast of Maine in the early seventies, it is obvious this "accelerated design evolution"—or revolution—has come a long way.

> That, with sun energy wealth (in one of its many conversion phases) leaking in from a myriad of new sources from which, by any recognized feudal agricultural economic precedent, wealth was not supposed to gush, the astonished discoverer of each latest leak could stand in front of it and fill his back pockets without question of his legal proprietorship to that wealth.
>
> *Ideas and Integrities* [1942], p. 135.

A half-century later we are witnessing alternative energy front and center on the strategic landscape of current world affairs—a re-design of our world before our very eyes, in a cosmic instant. The *New York Times,* citing a study by the United Nations Environment Program, recently reported that "Global investors spent about $250 billion building new power capacity in 2008, and for the first time the lion's share of that money went to renewable sources."[5] Think of it.

> Man now enters the phase of meager yet conscious partici pation in the anticipatory design undertakings of Nature. This conscious participation itself is changing from an awkward, arbitrary, trial and error ignorance to an intuitively conceived, yet rigorously serviced, disciplined elegance.
>
> *Ideas and Integrities* [1960], p. 323.

In 2006 I first heard one of the world's leading climatologists, James Hansen of NASA, on television conveying his assessment that we had only ten years left to turn around the climate crisis—in time to avoid a planetary ecological tipping point of no return. This stark wake-up call could only begin to be digested by reflecting upon Bucky's design science decade proposal—which provided some

5 James Kanter, "Clean Energy Funding Trumps Fossil Fuels," *New York Times,* June 3, 2009, http://greeninc.blogs.nytimes.com/2009/06/03/clean-energy-funding-trumps-fossil-fuels/ (accessed August 20, 2009).

sense of a possibility that there was a way to turn the ship within ten years. Even though Hansen's "clock" is now down to seven, perhaps we have a running start, since a silent design revolution is well underway. Clearly we do not have the time to wait on some leader to officially launch a comprehensive initiative to address the complex of crises facing us, as John F. Kennedy did in 1961 when he set a goal of putting a man on the moon by the end of the decade. Instead, each of us individual trim tabs will have to declare this project "started," one by one. But with time so short, and the crisis so far beyond just climate change, it is essential we are crystal clear on this "project's" mission.

In the eighties and nineties I was engaged in developing and teaching courses on Bucky's problem-solving approaches in corporate settings. In those days and in the corporate environment, I took note of the fact that the latest *rage* was the "new idea" of "mission statements." For years it seemed like everywhere in the world I went, organizations, institutions, and even individuals had or were developing mission statements. "What is the mission statement of humanity?" "Has one been done?" I wondered. Almost instantly it dawned on me that throughout his career Bucky, through countless statements about "making the world work," had been drafting, developing, and refining just such a statement. And somewhere along the way he had arrived at a version that provides the kind of clarity so desperately needed today. In much the haiku-like form we often associate with mission statements, he proposed:

To make the world work
for 100% of humanity
in the shortest possible time
through spontaneous cooperation
without ecological offense
or the disadvantage of anyone.

For New Fuller Readers

For those of you reading Bucky for the first time, I offer a few specific tips for your journey through his universe. You may find, with the pulsation from the *macro* to the *micro,* from the *comprehensive* to the *incisive,* that your mind is stretched and turned in a way that is, at first, disorienting. Think of it instead as a re-orientation—a real orientation that can at first be dizzying. Give yourself a lot of time. His books are thinking tools, catalysts for shape-shifting, for leaping far beyond *the box* of normal habitual thought processes. Perhaps a dose-a-day will be your pace, to thoroughly examine and digest the ideas as they come—paying attention to the changes in your own awareness ... daily, weekly, even monthly. Be encouraged: like learning a new language or a new computer program, I trust the current brain researchers would confirm that reading Bucky is just the kind of endeavor that can help us build brain cells and their interconnections.

Bucky also invents new words, or uses common words in ways that are new, precisely because he is attempting to steer clear of the limiting habits of thinking we all inherited. Starting at the age of 32, he made it a discipline, to think carefully about the words he used, resisting the temptation of saying things the way "everyone says them," dispelling the attempt to make them more palatable. For example, he would frequently point out "we still say the words *sunrise* and *sunset,* even though we have known for hundreds of years that the earth revolves around the sun!" In response, someone wrote him suggesting alternatives, *sunsight* and *sunclipse*—which he quickly adopted.

When reading Bucky I find it useful to apply a strategy I learned in foreign language classes: as you begin to converse in the new language let the words pass through without attempting to grasp every one individually. Stick with the continuity, even if it means that on the first time through you miss a number of details. For if you get the continuity, and are able to stay focused on the big picture and the underlying principles, you will glean a sense of the context, even if all the details are not yet clear. And with this general *sense* of what he is saying, you may discover the inspiration that draws you back a second time, to begin progressively examining the details. Bucky suggested this was in fact a principle of universe: there is a fundamental advantage in any problem solving or critical thinking when one "starts with the whole" (or overview), "and then proceeds to the parts" (or details).

A long-time friend and close associate of Bucky's, Don Moore, a gifted systems analyst and engineer, always used to say, "Bucky is the one person I ever met for whom nothing was ever out of context." And for Bucky the context, the way to see clearly our way through the challenges facing humanity, is always by "starting with the whole universe." For Bucky the answers to the problems of our world are all around us in the beautiful design of the universe. And in the end, more than the facts, figures, particular predictions, or solutions he developed, were the underlying principles of universe to which he was pointing. Thank goodness, nature reveals to us the state of the art in design and technology, if we will look.

Jaime Snyder

California, September 2009

Preface from first edition

This volume represents Buckminster Fuller's most incisive ideas and most intimate personal testaments. Like all of his verbalized thought, it is extensive, totally revealing, technical, and complex. It assumes a committed earnestness on the part of the reader. It assumes that the reader shares his concern for what is basic in society and cosmology, and that in the nature of things microcosm and macrocosm are inseparable.

The chapters vary in vocabulary and style. Some are papers that Bucky has worked and reworked to compress a maximum of content in a minimum of space. The latter reflect positive feedbacks, in which initial thoughts have acquired cumulative growths. Bucky is the one man in this age who, with no deviation, has met Matthew Arnold's sober challenge: to see the world whole and keep the vision constant.

The reader is urged to follow closely the implications of each line in this book; to reread, if necessary, and discern the subtle intent of lines that seem difficult. In Bucky's writing there is no waste, no phrase empty of content, no allusion not made to sharpen the edge of an idea. And there is no one today who has more trenchant things to say.

ROBERT W. MARKS

1 Influences on My Work

Many people have asked if the Bauhaus ideas and techniques have had any formative influence on my work. I must answer vigorously that they have not. Such a blunt negative leaves a large vacuum and I would like to eliminate that vacuum by filling in with a positive statement of my initial teleologic preoccupations and their resultant proclivities.

By "teleologic" I mean: the subjective-to-objective, intermittent, only-spontaneous, borderline-conscious, and within-self communicating system that distills equatable principles—characterizing relative behavior patterns—from our pluralities of matching experiences; and reintegrates selections from those net generalized principles into unique experimental control patterns—physically detached from self—as instruments, tools, or other devices admitting to increased technical advantage of man over environmental circumstance, and consciously designed to permit his modification of forward experiences in preferred ways.

My teleologic stimulation first grew out of boyhood experiences on a small island eleven miles off the mainland, in Penobscot Bay of the state of Maine. There, floatable at will, in and out of nature's tidal dry docks, with a fifteen-foot flood rise twice a day,

---

January 1955. The original is a letter from Fuller to John McHale in reply to questions about the influence of the Bauhaus on Fuller's work. First published in *Architectural Design*, July 1961. Editor John McHale. The diligent research work into the background of most of the essays which comprise this work (chs. 1–6, 10–12, 15, and 18–19) was carried out by James Meller, a dear, long-time friend and associate of Bucky's, in preparation for his influential 1970 anthology, *The Buckminster Fuller Reader* (London, 1970).

boat-building was the parent technology, and the devices for its original design and fabrication, together with its subsequent sparring, rigging, beaching-out, wintering, cradling, rebuilding, launching, and upkeep in general were so broadly effective as to govern spontaneously almost any technical tasks to be effected on the land, whether this was building of dwellings, barns, well houses, or water-course controls (for water conservation on the island was as essential to survival as was our ability to pass successfully over the waters around the island, away to other islands, or to the mainland). Fishing was the primary local industry, and such tension systems as seines, trawls, weirs, scallop drags, lobster pot heads, and traps, together with all their respective drag and buoy gear, insured an ever-present abundance of stout cordage and light lines as well as experience in net-weaving, tying, splicing and serving. Here men "passed a line" and "took a turn" in deft tension techniques as spontaneous as those of spiders.

This boyhood experience on an island-farm included those first turn-of-the-century days of individual, or family, small tonnage water transportation almost exclusively by sail or rowboat, leading to the experimental inclusion of the newly-invented internal combustion engines. We had in our sloop one of the earliest auxiliary gasoline engines within many miles, and this induced a whole line of inventiveness, along with gallons of sweat, relevant to priming the engine, testing the spark, and rolling over a flywheel. But the rowboat had to serve its complementary tasks, and as I had to row each day on a four-mile round trip to another island for the mail, my first teleologic design invention was a mechanical "jelly fish," or teepee-like, folding, web-and-sprit cone which was mounted like an inside-out umbrella on the submerged end of a pole. This pole could be hand-pulled through a ring over the stern, drawing the self-folding cone on the pole's water end through the water with little resistance. When pushed by the pole, the cone opened and gave inertial advantage, almost as though touching bottom, to push-pole the boat along far more swiftly and easily than by sculling or rowing.

These trips were frequently rowed in the fog and across strong tidal currents which involved complete dependence upon calculations and compass. The push-pole made it possible to see ahead, having been frustrated in back-towards-bow rowing.

Our island had a rich resource of beach-dried driftwood and standing timber, the use of which required permission of no one. With a pocket knife and a few other tools I designed and produced many crude, scale and full-size, experimental designs in planing boats, valvable houses, and rolling or soaring transport devices at Bear Island between 1904 and 1914. There were also a number of invented and produced furniture items. These also included a set of vertical Victrola record roll-in-and-pop-out storage cabinets which have been in use now for a half century. The first Victrola records of 1904 and 1905 stored in these cabinets are still in fairly good condition, due to their standing on edge rather than on face. These record storage units were tensionally partitioned, which made for great space economy. They were the prototype for the crop of welded wire devices which appeared on the market a quarter of a century later.

My next series of important design-influence experiences came at Milton Academy in Milton, Massachusetts. Here I received a good private school's theoretical education, coupled with enthusiastically broad experience in the historically differentiated family of controlled physical principles known as "athletics." Athletics greatly heightened what I call the "intuitive dynamic sense," a *fundamental,* I am convinced, of competent anticipatory design formulations. This organized primary education brought me into Harvard with good marks in all but Latin. My first serious objective adolescent experience grew out of being fired from Harvard, officially for cutting my classes, but in fact for general irresponsibility.

Fortunately, I landed in Canada as an apprentice to a group of English (Lancashire) and German cotton mill machine fitters. Here I learned to assemble and erect cotton mill machinery.

I finally mastered on my own the assemblage and installation of each and every type of cotton manufacturing machine. The installation included running of the pulley-shafting throughout the buildings and its over-all alignment from the power house takeoff through to each belted-in and aligned production machine. I stayed on to help put the mill into operation.

Starting with a bare new building in a new land and taking part in its mechanical installations and subsequent running I gained, at first hand, a dawning awareness of a major economic pattern factor—that of effective "addition of value (or wealth) by manufacture," effected between raw and finished goods, and gained by the rich synergetic admixture of *technology and energy*. Both the latter, I could see, were fundamental assets that defied exhaustion in *apparent universe*. Technology was a basic resource that improved, or self-multiplied, with each repeated opportunity of its application. I could see from all this fundamental wealth augmentation—without resource depletion—that there was arising an important reorientation of mankind, from the role of an inherent "failure," as erroneously reasoned by Malthus, and erroneously accepted by the bootstrap-anchored custodians of civilization's processes, to a new role for mankind, that of an inherent success.

But I could also see that this magnificent reorientation was occurring only through knowledgeful, and experience-rich competence in teleologic designs, integrating transcendentally man's conscious planning, but by virtue of physical laws, as an organic workable complex—*industrialization.*

Machines of the cotton mill in my 1913–1914 experience were as yet primarily *imported* by the Americas. The importations were mostly from England (Dobson and Barlow) but they were also brought in from France (Combers). The French machinery was of far better metallurgy and engineering refinement. The cotton mill machinery was shipped from Europe to America in cases of completely disassembled parts. Frequently the English machine parts were damaged or broken in transit, and it became my special task to find ways of obtaining replacement parts in a hurry within the small industrial town of Sherbrooke, Quebec. This involved me in a self-tutored course of engineering exploration in rediscovering the original designer's strategy of determination of the respective functions and stresses of each of the parts, which in turn had occasioned their appropriate dimensioning, and metallurgical specifying.

I also had to rediscover the economic considerations and production strategies originally used in determining the forming procedures for final realization of the parts. This experience involved, too, the discovery of the whereabouts of local resources for reproducing such items. It was an all-important phase in my life, when I came to know shop foremen, molders, machinists and their respective tools, and the beginnings of metallurgical procedures in general. Sometimes I succeeded in designing better parts.

The chief engineer of my company wisely persuaded me to keep an engineering note and sketch book of my experiences. So well did I enjoy and therefore carry out my new phase of learning that I was invited to return to Harvard and quickly accepted, only to be dismissed again for lack of sustained interest in the processes within the University.

Once more I resumed my real lessons, not without deep anguish and shame at having brought hurt to my family, but also with a sense of deep enjoyment in the opportunity to get into the live economic pattern. This time it was with one of the great packing house industries—Armour and Company—where I worked successively in twenty-eight branches of that company in the New Jersey-New York City area.

I went to work in New York City's pre-World War I daily market routine of 3:00 a.m. to 5:00 p.m. My experiences included physical tricks of lugging beef quarters into export ships, gaining knowledge of the economics of abattoirs, refrigeration, by-product chemistry, and high-speed, cross-nation perishable tonnage movements impinging endlessly on sidewalk market-trading. I learned of distribution shrinkage, of comprehensive premechanical accounting and auditing methods, and, most importantly, of broad scale, high-speed, behind-the-scenes human relations in the give and take provisioning of men's essential goods.

During the war I entered the Navy and took a course at the United States Naval Academy at Annapolis, which gave me an enthusiasm for scientific methodology, not only as witnessed in the large patterns of shipbuilding, but also as experienced in their handling and navigating, under a multitude of conditions. I found all of these ship-complexes to be the most superior tools of their respective historical moments, providing standards of effectiveness undreamed of in my boyhood's island days. The new tools of the Navy experience were the more deeply appreciated by me because of my earlier, limited success with self-improvised tools, which so often were realized only through successive stages of spontaneous designs and inventions.

My second derivative Navy experience, in conceptioning of patterns, gave me an exquisite confidence in the superior effectiveness potential to the individual in the direction of competently apprehended, analyzed and design-applied principles integrated to anticipate forward needs by physical translation of the associable principles into event-control mechanisms. Tools were consummately wedded *principles,* as function couples, as variably functioning couples, differentiated out of experience, abstracted (or generalized), in terms of ratios of advantage and ratios of anticipated stress proportionment—all objectively translated into the mathematically manageable but infra-sensorial principles governing synergetic chemical structures.

I learned the process of conscious self-attunement toward the understanding of principles and their subsequent teleologically translated anticipating effectiveness, as demonstrated in: navigation, ballistics, logistics, ship-squadron and fleet handling (at sea and in port), all of which attuned comprehension of principles invariably was reduced to generalized complex equation by a process of incisive and swift differentiating-out of the problems' complementary functions, *not only from one another but also from all of the entirely impertinent and unfavorable* a priori *association factors*. Then came the effective reassociation of the selected and separated pertinent factors within a reciprocating, dynamic totality of now relevant but complex interactions which methodically processed the variables in respect to the constants.

I was fortunate in having Navy commands and very live experience in exercising comprehensive responsibility for the safety, comfort and organizational effectiveness of large numbers of men, as associated with, and advantaged by, a complex of exquisite tooling. This tooling, it was clear to see, had accrued only to the whole history of man's experiences and subsequent irrepressible teleologic reflexes toward further anticipatory design.

Thus I saw that the teleologic design process was ever *regenerative*—within the plurality of progressively harvested physical principles of experience which could be converted, through initiative, to articulatable advantages, thus in turn progressively modifying man's *a priori* physical environmental-hazard patterns, and thereby bettering his effective survival chances. The teleologic process was therefore regenerative because its new patterns created restimulus toward further teleologic conversions of subjective, *a priori* design experiences into objective design formulations—as man took on increasingly conscious functioning in the evolutionary processes.

My Navy experiences ranged all the way from those small commands to subsidiary functions within much larger command patterns. The assignments and commissions brought, for instance, incidental participation in the first development of ship-to-plane radio-telephony. They also brought subsequent participation in the conversion of radio-telephony from seventy-mile-range spark sets to long-distance, arc-type equipment. The first instance of the above electronic experiences occurred when a small ship I commanded was selected for the experimental work of Dr. Lee de Forest. While aboard, he established the first successful voice communication ever heard between a ship and an airplane.

I was later fortunate to be Force Radio Officer for the Cruiser and Transport Force of the United States Atlantic Fleet which carried and escorted the American troops across the Atlantic in World War I, and, as personal aide for secret information to its commanding admiral, had intimate experience in large teamwork maintenance of colossal dynamic patterns: for instance, that of maintaining the high velocity trans-Atlantic turn-around of 130 major troop-carrying ships, together with their cruiser and destroyer escorts. Here was the pattern of secret high-speed exact communication and the strategy of sea group formation, all logistically maintained by expertly scheduled supply and maintenance men at their inspired best, accomplishing the *impossible* under war-induced spontaneous cooperation. After the war I compiled the official Navy statistics of that operation. During the war I had been editor of its sea-printed publication *Transport,* which had monthly circulation in our fleet of 130,000 copies.

Immediately after the Armistice of World War I, the U.S.S. *George Washington,* one of our ships, was selected for President Wilson's trip to France to attend the Versailles conferences. In the *George Washington* we installed the first long-distance wireless arc telephony which dramatically graduated the ship-to-ship telephone from a seventy-mile-range spark set squawk to an effective two-way trans-oceanic voice communication. On President Wilson's second trip to France, the human voice was transmitted trans-oceanically for the first time in history, as man was heard through the receiving instrument in Arlington, Virginia, speaking over the transmitter in the radio shack atop the U.S.S. *George Washington* at anchor in Brest, France.

This Navy experience also involved a tour of duty with naval aviation and short assignments escorting underwater craft. In our first naval aviation training program of 1917, seaplanes crashed daily, usually "stubbing" their floats, tripping and capsizing as they hit the water. A seaplane rescue mast and boom which I design-invented and mounted on high-speed patrol craft for yanking the usually-capsized crashed planes from the water, with the intent of saving the belted-in, stunned pilots from their usual fate of drowning, won me an appointment to the special course at the U.S. Naval Academy in 1917.

Such pattern-experience continually excited conceptioning in potential advantages accruable to new complex design integrations, and subsequent conceptual experimentation with forwardly conceived and theoretically designable entities. It made possible, for instance, a clear and reliable prevision of an entirely new type ship, and a well developed prescience of handling that ship in action; but all, of course, prior to its actual experimental development, physical building and final sea trials, as proof of the original conceptioning's validity.

This coordinate predemonstration conceptioning and integration is a mental functioning which must for millenniums have been common to those men who have undertaken new phases of ship design and building techniques and who today also lead the accelerating-acceleration in design evolution now characterizing air-ocean craft, which is developing at an exponential rate of growth without precedent in, and unanticipated by, history.

In their teleologic treatment of omni-oceans architecture—operating within, upon and around the liquid and gaseous envelopes of earth—the clear prevision of comprehensive designers integrates, perforce by stark physical limiting factors, a synergetic reality so organically persuasive as to induce its spontaneous identification in the communicating minds of men by the vital pronoun "she." Such man-conceived dynamic "shes" are parented by a whole inventory of newly evolving technical potentials, which individually break through barriers of yesterday's practicable limits, all married, by competent integration and intellect wrought with the whole history of acquired ship building and handling experiences.

In this intuitive formulating the aesthetic perspicacity—sensorially tunable by man—is specifically trained to process those borderline nuances of dimensional ratios of the envisioned system's interacting sub-system component functions.

So *invisible* are the important teleologic initiation processes of the designer's intellect, yet so dramatically visible are the sequitur processes and systematic phases of translation into reality of such ship-design-evolution envisioning, and so scientifically prosaic are that envisioning's ratioed criteria of required performance improvements per units of invested resources—over any previous results of undertakings within the respective categories—that it has been erroneously predicted throughout the original years of industrialization that the science, technology and industrial evolution must eventuate inherently in a vast stereotyped monotony.

In historical refutation of such inadequate surmise, it is now in startling evidence that no evolutionary era of biological mutations has ever proven so prolific in accelerated multiplication of species, types and sub-variety nuances and regenerative by-product aesthetic stimulation as that which now accrues to omni-medium ship architectures.

I will here trace briefly a forty-year sequence of episodes which quite possibly were delay detonated from delighted watching in 1904 of the jet-propelled white jelly fish in the clear Maine water. This experience inspired my push-pole propulsion device probably by the innate ability of children to practice, without knowledge of the mathematics discovered in generalized patterns and formalized by maturer minds—the spontaneous teleological inversion—or transformation of relative action-and-reaction behaviors.

The sequence which I shall now briefly trace starts in 1917. This conceptioning development is in turn woven into the warp of contiguously overlapping conception-to-reality threads which I have also served throughout a half century. The fabric thus woven adequately demonstrates my major preoccupations—and consequent orientation—to the important exclusion of, and immunization to, secondary value influences of post-maturing life.

During 1917 in exploratory conversations with my commanding officer, Commander P.N.L. Bellinger, later a vice-admiral and one of the Navy's first four aircraft pilots, I started my theoretical conceptioning and development of a wingless, amphibious "jet-stilts" elevatable aircraft which would plummet aeronautically in tetravector guidance. This aircraft would be powered by twin *combination plants,* consisting of gas turbines, jets and rocket assist thrusts, universally hinge-mounted, on both starboard and port sides, abreast the maximum beam section. Each thrust would be angularly orientable throughout a spherical-tetrant sector: vertically, outwardly, forwardly, backwardly, inwardly, with the geometrical degrees of freedom characterizing a wild duck's full maneuvering range of wing-thrust angles. The gas turbines would also be clutchable with breast wheels, or paddle wheels, for original ground or water taxiing, or for takeoff and alignment skittering.

This slowly gestating jet-stilts flying concept brought me to a paper and model-making design stage of a conceivably workable ship in 1927. It was, however, impossible to consider its full-scale realization in 1927 (even had I the necessary capital or technical accrediting, which I did not) because of then-prevailing metallurgical heat limits which, however, have since been advanced to permit practical realization by others of the principles involved, first as jet ships in 1943 and now as vertically orientable jet ships, "flying bedsteads," etc.

I published the concept with a sketch in a two hundred-copy, privately distributed monograph in 1928, and publicly in *Shelter* magazine in November 1932. In December 1932, I was invited to show the models of the jet-stilt "4D transport" in the Grand Central Building windows of the Engineers' Book Shop in New York City. In January 1933, I demonstrated them in a feature booth throughout the National Automobile Show in New York City's Grand Central Palace.

However, in February of the same year I was so sure of the eventual successful jet and rocket power plant development that in anticipation of its imminent realization I built three full-scale experimental transports of appropriate aeronautical conformation, embodying strategic steerability controls in respect to eventual omni-directionable steerability, loadability and maneuvering as these related to centers of balance, effort and stress. I hoped that these experiments would hasten man's practical realization and enjoyment of all-medium navigation by hoverable, yet swift, spot-alighting and spot-take-off transportation, thus opening up vast new ranges of preferred earth-dwellability, when extension of chemistry of the metallurgical heat-level strength ratios appropriate to thrust-supported, plummeting, air-land-water craft should be realized.

I felt that the ground taxiing and cross-wind travel problems of such wingless "fish" would be more difficult to solve than the aeronautical maneuvering problems to be encountered. This proved a worthwhile assumption, for the ground contact maneuvering problems proved to be many and difficult to overcome, as the land contacting problems of vessels of all types of either the sea or air have always been. Where there is plenty of sky room for the plane and sea room for the boat, time is afforded to reestablish controls when breaks in regular functioning occur. The liquid and gaseous mediums are chemically bonded in flexural freedoms, permitting energy-event contact stress distributions to innocuous magnitudes, but the crystalline state concentrates its energy effect. Crystalline-structured ships in liquid and gaseous mediums provide convergent-divergent systems in equilibrious balance, but crystalline ships and crystalline earth converge all their potential contact energies at point of contact. Pneumatic tires are packaged sky oceans to insulate earth and ship and to distribute their potential energies of contact. I chose this landed phase of the omni-transports experimental development, not only because the metallurgy was not quite ready, but because this was the hazard zone where lurked the preponderance of frustrations to be overcome on the way to important new freedoms of man, in exponential degrees of his present, first-dimensional linear, crowding along streets.

My three experimental units of 1933, 1934 and 1935 were called the Dymaxion 4D transports. As a result of building and testing these three successive types of the 4D transport I learned of the primary cross-wind, cross-furrow, in-rut, on ice, in-traffic, in-parking, ground looping, cornering, high-speed accelerating and decelerating problems and answers and, to the best of my knowledge, am at present better prepared than others for initiating the successful prototyping phases of this new era transport.

Prior to the arrival of the opportunity to make such initiation of the jet-stilt transport, I had ready the conception-processed designs for application of the tetra-vector thrust support and plummet principle to twin miniature-combination, jet-rocket power plants of a few pounds, each mounted in "crutch-like" assemblies, harness-able under and to the two arms of an appropriately clothed man, and providing practical means for the man's personal free hovering and swift flight, and bird-like landing and take-off, independent of fuselage or skeletal frame.

We now jump a long way back from such thoughts to resume tracking of my design stimulus and its complex of conceptioning trends. These have integrated most comprehensively in a search and research preoccupation which I have named *synergetic* and *energetic geometry*.

My attunement to this preoccupation was spontaneous and of possibly native interest, for I can dimly recall a happy experience in kindergarten about 1899 or 1900 when I made a complex tetrahedron structure of toothpicks and semi-dried peas, whereupon the teacher called another teacher to look at it. Together they expressed either feigned or true surprise and pleasure. Whichever it was, I had made an impression on the ladies and the whole affair was vivid enough for me to remember.

I do know, however, that I began my systematic search in synergetic and energetic geometry in 1917 and the omni-directionally regenerative octahedron-tetrahedron complex, or vector-tensor-equilibrium, was first assumed as probable to Avogadro's Law of gases, and then glimpse-discovered as constructionally possible some time in the 1920s and proven in the 1930s.

My discovery of the "Octet" truss was synergetic-intuitively avoiding special case tactics. I define "synergy" as follows: Synergy is the unique behavior of whole systems, unpredicted by behavior of their respective sub-systems' events.

I was seeking in the whole of experience and knowledge, rather than in specialized isolations, for a comprehensive mathematical scheme of patterning.

My energetic and synergetic geometry exploration has since proven the "Octet" complex to be a precessionally non-redundant, isotropic vector-tensor evolutionary relationship whose energy transformation accountings are comprehensively rational—radially and circumferentially—to all chemical, biological, electrophysical, thermodynamic, gravitational and radiational behaviors of nature. As such, the discovered synergetic system is probably nature's spontaneously employed coordinate system, for it accommodates all transformations by systematic, complementary symmetries of concentric, contractural, involutional, turbo-geared positive-to-negative-to-equilibrium-to-vice-versa coordinate displacements.

Subsequent to my Navy experience in World War I I made re-entry into the world of commerce as an assistant export manager of Armour and Company in 1919. With that re-entry into commerce came a whole new pattern of experience which integrated not only my theoretical conceptioning, but also the whole previous navy transport experience in maintenance, supply, and coordination of swift *turnaround,* with my pre-Navy packinghouse familiarity in high-speed continental distribution of essential and perishable goods, to all of which the factor of accelerating *turnover* seemed the key to success.

Thus came a dawning conception of an enormous over-all and world-around accelerating integration of those two land and sea processes—turnover and turnabout—turnover of the landed biological metabolic process cycles, and turnaround of the waterborne and later airborne vessels of distribution of the advancing process standards to the most people in the shortest time. The accelerations were obviously keys to the economics of wealth augmentation and its concomitant improvement of the over-all advantage of man. By acceleration more of the total energy relaying in universe may be shunted into a complex of earth-emerging patterns within a given time interval.

Towards the very last of the war my first daughter was born. She subsequently contracted each of the war-aggravated epidemics of influenza, spinal meningitis, and infantile paralysis. I was increasingly resentful that the effectiveness of teleologic processing of man's all-history experience came only to maximum projected design effectiveness in turnover and turnaround exploitation patterns arbitrarily selected at sub-total experience magnitude. This subcomprehensive undertaking invoked carelessly nonanticipated byproduct emergencies. The emergencies were resultant to irresponsibly neglected contiguous displacement accelerations inherent in the arbitrarily undertaken patterns. The contiguous displacements caused important economic gear strippings, which in turn induced economic and social impasse. Impasse meant war and inversion of the right-makes-might equation—consisting of exquisite teleologic processing of experience-into-design—inverted mathematically into might-makes-right and thereafter manifested through the teleologic processes only as an emergency rationalized, essential hitting power, with which to slug out the answer as to who should be held responsible for stripping the gears, which stripping could all the while have been avoided by an earlier and relatively small comprehensive investment of wealth advantage in the contiguous but disclaimed responsibilities for displacements.

However, it was clear that if those in responsible positions had been willing to underwrite contiguous displacement controls, even then such avoidance of evolutionary gear-stripping could have been effected only by an engineering-initiated and designed gradual transfer of the full load through progressively decommissioned apparatus synchronized with progressively commissioned new apparatus. This would be so only if the ramifications of individually assumed teleologic design responsibility were upped to include the looming minimum configuration of full world industrial network integration, on a realistic basis of omnibountiful advantage acceleration, in turn to be gained only through total commonwealth regenerative cycling advantage, itself in turn accruing only to an adequate statement of the original design problems—a big order, but a fundamental and therefore conservative minimum.

It was visible to me that the death of our child on her fourth birthday, 1922, resulted from then-unheeded environmental process integrations of comprehensively unattended yet design-preventable factors. This premise has been adequately proven to be correct by the interim elimination of those epidemics from the "fatal" list. Potential preventive success was visible to me as inherent in the advanced practical technology of the premium water and air-ocean tooling and their related ballistics and navigation sciences, in all of which I had experienced an intimate fore-imagining of their implied land-life applicabilities. Because the possibility was visible to me, when the unattended factors impinged on the life for which we cared the most, there then occurred the important beginning of the negative stimulus or vacuum into which my increasing pressure of teleologically-induced design increment tended to explode.

This pressure differential grew finally to a critical detonation point in the subsequent five years' experience within the most ignorant and most prodigious of men's fumbling activities—that sub-industry activity of men, in fortuitous agglomeration of sheltering and dwelling facilities. I learned how these were gleaned out of the industrial and defense left-overs, without benefit either of science or of advanced technology; how all building enterprise was exploited on a gross trial and error basis; how all building was beset with arbitrary rules designed to avoid political misfortune while promoting corrupt exploitation of economic monopolies staked out in the rubble and weed traffic; how building activity was nurtured with superstition, busybodiness, vain reflex patronage and, above all, fixed with the prior necessity to design ways to make money first, with which hopefully to buy living means afterward, rather than making better living itself through directly applied design competence and unpatronized designer initiative, undertaken in exploration for an art and science of a generalized anticipatory design competence that would convert social cycling from an emergency and cure sequence to an anticipating and laboratory experimenting, complex design, development sequence, akin to ship-building, which when appropriate introduces the new-proven advantages into the complex before emergency sets in, even as today we replace aircraft parts prior to probable failures through scientifically evolved scheduling.

The building world which I met with dismay in the 1920s was the paradoxical world in which the patient diagnoses his own ailments and by virtue of his dollar authority commands the retained and muted physician and surgeon to perform, with the doctor's feigned pleasure and admiration for the client's sagacity, operations designed by the patient's own limited, personal, traumatic conceptioning.

Between 1922 and 1927 I took part in the building of 240 structures in the expensive residential and small commercial buildings categories, buildings erected throughout those of the United States lying east of the Mississippi River. During this time I organized five regional factories and invented the machinery for the production of those bulk materials which I introduced into the 240 structures. There I met with the chaos of the building and home-improvising world.

After five years of prodigious and informative wrestling within this arena of increasing inefficiency, my thoughts were suddenly brought into new focus by an independent event. A new daughter was born to us and with her birth also suddenly was born my resolve to adopt a whole new strategy of thought and action predicated upon the assumption that if an as-yet-unattended but integral function of the industrial complex be adopted for responsible attention, and if design competence is demonstrated in the original statement and pursuit of that unattended problem, then even though the whole search and development was undertaken without any recognized public or private credit and economic authorization, its husbanding would induce spontaneous and unpredictable support by society.

My blind date with principle seemed the only way for me to serve those processes most potential of accelerating the overall technical advantage network toward realization for our new child and all new children of commonly gained participation in spontaneous, anticipatory, economic and technical pattern adoptions, by industry and by society, which would erase from probability the reoccurrence of the unattended environment-bred hazards fatal to our first child. I resolved to apply the rest of my life to converting my pattern sense, through teleologic principle into design and prototyping developments governing the pertinent, but as yet unattended essential industrial network functions, necessary to removal of such housing chaos by physically effective and lasting technology. As a corollary I resolved to eschew further acceptance of conventional recourse to political or moral reforms which, lacking physical energy effectiveness, must in the fact of physical inadequacy adopt peaceful or forceful palliation through political action.

It seemed clear to me that only a transcendental engineering design and technical process pattern predicated upon a world around dynamic town plan could here succeed. It would have to be a pattern of accelerating and anticipating design evolution to supplant by economic superiority the constantly innocuous design revolutions accruing at increasing expense through the substitution of new materials in the production of parts for old functions within an increasingly obsolete totality, *ergo,* by more expensive chemistry investment in less valid functions.

My envisioned transcendental world design plan would be inherently nonpolitical, because it would be utterly independent of any need for authority beyond that to-self-by-self for initiation of its study and development. It permitted on the individual's own initiative, convening of all the appropriate, documented knowledge of man and universe in integrated teleologic objectivity. It permitted priority of attention to designing the establishment of a whole new world industry concerned only with man's unavoidable needs and implementation of his inherent freedoms. Such an industry could well be the most important phase of application of the very phenomenon "industry," itself. To wit: the first-hand application of all advancing facets of knowledge to the design of implements for direct support of the regenerative process "man," within the known and economically realizable resource limits.

By industry I meant in 1927 and as yet mean the following: *"The integrated, teleologic objectivity of the full gamut of the exact sciences,"* no more-no less.

Clearly it would be essential to such comprehensive performance that structural and mechanical complexes be design-adopted whose high performance, per units of invested resource, would render the total tonnage of world resources effectively distributable to the physical advantage of the total world population, in improving waves of standards of satisfaction. This could be brought about only by the synergetic (behavior of the whole unpredicted by the behavior of the parts) effectiveness accruing uniquely to the relatively large art of sea and air-ocean vesselbuilding. Keels and ribs, though independently inadequate to subsequent stress functions, gain adequate effectiveness only through means of assembly within jigs, or cradle, which locally and temporarily position the components until the complementary interactions and shortened modular bracings are completed, whereby the structural behavior pattern of the respective single components is altered into coordinate action of associated vectors, interacting to exponentially augmented total advantage. Vessels, as a totality of differentiated and reintegrated functions, coactive as a complex of efficiently resolved functioning, may, when completed, be launched into a tolerable stress-distributive medium and brought thereby to an adequate plurality of appropriate work focuses within the great turnover-turnaround precessional gearings of total world patterning, thereby also to effect further augmentation of the world's tapped ratio of universally available energy—valuable only when valvable—and when valvable, accountable as explicit "wealth" increase.

The transcendental participation of the sheltering structures and dwelling mechanisms in the comprehensively gestating advantages of the industrial network of world design evolution could be effected through the teleologic designing processes of man which progressively convert his pattern participating from subjective to objective, i.e., from subconscious to conscious adoption. For the transcendental plan to be consistent with lessons of most profitable synergetic and physical experiment it had to involve direct airborne deliveries of jet-stilt transports, coming as an eagle to firm poise at loci of progressive advantage, within the regenerative man-patterning of geography, while ever increasing man's concomitant degrees of freedom and prospective advantage.

To such a comprehensive transcendental dynamic design complex, the sub-system problems, governing local differentiations of design functioning are sequitur but not inferior to considerations of the design evolution of the surrounding plurality of energy-valving mechanisms of the total industrial process. This is to say that the dwelling devices are essential and attention-worthy and only subsidiary in schedule of priority-for-development consideration within the greater pattern of dynamic turnover and turnabout of the mechanisms' tools-to-make-tools evolution. This "tooling-up" evolution is emergent in intermittently progressive wave peak congruences historically detectable as uniquely visible eras of the perfecting efficacy of the total network service integration, as the integration impinges upon the conscious reflexes of man, as periodic frames of infocusness of objective men upon subjective economic man. But between such glimpsed frames men are prone to return to irresponsible preoccupation with minor, local aspects of the reciprocating mechanisms.

However, the subsidiary system's dwelling devices, resultant to comprehensive processing, are equivalent to electronic tubes which may be plugged into the greater regenerative circuits of the electronic communicating systems. "House," in comprehensive designing, would be as incidental to the world-around network dwelling service as is the telephone transceiver instrument to the energy processing in communication systems, which are in turn within the larger systems of industry. Industry is subsidiary itself within the universal systems of macrocosmically and microcosmically pertinent evolution.

The Dymaxion technology and design formulations of 1927 were examples of such incidental design events within the frame of designing a new industry, a concept which I published in May 1928.

In 1929 in Chicago, student designers, excited by favorable results already visibly accruing to experimental tests of the economic efficacy of my nongeographical and generalized theories, informed me of a seeming revolution in European design activities in Sweden, France, Holland, Denmark, and in Germany at the Bauhaus. It was evident in the pictures they showed to me that the European architects were beginning to experience with cogency those same vital stimulations, through privations persistent within the paradoxical environment of high potentials, which had come flooding upon me a few years earlier, as I came to maturity in the accelerating industrial frontier economy opening chapters of new magnitude upon the shores of the American continent.

The industrial frontier wave on the American continent had been regenerated from its former European and even earlier Asiatic beginnings. On its American rebirth the industrial equation was approximately disembarrassed of the progressively paralyzing secondary credit-breaking devices which had been put upon European industrial facilities by cartelism's staticizing exploitation schemes. These sought, of course, to perpetuate security of income patterns, though those patterns were inherently incidental to passing phases of fundamental, universal, and evolutionary transformations.

The new cartel-shunning industrial wave, advantaging America's highly competitive early twentieth-century economy, was also a trend within which I underwent my unforgotten experiences with broken parts of industrial tooling received from Europe. It put me on notice that there was much room for original design improvement, made increasingly reasonable and possible by the evolving inventory of potential design resource growth within that part of the world in which it was my good fortune to be living.

It was also evident to me that the 1920–30 wave of architectural awareness regarding important design potentials, realizable as design simplifications and improvements, had been generated in Europe in the post-World War I decade by the European's 3,000-mile perspective-clarifying review of architecturally-unencumbered, giant silos, warehouses, and factories in the cleanly emergent United States-structures which had been disembarrassed in unique degree, in the space-rich American scene, of economically unessential aesthetics. This American inspiration was well documented by the European style protagonists whose original publications invariably fortified their arguments for design reform by photographic examples of American silos and factories as constituting sources of their European inspiration.

They still further fortified their argument with pictures of the generalized morphation in design complex, demonstrated by the nakedly functional superstructures of ships of the all-ocean all-sky categories.

For instance they built tiered, outstretched, cantilevered, conning-bridge wings, developed a half-century earlier with the first iron torpedo boats and subsequent battleships (the "bridge" having originated much earlier in gunwale-to-gunwale bridging superstructure-walk-ways over crowded decks). It was also amusingly clear that the European designers of the 1920s had glimpsed and comprehended the design paradox within the American continent. This was the aesthetically pure silos' and factories' coexistence with the aesthetically impure architectural nonsense beshrouding America's dwellings and patron-occupancy buildings, as the latter wallowed hypnotically and superstitiously within the European-originated architectural garmenture.

It was also evident that the going design blindness at the lay level in the United States afforded European designers an opportunity in Europe and America to exploit their farview discernment of the more appealing simplicities of the industrial structures which had inadvertently earned their architectural freedom. This had been accomplished not by conscious aesthetical innovation, but through profit-inspired discard of economic irrelevancies in non-popular occupancy structures. This surprise discovery, the European designer well knew, could soon be made universally appealing as a fad, for had they not themselves been so faddishly inspired? The international style thus brought to America by the Bauhaus innovators demonstrated a fashion inoculation effected, without necessity of knowledge of the scientific fundamentals of structural mechanics and chemistry, whose upped performance abilities had brought about, through economic spontaneity of engineering cost limits, that new factory design revolution which had a quarter of a century later such superficial appeal to the European architects as a functional style formula.

Paradoxically, the introduction of Bauhaus international to America was accompanied by a school routine of manual sensitivity training, whereas the fundamental of the design revolution inherent in industrialization, whose superficial aspects had inspired the international stylism, were predicated upon graduation *from* manual crafts, and "seat-of-the-pants" controls only within the sensorial sensitivity limits. The international style's simplification was then but superficial. It peeled off yesterday's exterior embellishment and put on instead formalized novelties of quasi-simplicity permitted by the same hidden structural elements of modern alloys which had permitted the discarded *beaux-arts* garmentation. It was still a European garmentation. The new international stylists hung "stark motif walls" of vast supermeticulous brick assemblage, which had no tensible cohesiveness within its own bonds, but was in fact locked up within hidden steel frames supported by steel without visible means of support. In many such illusory ways did the international style gain dramatic sensorial impingement upon society, as does a magician the attention of children. As with the magician, this new architecture and furnishings fad contrived semantic deception by using fake words to describe this design as being "tensed" or "suspended curtain" walls.

As the prestidigitator puts over his tricks by focusing attention of the audience's sensorial reflexes upon his decoy functions, in order to render the true functions invisible, so (despite the individual exploratory integrity of the artists themselves) were international style architecture and the quasi-abstractions of modern art aesthetically propagandized and patronized by those whose larger pattern security seemed challenged by the science-initiated transcendental transformations of the industrializing world's unhaltable trend to constantly accelerating change. Paradoxically, the extreme left and the extreme right (with no fundamental sympathy for the artist-explorer) both, hopefully, promoted the attempt to detour America's dynamic-function designed philosophy of evolutional acceleration into what they hoped might be an innocuous *cul-de-sac;* the extreme right because it hoped to keep the design change superficial in order to prolong the tooled-up pay-off, the extreme left with the hope of slowing down the industrial evolution within America and possibly even causing its breakdown through resulting common ignorance regarding fundamentals of the times camouflaged by the nonsense.

History shows that all those periods of faddish nonsense which promote "getting into the know regarding naught" eventually bring about comprehensive vitiation of a whole society, as is related in the tale of the emperor's clothes. What was going on in a fundamental way in the second quarter of the twentieth century was that world-around economics were shifting from the static norm of classical science to the dynamic evolutionary acceleration norm of relativity's realistically reappraised physical experience. The present economic revolution that renders income from capital gains more universally attractive than income from dividends, and converts yesterday's foolhardy into this day's sagacious, demonstrates that negative strategy has been abandoned and the dynamic relativity of values espoused. The prospects of society are now propitious to a re-welcomed evolution in fundamental design, which in turn promises advance in world design of economic affairs.

However, in the meantime, the momentum of this superficial modern fad nonsense has inflated the American success category of suburban "international-ranch" construction, from the $10,000 to the $50,000 range for equivalent cubage increments. This has heightened the emotional confusion of these dwellers in nonsensical structures who are already dizzied enough by the paradox of the augmented buying power of an industrially advantaged commonwealth, succeeding despite the commonly accredited Malthusian assurances of inevitable failure of the invention, "man," within an alleged inherently hostile, man-destroying universe.

I had to conclude when confronted by it in 1928 that as far as the international style and its influence were concerned, we were in for new educational decades in which we must learn to do all the little wrong things first in order to learn by direct experience that we must take broad, comprehensive and incisive responsibility in the formulation of our over-all strategies, if we in America are to maintain our responsible growth husbanding function in the history of man.

If we have not already scuttled our own historical ship in the process of learning how not to operate it, we may be able to bring it into port despite all the vigorous nonsense organized to redirect man's emergent competence into bypaths of vanity and self-inferiority coddling, which squander the potential advantage in superficial irrelevancies.

In speaking in such a directly critical and unfriendly way of the international style, I do not hold myself a paragon and am sure that there are many who feel that they can shoot more holes into my domed-over gardens of Eden or mountain-top, moorable, sky-houseboat kind of philosophy and record than I can in theirs or others.

I have written in this blunt way to demonstrate the remoteness of Bauhaus concepts from those I hold. However, the simplest demonstration of the fundamental remoteness of our ways is the lack of schedules of ratio of invested resources per units of performance abilities concerning structures designed by Bauhaus international school architects. Do any of them publish what their structures weigh and what their original minimum performance requirements must be, and later prove to be, in respect to velocities of winds, heights of floods, severity of earthquakes, fires, pestilence, epidemics, etc., and what their shipping weights and volumes will be, and what man hours of work are totally involved?

What convinced me that the Bauhaus international designing was of secondary rank and limited to interior furniture sculpture, fabrics, and bric-a-brac pattern variations, and to exterior rêdecorating to reveal the structural facts that had been insinuated behind the old-time facades, was the fact that their designing consciously limited itself to formulated employment of the component items manufactured by the going old-line building materials world. The Bauhaus international school used standard plumbing fixtures and only ventured so far as to persuade the manufacturers to modify the surface of the valve handles and spigots and the color, size, and arrangement of the tiles. The Bauhaus international school never went back of the wall surface to look at the plumbing, never dared to venture into printed circuits of manifoldly stamped plumbings. They never inquired into the over-all problem of sanitary functions themselves. They settled upon the real estaters' sewers like hens on glass eggs. They did not inquire into the economic patterns governing research, production, tooling, airframe and power plant, and distribution. In short, they only looked at problems of modification of the surface of end products, which end products were inherently subfunctions of a technically obsolete world. Finally the Bauhaus international undertook design only as commissioned by direct patronage and essentially for crafted production of limited edition products claiming that because the craftsman used modern machine tools (designed to make mass-production tools, not end products) the design must be modern.

This direct patronage designing was in contrast to the kind of "generalized case" designing effectiveness to which I subscribed. The generalized case designing had to assume complete lack of direct patronage in order to find through scientific competence the way in which ultimately to serve the general public in the manner most effective toward general man's improving survival and happiness. It was clear that the generalized case meant forswearing opportunism, and strict adherence to the programming indicated by the full gamut of laboratory-produced data covering the problem of effecting higher standards for all realizable from the full inventory of history's and geography's resources.

I could see as implicit in the generalized case that not until the comprehensive problem had been worked through in such a manner that the going resources could match the complex of required tasks and the economic criteria had been graduated from mystical hopefulness to demonstrable adequacy that the first presentation of the concept, in its entirety, could be made. When it could be made it must be so obviously of general advantage that it could be and must be brought in through the front doors of civilization because it would be too big for the cellar-way or side porch. It was clear that the front door introduction would be reachable only by the "hard way avenue" of broad integrity, universal tolerance, education by experiment, and due (i.e., thoroughly integrated) process.

Now that I have finished stating all the hows and wherefores of my primary design-influence-environment, I must also say that I always hold in deep respect, oft-times with enthusiasm, and sometimes with great affection all those of whom I am at times most argumentatively critical. It is they in particular who have taken the design initiative after the urgings of their heads and hearts. I warm to all such initiative. I find no men "bad." I am convinced by my own frequent stupidities that the hell's-fire-to-be-known by him who calleth his brother a fool is a hell-of-the-mind right here immediately upon earth. I am convinced of the utter integrity of the *total experience,* and of the indicated extensibleness of the comprehensive integrity-apparent universe-extensible further to man, as always, only through the congruent integrity of the individual. *Ergo,* I am convinced of the integrity of the infinitude of complementary functionings identifiable in principle.

In all our case histories are those unique cases where none may trespass and wherein all may profit through the increasing lucidity of the operative principles of the comprehensive integrity implicit in every self-error-revealed stumbling.

2 Later Development of My Work

I have been concerned for a great many years with the potential functioning of the individual in the presence of swiftly integrating world affairs and the increasingly massive states and corporations, and their respective enormous capital advantage in respect to the accrediting of initiatives in any directions. I am sure I am but one of several millions who wonder how much the individual can actually affect the evolutionary processes of his day, while starting only upon his self-accrediting of his own initiative, enterprise and effective transformation capabilities.

In 1927 I decided to experiment and probe in this direction by gathering data on how much the contemporary individual might be able to effect. That year I had come to the end of some very vigorous experiences in the world of building activities. I had taken part in the building of 240 buildings between 1922 and 1927. I had had a very vigorous experience in the American scene regarding this kind of activity. And that building activity followed directly upon experiences in the Navy with its then new world of flying and of radio and other experiences in mechanical activities. My conclusions after five years in the building world were that it, through no fault of its own or of its choosing, did happen to be the last primary area of man's activity yet to come importantly

---

June 5, 1958. The original was delivered by Fuller as the Annual Discourse to the Royal Institute of British Architects under the title "Experimental Probing for a Comprehensive Architectural Initiative." It was subsequently edited and published in the *RIBA Journal* in October 1958.

under the effect of the industrial equation which had been coming over all other world technologies and economics for at least a hundred years.

It was also very clear, I thought, that the superior capability of the industrial equation was approaching inexorably an embrace of all of mankind's productive techniques and therefore would in due course come into availability for direct solution of men's immediate living problems rather than as an aftermath diversion of war-born technologies. Industrialization had been applied at first on very high priority, due to its relative scarcity and enormous initial cost, only to great emergency problems of war and the annihilation of life. Because I had had high-priority industrial technology experiences in the mechanical, Navy and aircraft worlds and then subsequently non-industrialized experiences in the building arts, my experiences had taught me to see the differences between these industrial and non-industrial capabilities. Inasmuch as I saw those differences, there seemed to be some responsibility for personal taking of initiatives.

In 1927 I decided to peel off from conventional livelihood preoccupations and to enter into a period of research and development, the minimum limits of which turned out to be of many years' duration. In fact, the first prospecting into the ramifications of such a researching initiative pursued alone as an individual, indicated that there was a minimum of twenty-five years of detached reconnaissance activity before the individual might be able to bring into industrially useful economic harvest any of the kinds of initiations that he might undertake within these vast new evolutionary premises. Feasibility studies I originally found myself making showed that there were many different kinds of unfamiliar gestation lags in respect to final birth patterning within the industrial equation. Whereas in the agricultural world we tended by historical experiences to think of crops coming in annually, we also tended to expect profits annually in respect to the industrial equation. However, I found that there were a variety of multi-year lags between the various industrial inventions and their respective active introduction into the industrial world as new tools, structures and processes. For instance, in the railroad arts, there was an average of fifteen years' lag between invention and the incorporation of that invention in the railroading arts.

The lag was much shorter in the radio world—only about two years—and in the airplane world about four. In the world of building I found an enormous lag—approximately forty-two years. Typical had been a building arts invention at the time when mass production of steel by industrializing man began. Mass production steel was very different from the previous making of steel by man, which had dribbled along for centuries as a fine art. Production steel ushered in the civil wars of the mid-nineteenth century. In the mass production of steel Portland cement became a fundamental by-product of the complex steel-making activity. It was, however, forty-two years after the production of Portland cement as a by-product of the steel industry in America that anybody thought of putting a piece of steel into the cement to make reinforced concrete. This is very typical of lags in the building field—as well as of the latter's blindness.

Integrating all the different kinds of lags in the industrial equation ranging between forty-two and two years and weighting the total inventory of categories in the terms of their respective total dollar volumes in respect to the total annual activities, it appeared that there would be a twenty-five-year lag instead of a forty-two-year lag to be anticipated in relation to shifting "building category" over into the industrial equation columns and out of the craft arts columns.

I am going to examine the craft arts in contrast to the industrial equation in search of working definitions. There may be other definitions for *craft v. industry,* but when I use these words I mean the following:

Both craft and industry deal with extra corporeal work capabilities greater than those that are integral to the human organism.

Therefore, both deal with tools. The craft tools I define as that class of tools which can be spontaneously fashioned and adopted by any one individual starting nakedly in the wilderness—for instance, his picking up of a stone to do work at a distance greater than his arm's length; or his picking up of a stick, using the stick either as spear or as lever. Industrial tools I define as those which cannot be produced by any one man.

Those definitions seemed to me to provide a rather sharp differentiation. But adoption of the definitions brings surprise lines of cleavage. Let me take the case of the hammer: The man in the woods certainly would be prone, having thrown stones and probed with sticks, to take a crotched stick and lash a stone in it, making a hammer with which he could deal a blow greater than that accomplished with his fist. So we might say a hammer belongs categorically to craft. However, I looked at a modern carpenter's hammer and I found that this instrument, made out of forged alloy steel, does involve finding iron which would probably not be in the vicinity of the man in the woods. It involves a knowledge of how to mine the ore, to render and produce the iron, to find and render the manganese, nickel and molybdenum in faraway lands and to bring them all together. Therefore, invention of ships is involved in the bringing together of many metals, and there is also requisite the invention of blast furnaces, forges and so forth. Obviously, the modern carpenter's hammer cannot be produced by one man, and is therefore industrial—so there are both craft and industrial hammers.

While hammers demand a little exploring, we can take other cases, such as a steamship like the *Queen Mary,* which obviously cannot be produced by one man, operated by one man, or used by one man. What I mean by the industrial tools are those which only relate to the integrated capabilities and initiatives of a plurality of men. With that basic distinction I then discover many other and very important differences between the crafts and industry, as, for instance, craft is inherently local—local in time and in the generations of man. It is local geographically in the small ecological roamaround of the individual; it is very local, then, in knowledge.

In contradistinction then to this local time and geography and knowledge aspect of craft, we find the industrial equation does represent an integration of all the knowledge of all human beings, as gained from their plurality of experiences, and as relayingly communicated by one man to another. Industrialization represents an employment of all the resources of the earth, wherever they may be. It is inherently comprehensive and universal, in contradistinction to local. This is the reason why I have adopted the word comprehensive as unique to my kind of exploration.

The industrial equation goes inherently, *ergo* inexorably, around the world to find the various excellences of unique behaviors of respective elemental resources, because tools are only adopted by men to help them to do greater or more incisive work than that to be accomplished only with their integral physical member capabilities. Out of men's integrated experiences, there is regenerated an accelerating realization of ways in which they can improve a workable advantage over the progressively evolving physical environment.

In no time at all we begin to discover that not only in our own wanderings, but also in the reports of other men, there are unique materials elsewhere, which, if added to what we have locally, could give us greater performance capabilities, such as unique lightness combined with a unique new degree of hardness. We also begin to discover that by travel and commerce we might be able to bring together extraordinary new complex capabilities. Thus industrialization, as the total integrated complexity of advantage gains, grew slowly out of the progressively and regeneratively integrated information of man.

Unquestionably, we would say that words are the first industrial tools, for inherently they involve a plurality of men and are also inherently prior to relayed communication and integration of the respective experiences of a plurality of individuals. Due to the fact that nature has disposed the chemical elements around the earth in a very uneven manner, recourse to the total physical resource inventory of unique behavior advantages to be earned by integrating the totally relayed information does involve man's going all around the earth. Starting from any one point he has to go half around the world—which is always the length of his journey to reach the furthermost earth surface point. The industrial equation involves at maximum going half way around the world and then separating out the desired resources from their matrix, and thereafter a set of progressive separations and progressive forwarding movements of the unique resources towards the special area where you would wish to bring about the highest separation where you have already established a complex of high advantage tools.

Finally, on reaching the home tool complex, the resources from far and near are separated out to the maximum degree. Men then begin to reassociate the various preferred performance characteristics of these resources in preferred complex patterns, thus accomplishing greater or more incisive tools. Having done so the environment itself becomes permanently altered. The world never returns to the shape that it was before.

It is important to realize that the industrial equation has really altered our physical world relations, the major geophysical patterns, in ways and degrees possibly greater than are popularly realized—as, for instance, England was first exploited by foreign men, the Phoenicians, who discovered England's tin. This low-melting-point metal suddenly opened up new technical capabilities—therefore, economic wealth—and attracted the Romans. The tin ore was finally exhausted here, yet so much machinery of reduction, production and commerce had been developed around it, that tin was sought elsewhere by Englishmen who, going half way around the world from England, found tin in the Malay States, Bolivia, Tanganyika and so forth.

In America we have no tin ore of workable grade or amount. In the industrial equation we need enormous amounts of tin for many kinds of special abilities and tin opens up over and again all kinds of new ventures in industry. For instance, as babbit or bearing metal it first permitted the industrial wheels to go round.

So much tin has been gradually brought into America, and so easy is it to recover, that America's cumulative inventory of available tin has finally become a major world body of the tin reserve. In our aircraft industry today, because it is predicated on very swift changes of design and is a swiftly evolving art, we have so-called soft tools to make possible short runs of entirely new designs, and we learned from England how to make our Kirksite tin-forming dies. Back of every aircraft company in America will be found an enormous store of tin in the form of obsolete dies soon to be melted to form new dies. These tin die storage yards look exactly like large graveyards but are far more useful. In fact the largest inventory of tin in America is back of our aircraft plants. And there is so much of it there now that the actual tin in concentrated form above ground in America is so great that it is approximately equal to that below ground in Bolivia and the Straits Settlements. That is to say we have in America the largest tin mines in the world, all above ground.

So here we see major geophysical patterns of man's earth irreversibly altered. I have only given one typical case of a myriad in which the earth will never be restored to its previous patterns.

It was perverse in my youth young people were not supposed to know anything. All the grownups seemingly knew all the answers and you were simply told to shut up and learn. I was willing to shut up and learn. I decided that if I didn't like the smell of the building I'd better shut up—that I was stupid and squeamish. I stuffed back natural reactions pretty hard. It wasn't very long before I was suddenly out of my home. My father died when I was twelve. He went through a lot of sickness in our home, and I looked out for him. He had strokes and he was out of his mind for the last three years of his life. I had to lead my own father around by his hand, a man I had loved and revered. When I finally got through high school and went to college, I got into a lot of trouble, because I was suddenly on my own. I thought I was going to be a great athlete, and then I busted my leg playing football so I couldn't be an athlete. I was given some money–my year's allowance–and I didn't know anything about money at all. I spent my whole year's allowance in one week. I obviously couldn't stay at Harvard very long, so I got fired. They can't fire you for spending your money–it's your money–but they could fire me for not going to my classes. I got into trouble with Harvard two times, and if World War I hadn't come they would have let me back in again for a third try because I had high scholastic grades.

Each time I was sent out I went to work. I liked the people I met at work and I liked mechanics. I found myself employed as a machine fitter and I made a good mechanic. I worked hard and everybody said, "We've made a mistake about this boy, he really enjoys work and he's a very sane boy, so let's let him back in again." Then I would get in trouble right away. What I was getting in trouble with was not the college at all. In fact, I hardly knew the college existed. What I was really getting into trouble with were the social institutions: the club systems and things like that. I didn't like the feel of fraternities and clubs and patterns that were being formed on a basis I couldn't understand. They had nothing to do that I could see with the merits of individuals. I felt there were forces operating that were unreasonable and this was affecting me the same way those buildings originally had when I didn't like the smell of them or like the looks of them. I didn't like the smell or the looks of the patterns that seemed to move some people into power and some people into non-power that you couldn't see and you couldn't seem to deal with.

I've heard people say that I was a rebel; I wasn't a rebel at all. I just didn't know what to do about it and I dropped out. I had a genius for getting into trouble and then getting out of trouble when I had been displaced and moved into an area where there was something I could get hold of, like a piece of machinery. Anything you could weigh or feel or apply yourself to was fine, but not the dealings with the patterns of arbitrary customs and ways in which people were evaluating what you couldn't be—such as some old lady who didn't like your looks or whatever. At any rate, those were the things I had trouble with.

We all have certain tactical events that happen in our lives. A certain thing happened in my life that was tactically important enough to force me to make utterly vital decisions about my life. I was married during World War I and I was in the Navy. We had a little child born and she caught the flu, then spinal meningitis and then infantile paralysis. We seemed to be able to overcome these attacks more or less. That is, she seemingly was cured though she had many traces of paralysis left. Just before she was four years old she caught pneumonia and died.

During those years with a new life whom we loved so dearly, we were continually frustrated with physical inadequacies, such as the kind of apartment we could have. The physical environment conditions seemed terrible. By this time I had had a great deal of experience in flying and new technology. We didn't speak of "electronics" in those days—we spoke of it as "radio" or whatever it was—but I had had excellent experience in the Navy. I had been sent to the Naval Academy and I knew how to make big ships work. I knew a whole lot about mechanics.

The fact that the housing that we were in was very poor made me feel many times that the conditions which we were operating under were in many ways responsible for our child's sickness. The fact is, I was right because spinal meningitis, infantile paralysis and flu have since been brought under control in recent years. But in those days they were considered lethal and there was nothing you could possibly do about them. Nobody even tried to do anything about them. So Alexandria died just before her fourth birthday.

Before going into the Navy and in and out of Harvard twice I had been in a cotton mill where, as recounted earlier, I finally learned how to put up each type of cotton manufacturing machine. The second time, I went into the packing house business with Armour and Company. I went to work in New York and I worked in twenty-eight branch houses around New York—as I now review psychologically rather than technically.

In those days the packing house was a very tough business, along with all the other businesses, as far as hours went. We began work at 3 a.m. and perhaps were through at 3 p.m. because markets had to open before the rest of society to get foods distributed around the city. I learned a lot about New York on that job. I really knew something about the patterns of society there. From there I went on, as I said, into the Navy and I did well in the Navy. I got all the experience I could want with all the new technology—with the new airplane, the new radio, the new big ships, the new turbines and so on.

After I finished in the Navy I came out and they took me back into Armour and Company again because I had done well. They gave me a very good job; I was made assistant export manager. It was under these conditions that my child went through her sicknesses.

Despite the fact that I was assistant manager of Armour and Company, the pay at that time was $50 a week, which would not be considered very good today. There wasn't much for rent, particularly when we had two trained nurses. We had very tough going. I did well enough at Armour and Company so that an old Navy friend asked me to get out of there and go into a big truck company, and I was equivalent to national sales manager. My father-in-law was an architect and had invented a building structure. I liked this man very much—my own father having died—and I liked the invention he had. It seemed to make sense and I thought it would be useful if somebody did something about it. He didn't seem to know what to do with his invention, so I decided I would do something about it. I learned a great deal about corporations, and I finally organized five small factories around the country making this material.

Those years came immediately after Alexandra died. I worked very hard and I did build 240 small buildings in the eastern United States.

This building system was good for any filler wall. It was a light reinforced concrete structure and it would do for garages and residences or small buildings or filling in the walls of big buildings. During these years I worked terribly hard, but the minute I was through work for the day—I guess I was in a whole lot of pain about our child having died—I would go off and drink all night long and then I'd go to work again. I had enough health somehow to carry on.

Suddenly, I lost control of my company. I'd found myself becoming powerful through it. I met the prominent businessmen and the powerful bankers in the country who were all terribly interested in the idea of building. If you had something that was really going to be a breakthrough in building, you had people coming around looking at it with investment in mind. By 1927, it looked good enough so that others were ambitious enough to try to take it away from me.

I was very unguarded in my own personal life and suddenly I found that I had lost the company. When a person happens to play tough games he may be surprised to find himself not only in an embarrassing position, but also in a difficult position. I was in a difficult position, and just at that moment a new child was born—five years after our first one died. Under those conditions I was utterly broke, in Chicago, and I had lost much vitally important confidence in those whom I had thought to be my friends—and I was in a mess.

But I had had a terrific amount of experience. I came to a point where I found myself saying, "Am I an utter failure? If so, I had better get myself out of the way, so at least my wife and baby can be taken over by my family and they will do the best they can with them. Am I going to be a drag on them, or is there possibly any reason I can see why I ought to go on?"

I was forced by these circumstances to start doing some thinking on my own. It was at that point that I decided that there must be a certain first thought that I would have to go into. What is the first question I could possibly ask myself if I was going to do some thinking?

Standing by the lake on a jump-or-think basis, the very first spontaneous question coming to mind was, "If you put aside everything you've ever been asked to believe and have recourse only to your own experiences do you have any conviction arising from those experiences which either discards or must assume an *a priori* greater intellect than the intellect of man?" The answer was swift and positive. Experience had clearly demonstrated an *a priori* anticipatory and only intellectually apprehendable orderliness of interactive principles operating in the universe into which we are born. These principles are discovered by man but are never invented by man. I said to myself, "I have faith in the integrity of the anticipatory intellectual wisdom which we may call 'God.'" My next question was, "Do I know best or does God know best whether I may be of any value to the integrity of universe?" The answer was, "You don't know and no man knows, but the faith you have just established out of experience imposes recognition of the *a priori* wisdom of the fact of your being." Apparently addressing myself, I said, "You do not have the right to eliminate yourself, you do not belong to you. You belong to the universe. The significance of you will forever remain obscure to you, but you may assume that you are fulfilling your significance if you apply yourself to converting all your experience to highest advantage of others. You and all men are here for the sake of other men."

The next few thoughts had to do with the fact that I knew I did have many more types of experiences than most of my contemporaries, just by the good luck of being fired out of *this* and forced into that pattern. I had certainly had an extraordinarily broad pattern. Furthermore, I had known the most powerful people in the American world. I had dined with several of J.P. Morgan's partners, and I knew Al Capone. I was convinced that people on either side of the track in many situations didn't know or understand one another and yet somehow or other I did seem to know them both, and did seem to understand them both—and they seemed to understand me.

The next thing I concluded was that one reason I was in a great deal of trouble was that I had been extremely accommodating in my willingness to believe what the other fellow asked me to believe. I was over and over again in enormous conflict between what had seemed to be good rules given by one fellow who seemed powerful in his area and another fellow powerful in his area. Each one told me his little rule of thumb for things he thought really were important.

I was at an enormous pinch-point of pain in the great contradiction of many of these dogmas. Obviously, one had not thought the other's problems out well enough. The various kinds of tenets different people had were not comprehensive enough to anticipate the kinds of problems I was going to run into. So, it seemed to me, number one was, whether I liked it or not, that I was going to have to do some of my own thinking.

Having been told when I was young to shut up and learn, this was the first time I could possibly say the thoughts I had held for a long time might be valuable. My father-in-law, who invented the building system, was the first older man I had ever met who told me my own thoughts were valid and that I ought to pay attention to them. He encouraged me to go on with inventions, which I did. I took out quite a few patents. I invented the machinery that went into the manufacture of our product as there was none available to do the job.

I had become so impressed with the idea that I wasn't supposed to know anything that, when I wanted to get somebody to back my idea, I got some mechanic who was my friend, and I told him what my invention was. If he was enthusiastic enough about it, then I told the man with money that the mechanic had invented the thing, because I was pretty sure he trusted the mechanic's judgment. If the mechanic said it was good, then I was hopeful that the man would back it. But I didn't expect anybody to back my ideas. I don't know why I had this feeling, but I just didn't expect anybody to back me.

Anyway, in 1927, I decided that the way I had acquired bad rules and conflicting thoughts was through *words*—when somebody *told* me these things. Therefore, I became very suspicious of words. I said, "Words seem to me to be one of the most extraordinary tool acquisitions of men; I don't think men were born with words, but rather from what I have learned in education and of the educational system I suspect that men have evolved words. There may have been a time when they didn't have words. There are now many more words than there are birds or monkeys. I know of people inventing words, but most of the words were here before me and they are tools. They are obviously tools, and I'm enough of a mechanic to know that you can use tools in the wrong way. It seems to me that the facility with which we can make these sounds, as a parrot can copy a sound, is possibly one of the ways in which the trouble starts."

It was very tough on my wife, but I decided I was going to try to hold a moratorium on speech for myself. So for approximately two years I didn't allow myself to use words. I thought I would see if by doing that I could force myself back to the point where I would really understand what it was I was thinking and be sure that when I made a sound that I really meant to make that sound—that it wasn't something I was parroting and that was just coming off my tongue. I had learned how facile I was at popping off things that someone else gave me.

All this was pretty difficult for my wife because we were in Chicago and didn't have any money. We had an apartment in the least expensive fireproof tenement I could find, because we did have our baby. I really did stop all sounds, and then gradually started wanting to use a particular sound. I was finally pretty sure I would know what the effects would be on my fellow man if I made a particular sound. I wanted to be sure that when I did communicate that I really meant to communicate thusly and that this was *me* communicating and not somebody else.

In this time of isolated thought, I said to myself, "Out of all your experience what kinds of things do you know? For instance, what are the fundamental ways of looking at phenomena?"

I said, "Experiences themselves begin and end. When you go to sleep you can never prove when you wake up that you're the same fellow that went to sleep. You may feel quite a lot like 'him,' but there's no telling whether this is the starting of another kind of dream. At any rate, we certainly do have stop-and-go consciousness, and you might say that there is a finite period of when-I-started-to-think-this-morning and when-I-come-to-a-shut-off-tonight. So that's a package.

"Experience is something that very clearly begins and ends and is finite. Furthermore I don't think that anything I feel or think can possibly come out of anything except experiences. Do I ever think in terms that are not of experience?"

I could never catch myself thinking in terms that did not have something to do with experience. There's nobody around to "mark our papers" in this kind of a situation. So I decided that it was impossible for me to think except in terms of experience. This was my decision.

You might ask, how was my wife eating and how was my baby eating? I decided just to leave that to luck. I didn't know anything else I could do about it. I was confident that the one thing I had to do was think. I was also confident that if I really did think, that there would be a day-to-day survival, provided I really was working hard at this thinking.

If I were just trying to get away with something, I knew what I would do; I would simply jump in the lake. That would be easy and my family would take care of my wife and daughter. The family were not rich but they were comfortable, and would find a way to do something about them. But if I were going to stay around this show at all, whatever I was going to be able to do about it had to be by virtue of my dealing with the only asset I had, and that was my experience. So I had to do something about looking my experience over and though nobody had taught me how to think, I had to learn to think.

"I'm just going to take a chance," I said, "on the idea that if I'm working at it awfully hard—there won't be any margin here; nobody will be able to encourage me—but if we survive at all it will be because one of the rules of Nature is that she permits us each day the integrity of that day's thinking. I must learn to work this way"—and I did.

When I was nine years old the airplane was invented, and it was a very extraordinary kind of experience of fundamental change. I was among the thousands or millions of young boys trying to make some kind of a little device that would fly. And suddenly there it was. When my daughter Allegra was born in 1927 (the year of Lindbergh's flight) I was pushing her baby carriage—in Lincoln Park, in Chicago, because at this time I had started in on a research program. I didn't have any everyday business so I had time to push the baby carriage. The night air mail was not to be flown out of Chicago until two years later, 1929, so it was a rare event indeed that as I pushed my daughter's baby carriage a little light plane flew directly over and I said to myself: Isn't it amazing that, unlike myself, my child is born into a world in whose sky there is an airplane as an *a priori* universal event? How different that universal relationship eventually became, even though we didn't see another airplane there for the next two years. But a quarter of a century later my granddaughter Alexandra was born in New York. She was brought by her parents from the hospital to their apartment in Riverdale, just across from the northern end of Manhattan, which is quite a high point of land. This point was directly in the path of the take-off pattern for both of New York City's major airports, La Guardia and Idlewild,[6] with their westbound American continent flights. The planes were going over frequently, sometimes every few seconds. There was the familiar roar and, on such a high promontory, it was a very important fundamental event to a new life.

The interesting result was that my granddaughter's first word was not "Mummie" or "Daddy," but "air"—short for airplane. She was born in the fall of the year and though her parents had a little balcony on their flat, looking out upon some trees, the fact is that she saw many thousands of airplanes before she ever saw a bird, and the airplane was much more normal in her sky than was a bird. As I realized and thought about this, I wondered if there were other important *a priori* changes, and I looked at the books that were given to my granddaughter. These books were the same kind that I had when I was a child. They were full of donkeys and pigs and goats and cats—but my granddaughter had never seen a donkey or a goat or a horse! They were just as unfamiliar to her as if you showed her microphotography of germs and cold bugs. What had been normal to me was abnormal to her. She was very kind to us about it and was politely amused at the things we were showing her, but they had no relation to reality! This accelerated progression of *a priori* universe alterations is typical of the very swift alteration brought by the industrial equation. Disparity of the successive present generation's norms with those of previous and yet living generations is swiftly widening the gap between aspirations of the old and newer generations.

---

6 Originally New York International Airport it was renamed Idlewild Airport in December 1948. In December 1963, one month after President Kennedy's assassination it was renamed John F. Kennedy International Airport.
http://www.queenspress.com/anniversary2001-jfkairport.htm (accessed July 7, 2009)

To make this disparity and its potential solvability clearer for study, I made some figures that I now find useful in comprehending the enormous velocity of change wrought in our evolving relationship to our respectively altering *a priori* universes. I started with a sphere twenty feet in diameter as a model, was meant to represent the slowest relative rate of negotiability of the earth as gauged by the following calculations.

First, I supposed a path to be put about the earth, there being no dry path around the earth. But I wanted to allow a man to walk around the earth at the rate at which the Army says a man can walk daily, and rest and feed. The twenty-foot globe represented the rate at which he would be able to walk around the earth. Then I gave him a horse. The horse also had to sleep and rest and eat—and, using the Army figures again, I found man can negotiate the earth with a horse so fast that the relative size of the earth is reduced to a ball six feet in diameter.

I gave man a fast-sailing clipper ship and the earth came down to the size of a basketball. When I obtained these figures I realized the historical economic advantage that a man with a ship had over a man with a horse and how much greater advantage they both had had over a man on foot, throughout all history. The clipper ship, of course, was a tool; it was the first really large industrial tool that could not be produced by one man. And it did not have to stop to sleep at night like the horse, but kept on going twenty-four hours, day after day.

Now when you give men railroad trains and steamships, which can negotiate about the same distance daily, because the railroad train has to be replenished very frequently, we find that the relative size of the rate of negotiability of earth comes down to the size of an American baseball. Taking the jet planes, the relative size of man's negotiable earth comes down to the size of a ¾-inch marble. Projecting the present rate of acceleration of commercial air transport speed for just five years and taking the figures now adopted for 1968 by the International Aeronautical Union and the

American Air Force, the relative size of man-negotiable earth will be the size of a pea, and that is the smallest we need now consider, for it will inaugurate an entirely new era of man-around-earth.

Any who have looked at the jet plane schedules know that they can fly to the furthermost points around the earth from where they start in less than 20 hours, so that within the day they can reach the furthermost point of the earth. Projecting for only five years, you find the speed is such that you will be able to leave your home any morning, go to any part of the earth to do your day's work, and come home for dinner. And if our definition of a town is a place where you work and sleep, then in five years from today we can have a one-town world. What has been a theoretical and idealistic concept will be stark reality.

These are the consequences of altering the relationship of man to his environment as uniquely brought about by the industrial equation—an alteration utterly impossible to craft capability. While we in no way deprecate the extraordinary craft accomplishments of men, we do see the great difference in the relative economic and social effectiveness of the industrial and craft tools.

In 1927 I became interested in discovering in what way the enormous advantages of the industrial equation might come to bear directly on man's means of living, even as it had already been brought to bear on mass production of ways of dying. When first employed, this industrial capability was inherently very scarce—scarce in material, ships and men who would know how to employ it. Its scarcity and complexity of tool-up costs made its initial employment almost prohibitive in cost. Only in great national emergencies, underwritten by mortgaging of whole sovereign states, could men muster the capital credit to use the industrial equation. These national emergencies we know were the great moments of war, and under those war conditions high categorical priority of use was given to the application of those scarce industrial capabilities. In setting these priority schedules we hoped to keep the war to be joined as far away from home as possible, because if the joint of war reached home you had lost. Priority of industrial capability went to the establishment and support of the longest ranging arm of highly energized hitting power by the world-integrated network of comprehensively designed industrial capability, which first of all had to produce the navy and transport to rule the seas that covered three-quarters of the earth and divided all lands and therefore controlled the principle of longest arms of hitting power.

By making do with industrially unwanted, low-performance materials, men were able to solve non-war production problems. We praised the many ingenious make-do solutions we gave to home-front problems, quite independent of and out of sight of the alternate solutions we might have made with the industrial equation, were its capabilities grown so plenteous as to make universally possible the using of world resources in the most effective kind of manner.

There are several more fundamental aspects of the industrial equation. We have seen that because the industrial equation involves the enormous pattern of half-way-round-the-world resource-centralizing that by the time we have centralized the resources, the capital expenditure is enormous. In order to justify such enormous anticipatory expenditure, we have to reassociate the centrally dissociated chemical elements in such an effective manner that the temporary products of this activity will be so generally advantageous to the world around man as to win an actual commonwealth of a physically regenerative, or inherently increasing, advantage of man over nature's *a priori* patternings—which means the increasing ability to govern the ceaseless evolution of inter-patterning transformations. Therefore, in order to find the largest number of human beings who can be benefitted by the newly produced patterns we have to go half way round the world again—in all directions.

By discovering the highest possible numbers of users we find means of maximum division of initial costs and sharing of further capital initiations. Therefore, the industrial equation is inherently involved in underwriting two half-way-round-the-world network ventures. Next we see that the energies expended in doing work all around the world are enormous. We therefore begin to comprehend that the ratios of performances per foot pounds of work done by given units of resources invested or expended are vital data to the comprehension and scientifically designed employment of the industrial equation. In the industrial equation performance ratios per weight of products are very important to the success of the world-embracing economy that is being developed.

In our home front buildings, however, we do not think very much about weight. The engineers who must calculate the buildings, in order to implement their architectural designs, are forced to analyze and treat with their weights, but weight is not an original consideration of the patron and architect. Does anybody know what a given building weighs? I once asked an American symposium of architects, including Raymond Hood and Frank Lloyd Wright as well as the architects of Rockefeller Center, the Empire State Building and the Chrysler Building what the different structures they were designing weighed. Clearly, weight was not one of their considerations. They didn't know.

If we ask about the weight of one of our major ships, such as the *Queen Mary,*[7] which is obviously of the magnitude of one of our very large buildings, we find that these kinds of industrial pattern weights are very familiar to the public. Therefore, the fact that weight considerations are not primary in buildings tells us how far building is from the industrial equation. No one should think that because we build big buildings and use some industrial materials that industry has therefore embraced the building arts.

One principle governing the industrial equation is that the tools themselves can be used to make more tools. You can invest the industrial capability exclusively in the regenerative function of greatly enlarging itself. Industry really accomplishes self-lifting

7 The *Queen Mary,* commissioned in 1936, weighs 81,237 gross tons. http://www.20thcenturyliners.com/cl_queenmary.htm (accessed July 6, 2009)

by its own boot-straps. One lathe man can make ten more lathes instead of consumer products, and then ten men can go to work, each making ten more lathes, and each one can be a better lathe than the one before. Thus the whole world's overall tool capability is swiftly regenerated toward comprehensive and plenteous capacity.

Another aspect of the industrial equation is that it gradually discerns the various functions of humans and differentiates those functions out, developing tools which can carry out those functions. We find that industrialization is inevitably headed towards automation, that is towards disenfranchisement of man as a physical machine. The concepts of Karl Marx are typical of the erroneous and inadequate way in which men at first pondered the industrial equation. They thought of man chained to the machines and grievously exploited by the machine owners. With automation, an increasing economic reality, we now see that the industrial equation was all the time heading toward complete elimination of man as a worker. The industrial equation will bring about a condition where, within a century the word "worker" will have no current meaning. It will be something you will have to look up in an early twentieth-century dictionary.

How, then, does the industrial equation go on? What is man's relationship to it? The answer is that the larger the number served by the industrial equation, the more the unit costs are lowered and the more universally its regenerative pattern stimulations become distributed. This is to say that the greater the number of consumers, the more successful is the industrial equation. The more people served, the more regenerative industrialization becomes. Industrial equation works toward man having infinite significance in the universe as a regenerative consumer.

As a fundamental result at our present moment in history, men are becoming very swiftly disemployed as physical workers. On the other hand, men are now swelling the ranks of intellectually preoccupied experimentalists in scientific and industrial research and development and are getting ready for the launching of the next wave of evolutionary transformations. Men are increasingly concerned with greater anticipatory design of the use of the world-around network of industrial capabilities. Even unwittingly men are accelerating their capability to render the world's total inventory of resources adequate to the comprehensively advancing needs and growth advantage of all men.

I will cite one more pattern governing industrialization as it comes finally to bear upon the building arts. The kind of patterns that we are reviewing are obviously patterns that only come into apprehension, comprehension and reviewability through time and increasing inventories of the integrated experiences of all men. These are not patterns which were discoverable in advance by men.

In architectural circles we frequently speak of buildings as environmental controls, or the local controlling of energetic patternings of the universal manifold of high and low frequency events; we have local environmental controls on the land which we call buildings; we have environmental controls on the sea which we call ships; we have environmental controls in the skies which we call airplanes. These are each and all vessels of preferred pattern regeneration.

The environmental controls on the land are installed in the crystalline chemical structures' state. Environmental controls on the sea are installed in the chemical structures' liquid state and the environmental controls of the sky are installed in the chemical structures' gaseous state. In the crystalline state, the amount of energy necessary to disturb the chemical structures is enormous. The amount of energy necessary to disturb liquid phase chemical structures is but a small fraction of that necessary to disturb crystalline structures. The amount of energy necessary to the pattern disturbance of the gaseous phase of chemical structures is but a small fraction of the amount necessary to the disturbance of the liquid phases of chemical structures. Einstein's equation $E=MC^2$ directly governs these relationships. In a universe of energy in which no energy is created nor energy lost, the number of times that Nature has enough energy concentration to disturb the crystalline state at any one locality in the universe is relatively infrequent. The number of times the universe has energy available locally to disturb the liquid structure states is very much more frequent.

Even more often there are enough energies available locally to bring about very large disturbances of the gaseous states. If men are going to build a structure on the land as a local energetic environmental control (knowing the probability of an earthquake at any one point is so low that men for many generations were unaware of its even being a possibility) they certainly would hope to build in between the earthquakes. The number of times floods might occur is much more frequent but it is considered worth while, because the alluvial plain is so rich the inhabitants would rather climb to the high land as the floods occur and go back to the low land when the floods receded. The number of times that there are avalanches and fires are relatively few, so people build upon the crystalline state, oblivious to the infrequent challenges of earthquakes, hurricanes, floods, avalanches and so forth. They were more concerned with building bulky, inert fortresses which, because of the solidity of the earth, seemed to rest on top of the earth without sinking into it as men developed building arts.

On the sea we are immediately faced with flood all the time, and the best thing to do is to stay on top of it. And when we try to discover how to float, we find that stones don't but wood does. Thus men discovered floatability millenniums and millenniums ago. In dealing by designed actions with controlled environments suitable to the liquid state, men are normally faced with this floatability as a basic requirement, but are also faced with very frequent seaquakes. We probably have seaquakes every day in which the size of the waves will be greater than those of the earthquake. Therefore, we have to design for seaquakes or we won't stay on top of the water. Every time the great seas come combing over and smashing down on our decks, the actual tonnages involved are quite equal to the tonnages of the impact of an avalanche.

When controlling environment on the liquid state we also have to design for hurricanes because in fact upon the sea we are going to exploit the hurricanes to drive our ships. In ships we must design directly for structural behavior superior to all these very hostile behaviors of Nature, specifically regarding the foot-pound energies of Nature's limit behaviors. Once we have learned how ferocious Nature may be, then we ask: Is it worth while going into this very unfriendly, energetic world of the sea? We discover it is, first, because of those resources that occur remotely all around the world, and second, because of the fact that you can float such enormous loads of resources from here to there as to completely outclass the small loads that you can carry on your back or on the backs of animals. Therefore, the ships are potentially very worth while, and in order to make the ship realistically very worth while you have to learn how to establish ratios of preferable investments of the total floatability, how much is to be assigned to the cargo and how much is assigned toward each of the structural capabilities required to meet these enormous stresses, corrosive forces, etc.

Rationing of the performances per pounds per functions became the very essence of shipbuilding design, whereas such ratios were never thought of in respect to building environment controls upon the crystalline structured land. In fact, the first great buildings were only for fortresses in which weight was desired. They were preceded by nature's own caves, which were occupied and which were later contrived as local modifications of the solid earth and not thought of as separate buildings.

When we go into the air with man-designed environmental controls, we come into conditions where there is no floatability. To stay in the air at all, we have to stay there on sheer intellectual capability. We get out into the sky and stay there by integrating the experience of all men and by faithful consideration of the factors and measurements of the experiences. You cannot stay out there on a myth. First we must start flying at greater than hurricane speed. Hurricane speed is stalling speed, so the hurricane speed becomes minimum normal and in our modern airships we go into six, sometimes eight times hurricane velocities as a normal condition of environmental control designing.

Due to large-size disturbances of the air by very small amounts of energy, even the sun radiation reflecting from the surface of a small white glistening roof will bring about a spirally rising thermal column of air rising hundreds of feet, sometimes a mile high, into the air. In a plurality of these great thermals we get enormous air waves which might properly be called airquakes. The airquakes are enormous in size and of such high frequency as to be almost continuous.

When a great airliner moving along at five times hurricane speed runs into one of these thermals and rises and drops hundreds of feet, the physical dimensions and stresses involved are precisely those of taking the *Queen Mary* over Niagara Falls at full speed and doing it so capably that the passengers believe it's only a "little bump."

It is very important to realize the magnitude which man's scientific and technical capability has really reached. In both the airframe and power plant phases of industry today man has really reached astronomically augmented degrees of new advantage in respect to his ability to swiftly alter his *a priori* physical environmental patterning. When we learned of Sputnik's success, we were thereby informed of the arrival of the inter-continental missile rocket. With it, the airplane, which in the first decade of this century became the longest arm of striking power, was displaced as the number one weapon. For fifty years the aircraft had enjoyed all highest priorities of access to scientific industrial capabilities. So complex and swiftly evolving was the airframe phase of the industrial equation that its underwriting could only be financed by major nations and only under the mandate of omni-survival emergency anticipations. So great have been the nationally subsidized underwritings of the airframe phase of man's acquisition of the industrial equation capabilities that the fifty years of man-piloted aircraft development involved a total of international expenditure in the range of three trillion dollars, approximately one hundred times the value of all the gold in the world. It was an over-all undertaking whose magnitude could only be visible in retrospect, and as astronomically invisible to yesterday's private finance capital capabilities as was atomic power to optical foresight.

With the airplane industry rendered suddenly obsolete as the premier long-range, highest velocity, highest energy packing and hitting power—the great national subsidy of the aircraft industry automatically relinquished its half century of popular mandate support as the national emergency-anticipating defense measure. This obsolescence became simultaneous in all the major industrial initiative-competing nations. The aircraft industry should not be looked upon as one industry amongst a myriad of other independent industries. It should be regarded as the total industrial equation, accredited and operating at the highest level of historically augmented and integrated capability. In the aircraft phase of industry, the relative efficiencies of performance realizations as ratioed to invested resources are, for instance, ten-fold the efficiency realized when the industrial equation is operating at the automobile manufacturing level of comprehensive policy integrity. Shorn of its half century of vital subsidy—as a child grown to manhood and at full stature of capability is divested of further parental support—the aircraft phase of industry will now have to employ its superior degrees of capability with even greater discretion and comprehensive usefulness than under its bureaucratic governance. With its sudden reorientations first labeled recession, this release of a ten-fold greater capability into the home front undertakings will bring about manifold dislocations of the lower order of efficiency phases of industry—but nowhere will its world-around capabilities be more dramatically applied than to the long-time anti-priority area of the comprehensive building arts and to the swift provision of world-around accommodation of the new air-ocean, world-flown embracement of whole earth by all men—in their frequency-modulated, therefore approximately invisible, one-town world of 1968 realization.

In 1927 I undertook a thirty-year series of experimentations, not only in the direction of ultimate participation of landed environment controlling in the most advanced capabilities of industry, but also in relation to the individual and his functioning, and in relation to the questions of whether and how he can take the initiative in regard to various challenges. In searching for the functioning capabilities of the individual in the industrial equation evolution I saw myself as "any typical, fairly healthy individual." What impressed me about me in making the experiment with me was that I was so very average. I can say that whatever results are now subject to inventory, are the results of my basic assumption of "average individual capabilities" at the outset. I knew when I started in 1927 that I could not jump very high and I could not swim very fast and I hadn't earned the best marks in the class. Inasmuch as I was interested in what the average individual could do, I was a very good case for experimentation.

There was one *a priori* requirement to this third-of-a-century experiment, that I adopted to give it a cleanly controlled opportunity of producing unprejudiced results. I must forsake altogether the idea of priority of the necessity to earn a living. When I was very young my two grandmothers told me about the Golden Rule, and as a young man of four I thought it was a very excellent rule and I admired the idea. I had a shock later on when I joined the Navy, where it was suggested that this might not be the operating rule of the seafaring people. Later an uncle took me aside and said, "Young man, I am sorry to have to tell you that about a hundred and fifty years ago we had scientific proof that there is not enough to go around. ... and so it must be you or the other fellow and it must be your family or the other fellow's. Really, it's very tough, but Malthus and Darwin gave very clear proof of these facts. So I suggest that you learn how to acquire yours quickly and incisively and then get around to applying the Golden Rule as far as is expedient."

Even if born with an adequate income almost all of us are faced with the necessity of earning ourselves a living. I have visited many universities, and certainly the idea seems universal that the boys are preparing themselves first of all to be able to earn a living, hopefully within an area that is interesting to them. They hope they'll earn a good enough living and obtain early security so they may have time to do the things they would really like to do all the time.

Now, in 1927, when our daughter Allegra was born, we had no money, and obviously under those conditions I ought to have gone out to earn a living. But it was just at this moment that the kind of picture I have been describing was looming before me and I didn't see how I could escape doing something about it. I first tried to interest people I thought were much more capable than myself in respect to the problem, but I found none who were interested in spending the rest of their years on it. It seemed to me from my industrial lag studies it was a problem that was going to take a minimum of twenty-five years to bring into useful scientific treatability. So the question was: How could I peel off and forget about earning a living? I did finally detach myself from conventional preoccupation with living security, but I did not undertake this research and development as an idealist nor, I hope, as a crank. My conviction grew out of my discovery of the comprehensive validity and vitality of the industrial equation and the operative principles apparently governing its growth transcendentally beyond any directed ambitions of men.

I was impressed with the fact that in the primarily agricultural and craft eras the individuals in the little towns bartered directly with one another to arrange for their mutual security. One was a shoemaker, the other was growing potatoes, and so forth; each one produced more of his products than he could use personally and exchanged his surpluses with the other fellows. A man then bargained at 180° with the man in front of him. Each made his own deals and organized his comprehensive security within the visible horizon.

However, in the industrial equations, I saw the man standing or sitting at his production station and the nuts or bolts the machine was making at his station were not going off at 180°, but were going off sideways at 90° to his line of sight. I saw that it was futile for him to fill his pocket with nuts or bolts to exchange with the hamburger man. The industrial products tended to go off around the world until the nuts and bolts, for instance, each arrived in their respective logical relationship in larger industrial organisms, along with the myriad of other kinds of components; and finally some nuts and bolts would come back to that machine operator, but only as an organized technical complex such as an automobile or water pump or whatever it might be. His basic security was obtained through the increasing capability of all society, thus comprehensively advantaged by the universal tool network.

It occurred to me that it could also be true in the industrial equation that security need not be a local, 180° negotiation, but an around-the-world circuit-closing principle. If this were so it could also be true that if your experience actually discerned an industrial gap-closing task that needed your particular experienced attention, and no patron of the task could be discovered who was inherently concerned with such tasks, you might then assume you were being directly challenged by natural evolutionary process with doing something about that gap, which challenge and response were no more mystical than the spontaneous dodging from under a falling tree. It might prove to be economically feasible for the individual to apply himself to such gap-filling functions whose developed solution might then go multi-directionally around the world to find its right places in the network of integrating capabilities. Thus, the wealth advantage of man might be comprehensively increased and the gap-filling individual might find himself surviving by all manner of indirect means as integral functioning of the larger network equations.

So it was with the hope of discovering as soon as possible whether that really was true or not that I decided, in 1927, to forget forever the idea that I ought to earn a living. My wife really bore the brunt of that decision. But as months and years were passed safely, I watched young men become interested in my kind of research and development advantages and results. The minute you were not concerned with earning a living and really tackled problem after problem that the other fellow was not tackling, there proved to be a wealth of solvable problems. In fact the whole mass of problems that are worth tackling is so great that any average individual who goes into that kind of a paradise wilderness garden ought to make very good progress. If I have made progress that is mildly notable it is only because I walked into a vast, unattended, potential harvest.

Year after year I saw young men become fascinated with those potentials I was dealing with, and then suddenly say to me, "I'm sorry, but I have to earn a living–I'm different from you, I've got a wife and child. I'm sorry to have to quit you." Today I am still engaged in this experiment and while I have no right to certify that others may be able to survive working upon these same premises, the fact is that my family and I have weathered more than thirty-five years in search and development relating directly to the application of the industrial equation to shelter and shelter mechanics and their design, production and distribution.

We cannot say that this survival success is not coincidence, but I personally think it would be extravagant to call it coincidence. I think that the principle of indirect industrial realization of survival advantage is as well proven by my experience as is the indirect result of general good health that comes of an integration of a myriad of individual self-disciplines. I am not afraid to suggest to a young man today that it is possible to forget altogether about the priority concept of earning a living.

I had the great honor of meeting Dr. Jonas Salk not long after his vaccines had been acknowledged in America as providing immunity to the vast majority of infantile paralysis exposures. Dr. Salk said, "I've always felt that those dymaxion gadgets—cars, houses, maps, etc.—were only incidental to what you really are interested in. Could you tell me what your work is?" I said, "Yes, I've been thinking about that definition for a long time. I've been engaged in what I call *comprehensive anticipatory design science.*" And Dr. Salk said, "That's very interesting, because that's a description of my work too."

That statement by Dr. Salk fascinated me because I have long felt that (whereas medical doctors were at first accredited by society only when men were in trouble, and that whereas cures were difficult, doctors long ago discovered the excellent results to be obtained by anticipatory laboratory research that led to prevention as far more comprehensively effective than cures, and thought that whereas doctors are concerned with the internal organism of man) industrialization might be thought of accurately as the external organism of man. Man's external disorders could best be treated, therefore, not as local curative techniques but as comprehensive laboratory search and research leading to universally effective anticipatory prevention of maladies of the industrial organic evolutionary growth by appropriate comprehensive anticipatory design science.

Comprehensive anticipatory design science assumes that the client knows absolutely nothing about what he needs or what should be done about it. There is a word which I would like to introduce into our thinking, and that is *synergy.* Now the word synergy is as old as the word energy. By energy we mean the differentiated-out local behaviors of comprehensive universe or Nature, for instance as gravity or as optics. By synergy we mean the integrated behaviors of nature, and synergy is said to be *"behavior of a whole system unpredicted by the behavior of its components or any sub-assembly of its components."*

Men do not know the word synergy because they do not tend to need the word in their thinking patterns. Behaviors of whole systems, unpredicted by behaviors of their parts, seem to our accepted logic to be a sort of mystical concept. We tend to think in the terms of our elementary strategy of education, where we start by dealing with our local parts and learning how to handle these parts well. Because of our local elemental focus we tend to think it is logical to say that "a chain is no stronger than its weakest link"—which immediately is thrown out of validity when we first join the other end of the chain back on itself. When we break the weakest link there is still only one piece of chain and we are mildly confounded in our statement. "Well, chains are not supposed to be linked together at both ends," and the reason we say that is because we inherited the Greek concepts of linear and plane geometry as elementary and later those of solid and spherical geometry as "advanced."

The exclusively local aspect of plane geometry imposed the concept of an infinite surface and the infinite line as logical to the then-prevalent belief that the earth was flat and infinite—*ergo,* all "straight lines" were open-ended, or infinite. That is why we think a chain ought to be just an infinite line. However, in Nature all the lines are completely curved and all chains do eventually return upon themselves. This fact is reflected in, for instance, the very essence of metallurgical structuring.

Are there, in nature, behaviors of whole systems unpredicted by the parts? This is exactly what the chemist has discovered to be true. Moreover, he had discovered that, contrary to his elementary kind of experience at school, he did not come into the chemical laboratory and find a soda fountain with spigots for hydrogen and oxygen and so forth with which you mix up the universe as you go, and then begin to make it work. He found the universe already in complex working order. And every time he partially separated out any of the elements from the others, he always discovered that the behaviors of the localized elements never accounted for the associated behavior of the *a priori* complexes.

The chemist is thoroughly familiar with the word synergy, which is the only word in the dictionary for this omnioperative behavior of universe. Synergy is the essence of those great changes of man in respect to his *a priori* environment. The essence of the evolutionary realization of the jet airship is chrome nickel steel, by virtue of which the enormous concentrational energies could be released as heat, which would have destroyed engines of any pre-chrome nickel steel production. Because of the strength of chrome nickel steel, even under conditions of enormous heat, it prevents the destruction of the structural design integrity of the jet engine, which could then translate its thrust to the ship. And chrome nickel steel is very typical of synergy.

The predominant constituents of chrome nickel steel—the primary element components, iron, nickel, and chromium, and their tensile strengths per square inch of cross section—are their primary criteria of relative strength. Taken individually the chrome, nickel and iron square-inch sectional capabilities are in the approximate range of 70,000, 80,000 and 60,000 p.s.i. tensile strength respectively. In association, chrome nickel steel is a pattern, a constellation of behaviors dictated by Nature, not by man, and as a chrome nickel steel casting we will often realize 300,000 p.s.i. tensile strength, which is then five times as strong as its weakest elemental link and four times as strong as its strongest link.

Is this a mystical behavior or can we account for it? We discover of course that we can account for it in a logical manner. We knew, regarding organics in the previous century, that all the organic structures were tetrahedronally configured. Since 1933, we have also learned that all our inorganic structures are tetrahedronally configured.

3 Margaret Fuller's Prophecy

I am including here a quotation from my great aunt, Margaret Fuller. This quotation is important today, when considered in the light of C. P. Snow's book, *Two Cultures*. His two cultures are those of the scientists and the literary intellectuals, whose respective languages and interests in the last century and a half have pulled so far apart as to have created a chasm. Snow says that this is partially due to the fact that the intellectual writers of the early nineteenth century not only failed to comprehend the significance of industrialization but that its individual literary stars abhorred industrialization's every symptom. This occurred despite the fact that The Royal Society of Arts was formed in England in the 1750s by the literary intellectuals and learned scientists for the very purpose of anticipating and forestalling this dichotomy. Snow says that Emerson and Thoreau in America were typical of intellectuals with aversion to industrialization, and their popularity increased the academic divide between the literary and the scientific.

Margaret Fuller was co-founder with Emerson of *Dial* magazine, which she undertook as the first publishing medium to present the work of Emerson. She was also the first publisher of Thoreau's work and he, Emerson, and other *literati* of the time

---

Published by Buckminster Fuller in his Shelter Magazine in November 1932, and issued four days before the presidential election during which Franklin D. Roosevelt was first elected President and instituted the New Deal.

were her great friends. She alone seems not only to have been aware of the looming significance of industrialization, but also to have hailed and welcomed it as it came from England to impinge upon America.

In reading Margaret's essay, it should be remembered that two years before it was written she had spent the summer with the Indians outside Fort Dearborn, which had been established seven years earlier. She had reached that present site of Chicago via the sailing ships on the Great Lakes, and stage coaches. The telegraph had been invented a few years earlier, and at the time Margaret wrote her essay in 1842, the only railroads in America were the short twenty-mile line between Schenectady and Albany and the forty-mile track between Baltimore and Washington. There was nothing in the scene of her time that obviously foretold her "complete linking together of the great continent of America by the telegraph and railroad." Very little of America was as yet within the "United States." Not only did Margaret envision the coming and the important significance of industrialization, but she stated also the realization that it would bring a great cross-breeding of man. She foresaw the necessity for the public to serve as sole patron of mass production and she predicted the public's ripening ability to appreciate its responsibility to the regenerative functioning of the individual artists.

Some may think it paradoxical that the work of Emerson, Thoreau, Hawthorne and Poe has been acclaimed by history (though these writers were antipathetic to the subsequently realized evolution of man), while Margaret Fuller's name has remained obscure. In fact, her work has remained so obscure that C. P. Snow and his audiences are unaware of the extraordinary vision and cordiality to industrialization in America she had more than a century ago. Margaret Fuller, however, is well known academically in America. Her life and work is one of the leading thesis subjects for graduate school candidates for Master's degrees in early American literature.

When Horace Greeley founded what is now the *New York Herald Tribune,* in April 1841, he asked Margaret Fuller to be his literary critic. Heywood Broun, one of her many successors as literary critic of the *Tribune,* said almost a century later, "This was the first and last time a literary critic was regularly 'frontpaged.'" Because Margaret was devastatingly critical of popular American writers and poets who produced what would be today classified as "saccharine corn" imitations of English authors and pursued a far-sighted vision of an as-yet-gestating intellectual conceptioning for America's role in history, she lost her frontpage battle to establish the primacy of the regenerative individual to industrialization and the fundamental economic responsibilities of an industrially-instrumented society to its individual conceptual pioneers as the prime commonwealth initiators and augmentors.

Margaret Fuller's 1842 Prediction [8]

Some thinkers may object to this essay that we are about to write of that which has as yet no existence.

For it does not follow because many books are written by persons born in America that there exists an American literature. Books which imitate or represent the thoughts and life of Europe do not constitute an American literature. Before such can exist, an original idea must animate this nation and fresh currents of life must call into life fresh thoughts along its shores....

That such a genius is to rise and work in this hemisphere we are confident; equally so that scarce the first faint streaks of that day's dawn are yet visible. It is sad for those that foresee, to know they may not live to share its glories, yet it is sweet, too, to know that every act and word, uttered in the light of that foresight, may tend to hasten or ennoble its fulfillment.

---

8 Excerpted from her *American Literature; Its Position in the Present Time, and Prospects for the Future,* originally published in 1846 in *Papers on Literature and Art* (New York, 1846).

That day will not rise till the fusion of races among us is more complete. It will not rise till this nation shall attain sufficient moral and intellectual dignity to prize moral and intellectual no less highly than political freedom, nor till the physical resources of the country being explored, all its regions studded with towns, broken by the plow, netted together by railways and telegraph lines, and talent shall be left at leisure to turn its energies upon the higher department of man's existence. Nor then shall it be seen till from the leisurely and yearning soul of that riper time national ideas shall take birth, ideas craving to be clothed in a thousand fresh and original forms.

Without such ideas all attempts to construct a national literature must end in abortions like the monster of Frankenstein, things with forms, and the instincts of forms, but soulless, and therefore revolting. We cannot have expression till there is something to be expressed.

The symptoms of such a birth may be seen in a longing felt here and there for the sustenance of such ideas. At present, it shows itself, where felt, in sympathy with the prevalent tone of society, by attempts at external action, such as are classed under the head of social reform. But it needs to go deeper before we can have poets, needs to penetrate beneath the springs of action, to stir and remake the soil as by the action of fire.

Another symptom is the need felt by individuals of being even sternly sincere. This is the one great means by which alone progress can be essentially furthered. Truth is the nursing mother of genius. No man can be absolutely true to himself, eschewing cant, compromise, servile imitation, and complaisance, without becoming original, for there is in every creature a fountain of life which, if not choked back by stones and other dead rubbish, will create a fresh atmosphere, and bring to life fresh beauty. And it is the same with the nation as with the individual man.

The best work we do for the future is by such truth. By use of that, in whatever way, we harrow the soil and lay it open to the sun and air. The winds from all quarters of the globe bring seed enough, and there is nothing wanting but preparation of the soil, and freedom in the atmosphere, for ripening of a new and golden harvest.

We are sad that we cannot be present at the gathering in of this harvest. And yet we are joyous, too, when we think that, though our name may not be writ on the pillar of our country's fame, we can really do far more toward rearing it than those who come at a later period and to a seemingly fairer task. Now, the humblest effort, made in a noble spirit, and with religious hope, cannot fail to be even infinitely useful. Whether we introduce some noble model from another time and clime, to encourage aspiration in our own, or cheer into blossom the simplest wood-flower that ever rose from the earth, moved by the genuine impulse to grow, independent of the lures of money or celebrity; whether we speak boldly when fear or doubt keep others silent, or refuse to swell the popular cry upon an unworthy occasion, the spirit of truth, purely worshipped, shall turn our acts and forbearances alike to profit, informing them with oracles which the latest time shall bless.

Under present circumstances the amount of talent and labor given to writing ought to surprise us. Literature is in this dim and struggling state, and its pecuniary results exceedingly pitiful. From many well-known causes it is impossible for ninety-nine out of the hundred, who wish to use the pen, to ransom, by its use, the time they need. This state of things will have to be changed in some way. No man of genius writes for money; but it is essential to the free use of his powers, that he should be able to disembarrass his life from care and perplexity. This is very difficult here; and the state of things gets worse and worse, as less and less is offered in pecuniary meed for works demanding great devotion of time and labor (to say nothing of the ether engaged) and the publisher, obliged to regard the transaction as a matter of business, demands of the author to give him only what will find an immediate market, for he cannot afford to take anything else. This will not do! When an immortal poet was secure only of a few copyists to circulate his works, there were princes and nobles to patronize literature and the arts. Here is only the public, and *the public must learn how to cherish the nobler and rarer plants, and to plant the aloe, able to wait a hundred years for its bloom,* or its garden will contain, presently, nothing but potatoes and potherbs.

4 The Comprehensive Man

Education

Alfred North Whitehead, in a pre-World War I statement on education, noted that the processes of education were increasing the numbers and sizes of graduate schools and were at the same time selecting students of highest intellectual promise to enter into those postgraduate schools and thereafter into careers of expertness in specialized fields.

He then said this process would develop increasing numbers of exceptionally capable men as brightly shining stars in very special and remote parts of Heaven—but unworldly stars, precisely because as stars they would be "out of this world."

Whitehead went on to say that, whereas every action has its reaction, such selecting of the intellectually strong men for specialization must of necessity leave a weaker intellectual residue upon which would fall the task of coordinating the everyday affairs of man. The swiftly multiplying inventory of special capability potentials produced by the specialists would be harvestable only to the lesser limit of discernment and comprehension of the residual lower-mentality integrators of mundane affairs, regardless of how charming, loving, courageous, energetic or cunning the latter might be.

January 1959. Fuller's revision of a talk given to the faculty of the School of Architecture and Allied Arts at the University of Oregon. Published in the *Northwest Review*, Spring 1959.

Whitehead then foresaw an ultimate crisis in our society, wherein the people who were responsible for putting things together (though themselves subjected to improved educational techniques), would have fallen so relatively far behind the more swiftly regenerative reaches of the specialists in exquisite knowledge extension, as to be practically incapable of comprehending the integrable significance of the specialized findings. Thus, the integrators would be unable to coordinate and realize the commonwealth potentials opened up by the differentiators. Our society would come to technical and economic stalemate in the face of magnificent potential.

Quite possibly we have reached that era which might be properly indentified as "Whitehead's dilemma." Our scientists are worrying about the exclusively negative and possibly lethal uses of their various special discoveries. At the same time we find society unable to translate the scientific discoveries into realistic magnitudes of comprehensive commonwealth advantage. The macro- and micro-reaches of the physical universe, whose energy may neither be created nor lost, have been so successfully tapped by the scientists that the approximately unlimited energies of a universe capable of doing realistically unlimited work, thus of producing realistically unlimited wealth, now need only their social comprehension and orderly social initiatives for turning on the valves of unlimited wealth for all humanity. It is precisely the educated social comprehension and self-disciplined orderliness of coordinate initiative which are lacking. Only the profound inertia of ignorance, common to all of man's everyday preoccupations, and to all of his as-yet-known and employable means of solving problems by private or public enterprise (and by any and all of his political and cultural systems in existence around the world), now withholds the practical realization of successful physical survival of all of humanity, all at higher standards of living than have as yet been conceived by any man. It is indeed a comprehensive educational problem.

In unique exception to the over-all educational evolution depicted by Whitehead, there are a few educational undertakings of the last century that select the most promising students for advanced integrative capability. Notable among these exceptions have been architecture, international law and military logistics, particularly world-ocean logistics. But architecture since 1500 (Leonardo's time) has functioned only as an accessory after the fact of successful commerce and industry enterprise, which latter were entered into without benefit of architects in their initial conceiving. Comprehensive world-ocean logistical capability was dropped from the curriculum of naval establishments in World War I, when the autonomy of ships' captains and admirals vanished with the introduction of radio communication. This leaves only the international lawyers and hot- and cold-war militarists as halfway specialists exploiting extreme scientific specialists, while wrestling unilaterally with the comprehensive survival-destruction paradox and accelerating tempo of exclusively negative crises.

For many years I have had the intuition that in the world of architecture there lies the possibility of the development of brilliantly educated men capable of a generalized comprehensive anticipatory science of design, which both can and may be as effective in bringing about man's general well being as specialized education has been in bringing about only isolated successes within an otherwise general environment of chaotic dismay, frustration and high-frequency failures. I have believed that such a generalized architectural education could be accomplished by employing the comprehensive-academic and educational strategy exclusively reserved, prior to World War I, for the few most promising students found among the Naval Academy's midshipmen, and which, since World War I, has been nonexistent as an educational strategy. Such an academic and postgraduate strategy involves the working assumption that the individuals concerned may at some moment in their lives be confronted with the opportunity of taking the supreme initiative in the conscious and comprehensive formulation of mankind's critical participation in universal evolution.

Directions for the Student

I have often urged boys graduating in architecture to go into the aircraft industry, not just to learn the stress-analysis which they would immediately be taught, but, if possible, to get into production engineering and to learn about the whole family of tools and the chemistries, the alloys—all the strategies of very advanced technology. In other words, these advanced aircraft industry tools would be the builders' tools of our day, suitable to these innate integrators who really want to know what they can do in our moment of history.

Then, too, I have urged star architectural graduates to go into other economic experiences tending to give them a sense of world-around distribution patterning and the very high-speed deliveries with air transport. I have urged them to get experience in any and all patterns related to the whole world and to the most advanced tools. Particularly, I have urged them to learn what they can of chemistry, for I feel that chemistry is basic structure, *ergo* architecture. I really am surprised to find at the architectural schools that, despite the prevalent intuition that one certainly ought to know a lot about technology to be a good architect, the curricula tendency established to gratify that intuition is only to give much more mathematics. For instance, at M.I.T. architectural students do not have to take chemistry after their first year but do have to take five years of calculus, and I don't think any of those students after graduation ever again use the calculus. Architectural students are taught about a few dozen natural and so-called artificial materials, which are only the superficially identifying aspects of invisible chemical structuring.

With World War I, the great chemical revolution brought to availability a quarter of a million chemical substances. All of those substances were comprised of the ninety-two regenerative chemical elements. They were complex, structural behaviors permitted by Nature. They were not Nature substitutes, though many were called substitutes. Again, in World War II, when the large resource mobilization program started, it was found that the inventory of chemical substances known to man had passed two million in number. But many of these substances were as yet called "substitutes" in political, administrative and military Washington. Even today, despite interim development of fundamental knowledge to the contrary, we speak erroneously of "artificial" materials, "synthetics," and so forth. The basis for this erroneous terminology is the notion that Nature has certain things which we call natural, and everything else is "man-made," ergo artificial. But what one learns in chemistry is that Nature wrote all the rules of structuring; man does not invent chemical structuring rules; he only discovers the rules. All the chemist can do is to find out what Nature permits, and any substances that are thus developed or discovered are inherently *natural*. It is very important to remember that.

The Myth of Industrial Design

The name "industrial designer" was invented about 1926 by the professional advertising company forefathers of what is now known as "Madison Avenue" on behalf of large banking groups investing in the automobile industry. The banking groups were getting together all the machine tools, production tools, jigs, fixtures and buildings in Detroit that had originally belonged to 125 starters of the automobile companies' roster. The idea was that if they put enough tools together they might reach the point where the production capacity would be of adequate magnitude to sustain courting of the mass market price. By 1926, Wall Streeters had learned, after billions of dollars of trial and error failures of the early 1920s, the fact that 135,000 cars a year by any one company was the minimum production rate required to amortize capital investment and make a sustaining profit.

The bankers dismissed from Detroit all the inventors of automobiles. They didn't want any more inventing of automobiles. They wanted only economical production of transportation units from those tools which themselves were immune to the devastation of dollar bankruptcy. But the big investment banking houses knew that the American public had learned to go to automobile shows annually to see the new cars, and saw in the swift advance of automobile inventiveness that a new era of man was in the making. There was something emotionally essential and satisfying to the American in those new cars. The cars embodied whole constellations of ingenuity and invention and the users learned intimately about the parts. They understood thoroughly by direct experimentation regarding the significance of seven main bearings as against four; they knew because they were both the active laboratory workers and the underwriters of the costs. They could adjust their own carburetors and grind their own valves. The public was intimate not only with the cars but also with the methods used in making them. So the question the banking houses had to face was, "What are you going to do about the American public's desire to have a *new* car each year, now that the inventors have been kicked out of Detroit and production men put in as the managing authority?"

The pre-Madison Avenue public mind-molders then said, "This is very easy; there's a new invention called the airbrush. We will use it in our advertising work. Pictures of the automobiles are going to appear to be advanced—but as pure camouflage. The changes will be as superficial as fashion changes, but people will think they are looking at a new car. The public has now an appetite-momentum for automobiles, so all that is needed from here on in is a familiar lure for his conditioned reflex. This superficial rather than fundamental design function will be effected by a new industrial showman to be called an *industrial designer*."

This was the beginning of the greatest betrayal of mass communication integrity in our era of history. Progressively rationalized, it seemed to justify every manner of mass self-deceit of world peoples by their own self-ventriloquized corruption of their democratically tried and accepted institutions and their conventionalized characteristics and symbolic abstract beings. We are now paying the price. We have learned to kid ourselves in so complete a manner that we are liable to have a great economic bust—led by 400-horsepower, two-and-a-half ton chariots of guaranteed "supreme distinction." The self-deceit which we have practiced may cost democracy a major cold war defeat falsely to be charged to democracy's bamboozled account.

Obviously, I think industrial design is a very tarnished affair. I'm terribly sorry that many young students, fooled by the words "industry" and "design" (which independently are healthy words), think that because the words have been linked and there is a course called "Industrial Design," they are going to learn something about the fundamentals of design initiation in industry. I assure you that no aircraft company will let an industrial designer through its engineering front door. Industrial designers are considered to be pure interior and exterior decorators. And yet, I've listened to industrial designers assert that they designed the steamship, *United States*. If you were to exhibit schematically all the items that the industrial designers created for the *United States,* you would have sailing down New York Harbor an array of window curtains, chairs, paint clouds and bric-a-brac floating in space, with nothing really to hold it all together. To assert that these men designed the *United States* could not have been more dishonest.

Naval architects designed that ship—naval architects of extraordinary capability. No industrial designer was allowed near until the ship was built. The industrial designers were not even allowed to touch the exterior color of the ship, because the color depended on such things as whether the ship would be in northerly, temperate, or tropical waters—black if the former, and white if the latter. (The black absorbs sun heat; the white reflects it. The right colors saved thousands of dollars of air-conditioning costs.) The naval architects were not given control of interior decoration because they were not the operating riskers who decided to build the ship. And the people who put up the money wanted to be really sure they were going to be able to sell their rooms as against the other fellow's, so they didn't dare trust the engineer. After all, an engineer is inclined to say, "This bed will hold you up." Engineers are inclined to tolerate the crude but "safely adequate." So the advertising and public relations men say, "Go over here, boys, and hire the ones who know how to design the man of distinction's brothels." The sure-sale conditioning is really that bad.

A One-Town World

At our present moment in history, whether we in America like it or not, we are no longer geographically isolated. Within a few years we will be able to go in the morning to any part of the earth by public conveyance, do a day's work, and reach home again in the evening; and by the Treasury Department's income tax allowance for traveling expenses, we will not have been out of town. We will be realistically and legally in a one-town world for the first time in history. Not only that, but our world population will have tripled since the beginning of the century.[9] The design students who are now graduating are going to have to handle billions of additional people. Town planning is meaningless today if it is not also world planning.

So we must start comprehensively with all men. Mobility is man's first positive and negative kind of security—his innate ability (unlike that of a vegetable or a tree) to advance or retreat. Soon man will be able to advance and retreat all the way around the world, and will do so; he can both associate and disassociate to extraordinary advantage. Architects, if they are really to be comprehensive, must assume the enormous task of thinking in terms always disciplined to the scale of the total world pattern of needs, its resource flows, its recirculatory and regenerative processes.

---

9 **The world population grew from 1.65 billion in 1900 to 6.07 billion in 2000—6.83 billion in 2009.** Population Division of the Department of Economic and Social Affairs of the United Nations Secretariat. *World Population Prospects: The 2008 Revision; Highlights* (New York, 2009).

Comprehensively anticipatory design science architects will have to think in the terms of great patterning envisioned by Sir Halford Mackinder, the English geographer. Sir Halford told the high command of Great Britain in 1900, in effect, that the land railway is a surprise child of the age-old marine railway, which was invented to launch heavy ships upon the water. Until 1830 only ships supported by water could carry the large and heavy cargoes to be transported, which were greater than those that could be transported on the backs of men or animals. The grand strategy of the world-around British empire was predicated on the proposition that the world's waterfront is the terminal of heavy logistical mobility. But today if you think the "waterfront" is where the ocean stops, you are getting very much fooled, because the "waterfront" is now where you can carry the kind of cargoes that do the missions you used to do on the water. The marine railway in reverse finally launched the railroads upon the land, and the railroads are using the land for a new kind of ocean. Your "waterfront" is retreating to the terminal of the railroads, and even beyond, as the cargoes go in the auto-trucks, which are pneumatic-tired canal boats. Thus, in effect, spake Mackinder.

He scared the British into realizing that technology was indeed altering basic considerations, but after World War I the British were too physically tired to listen further to Halford Mackinder's theory. Mackinder, however, had developed some now-famous concepts, such as "heartland": *"Who rules the Near East rules the heartland and who rules the heartland rules the world."* He looked at the whole of the earth and at all the waterfronts and he showed how the people in the north had the highest stimulation to invention because they were exposed annually to many more severe climatic changes than were tropical peoples, and they tended to invent in response to the greater extremes. These were typical of Mackinder's comprehensive thoughts and they became the essence of pre-World War I British Empire's strategy. *Heartland* hid competitive treat east-west land routes.

The British, spent by World War I, had paid little heed to Mackinder's post-1918 ideas. He said, "Gentlemen, there's something very much bigger happening now. Airplanes, used up to now only for war purposes and stunting, are going to fly the world skies as passenger and cargo transports. In effect, the primary logistical ocean now flows completely up and over the whole land. Our dry land is simply the bottom of the world's one airocean. Your 'waterfront' is gone completely. How now are you going to hold your heartland? You had better change your strategy greatly and look principally to the air."

Though the British paid only scant amount of attention to Mackinder at this time, one student listened to him intently, a German named Karl Haushofer. Haushofer went back to Germany and became the great strategy counsel to Hitler and to Goering. He told them of Mackinder's unheeded counsel to the British, which he translated into German as "geopolitics," the word best known today as identifying Mackinder, its inventor. The Luftwaffe and *blitzkrieg* strategies were paradoxically predicated upon Mackinder's warning to their proverbial enemy, England. The British Empire collapsed as Mackinder predicted.

Mackinder's books dramatically emphasized a powerful discipline in treating whole-world problems. As we are now concerned with the whole world, architectural students must gain a working familiarity with the whole earth and its comprehensive evolutionary processes in all departments. Their home towns, or where they can get a job, the state licensing boards—all are secondary or lesser levels of consideration.

Long isolated from the rest of the world, we could get by despite our great ignorance; we could make bad mistakes without visible consequence. We are now only seven percent of the world's population [10] and we are gradually learning that at least fifty-one percent

10 **In 2005, the U.S. population represented 4.6 % of the world population.** Population Division of the Department of Economic and Social Affairs of the United Nations Secretariat, *World Population Prospects: The 2008 Revision*, http://esa.un.org/unpp (accessed July 8, 2009).

of the earth's population doesn't like us any more. They once loved us for our innocuous *naïveté;* today they are bored or disdainful of our irresponsibility. Apparently we are unable to formulate aught but defensive policy. It is now essential that we expose our students directly to the big show. What we need is positive design, which politicians neither dare to make nor are capable of making.

Inasmuch as we have the students with a proclivity for becoming advanced in the disciplines of architecture as resource integrators, it is evident that their highest capability may be developed only by exposure to the full breadth of economic geography and to the comprehensive array of front-line science and technology potentials scientifically comprehensive and economically effective in our day. But I figure it can be done only by applying our highest technical competence directly to the satisfaction of all humanity's needs and satisfactions, rather than giving priority to military preparedness incidental to which there follows the second-hand, inept conversion of war-production-born technology to peaceful needs, after enormous wasting of technical potentials in obsolete war goods. As we employ the total science and resource potential directly to world-man's peaceful advantage, the numbers of those participating in the total capability will swiftly increase from the present forty-four percent to one hundred percent, approximately speaking.[11]

A new, self-employed architect scientist is the one in all the world who may accelerate realization of a high-standard survival for all, as now completely practical within the scope of available technology. The self-commissioned architect is the obviously exclusive potential—for as at present used, or designed, the world's resources are serving only forty-four percent of humanity. Politics

11 **In 1981, 44% of humanity (1.9 Billion of 4.4 billion) were out of poverty. In 2001, 56% (3.4 billion of 6.1 billion) were out of poverty, using current notions of "middle income" and "high income" families. Note: "middle income" on a global development basis means "incomes of a few thousand per year," which is not equivalent to measures of "middle income" in wealthy countries.** Jeffrey Sachs, *The End of Poverty: Economic Possibilities for Our Time* (New York, 2005), chapter 1.

can only redeal the inadequate cards, but scientifically known principles may employ those same resources by new design in such a manner of increased ratio of performance per pound of resources as to make the same tonnage of world resources serve one hundred percent of humanity and at higher standards of effectiveness and satisfaction than any as yet experienced by their most hitherto advantaged of men. It is new design by architects versus world revolution by political leadership.

Architectural Research in Universities

In the terrific depression of the 1930s most architects were unemployed, as were the new architectural graduates. Many went to Russia and other world places trying to find something to do. Then the New Deal came in and socialized building by taking over the underlying mortgage base, the economic base of last recourse of so-called real wealth. The government put some new equity into building through technical renovation. The government has more than one hundred billion dollars worth of mortgages right now on its hands, and in order to keep inefficient building arts alive, has to extend payment to thirty years for homes which could be so economically produced (under comprehensive architecture) as to be paid for in one year. So in the United States socialization of building led socialization of industry, and all economic initiative is now led exclusively by the negative credit billions for defense undertakings. We should not be misled by this. Though the government allows its so-called private banks to issue the mortgage money, it is the government which underwrites the mortgage. The money has not been risked by the bank; it has been put up out of government guaranteed depositors' accounts as a convenience to a government by a people who like to pretend that they are against socialism. Nothing has been risked by the individual loaner, only by the individual as "buyer."

The fact that there has been employment for architects in the post-World War II years is a product of a socialism that has an increasingly bad risk, for which it has to give longer years and easier terms to buyers while paying higher and higher rates of interest on its government borrowings. Look at the times when the architects' offices may not be busy due to the inflationary spiral generated by government underwriting of continually more obsolete and relatively more inefficient building art. In order to contract with the defense-generated dollars, architects need a lot of draftsmen, and a great many architectural schools have been turning out architectural graduates only to be draftsmen. Extraordinarily talented boys become drafting machines or catalogue-searching machines. Architectural schools are then providing socialism with functions, which in the era of automation will become as obsolete human functions as are aviators to the guided missiles.

I am frequently invited to speak at regional conventions of the American Institute of Architects to discuss problems of the architectural future, and a member of a prominent firm will ask, "Do you advocate our inaugurating a research department in our firm?" My answer is, "I'm perfectly sure you do not have enough money to do so, as research and development cost far more than the money which could be saved from architects' profits."

There is an effective strategy open to the architects. Whereas doctors deal with the interior organisms of man, architects deal with the exterior organisms of man. Architects might join with one another to carry on their work in laboratories as do doctors in anticipatory medicine. Architects might solve design problems of world-resource use before people get into resource troubles. Architects might thus join forces, as do scientists, with the integrity of inter-self accrediting of the respective abilities of each individual on the team. Architects might begin the laboratory pooling of their resource capabilities at the university level.

At present, the architectural schools are under the impression that practicing professional architectural firms want them to produce draftsmen. Architects should tell architectural schools that they also favor research and development in the university (where society has already provided the multi-million dollar facilities). Architects might find themselves returning to participate in research, instead of dreaming about it in their offices.

Such a policy has already met with favor. A few years ago, at several regional A.I.A. conventions, I proposed such architectural participation in our university research program, which was later carried out as a practical matter with considerable satisfaction and enthusiasm. I have had sufficient experience in this direction to dare to say, without misleading the reader, that such research laboratory undertaking in the university will meet with increasing professional support. Possibly in their own non-busy times, professional architects could return as graduate students in that research and development. This would make it possible for the students to participate with men of experience who could say, "The hard facts of life are thus-and-so once you get out of here, and that's why I'm coming back."

5 I Figure

On November 1, 1942, eleven months after Pearl Harbor, the editor and staff of Pencil Points Magazine *which later was renamed* Progressive Architecture *proposed that I write an article on postwar housing. Chapter 5—"I Figure" which now follows was the result. When I turned it in to them in December 1942, they decided against publishing it. By then I was busy in the U.S. Government's Board of Economic Warfare and I put "I Figure" away in my File and Forget file—and did actually forget it—for twenty years—until, in preparation of this biography of my thought development, I recalled it and felt that its inclusion might permit a sense of realistic participation by others in the typical circumstances and intuitions that seemed to have uncorked my intermittent prognostic outpourings.*

I certify that no changes other than those of spelling or typographical corrections have been made in it and that I had not looked at it for twenty years.

Many of the predictions have proven premature, yet these seem more plausible in 1963 than in 1942 which suggests that they may be realized within another decade or so. Some of the predictions have proven surprisingly accurate not only in spirit but in factual magnitudes, for instance, of housing activity or other social developments.

I apologize to my many friends in the American Institute of Architects for my rugged treatment but they too will recall war engendered emotions and will, as they have so frequently in the past, once more forgive me.

It is only fair to this soliloquy that those who read it in the inevitably changed mood of the world years from this date—Sunday afternoon November 7th, 1942—take note that as I now sit down to my typewriter the radio program has just been interrupted with the announcement that "strong and modernly equipped American forces have landed on the Atlantic and Mediterranean coasts of North Africa."

Some day, probably not remote, we may have scientific measurement of the power regenerated in the individual by the telepathetic stream of emotions popularly propagated by such announcement as this. But certainly it is with a sense of unwilling personal remoteness from the excitement of the swiftly unfolding events that cerebral "I" withdraws to concentrate upon answering the earnest question put to me by a trade magazine publisher—half in apprehension, half in business necessity: "What do you figure to be the characteristics of postwar housing, speaking both generally and specifically?"

The suppositional setting of this day-after-sometime activity was not furnished. Many months, many years hence, never? Housing. That is an entirely irrelevant subject anyway. Or is it?

Could housing, for instance, have anything to do with whether it will be months or years to war's end? What nonsense! Haven't they shut down on priorities for that housing stuff until the show is over? Has housing, in fact, anything whatever to do with war? If we pass over newly created munitions production that was delayed for months while awaiting provision of housing to bring personnel within operating range as being a matter of poor management, could we say that "housing" in itself has at least something to do with how it happened that we are now at war? If only in housing's function as incubator of the social components,—the individual and the family group?

That is to ask: Is it possible that housing could have been originally responsible for war in its ignorantly rendered task as the environmental factory for mass-maturing the end product, man, which latter perplexing invention psychology is roughly estimated to be five percent a product of heredity and ninety-five percent a product of environment?

In view of the fact that the above assumption has been vindicated by scientific measurement, are we brought to recognize that houses are thus scientifically discovered to be incubators of relative degrees of race insanity—incubators of human "fowl," self-hybreeding for their self-invented lethal pit fighting, on the one hand as the sport of cartel-imperialism (which game they also self-invented), or on the other hand for the self-caged, mass egg-laying industry, or quite simply for self-stuffing, roasting, frying, or adulterizing?

If found materially contributory to the whyfor of war, would it not follow that the housing issue might have something important to do with how, when, and even where the peace might happen? Haven't we been taking an awful lot for granted about housing anyway, and an awful beating to boot?

Haven't we let opinions of every formal or informal pressure-generating group lead us in diametric directions, each for its own special easiest-way ends, getting us nowhere and ever dictating to us what we "want" or "need" as environment?

And must I not start my aroused conjectures about housing with consideration of the measure of sagacity implicit in the expression of the problem as "postwar housing"? Doesn't this sophisticated expression seem a bit patronizing, a little too sure, faintly insinuating a tomorrow unrelated to the vital issues of today,—an aloof pragmatism that has stood deferentially aside while men fought and which is now discounting the human family expenditure of twenty million of its lives, the most costly investment in its future mankind has ever been called upon to make?

Or even if postwar housing is expeditiously considered as just a temporary rebuilding program or an emergency resumption of inefficiency, does it not at least suggest further compromising investment in that outworn, though never trodden, backwards road to normal?

"If what man really wants," says science, "is to go backwards to all the troubles of yesterday, packaged tightly in cellophane and neatly labeled 'normal,' he had better turn around that crate that he has labeled 'civilization' and go back where he came from—because this particular highway that he has been traveling all these centuries doesn't happen to lead to a dead end of selfish limitations.

"The highway leads," says the referee, "with many a promising sign along the way for those who can read science's language, to broad green lands so vast that they may only be cooperatively husbanded by the brave and enlightened. In these broadlands directly ahead the selfish isolationists must starve, for the fruits are so large and are hung so high that they are beyond the grasp of the single-handed anarchist poacher."

May we not throw overboard that slavish "down-to-business-like" thought of a "return" to postwar housing, a phrase to which attaches the stigma, be it ever so delicate, of precious self-profit? May we not immediately undertake a solution of housing realistically underwritten with unlimited worldwide commonwealth credit, and with enthusiastic and complete self-commitment to the omniscient custody of the Almighty, so reliably bespoken by the orderly vastness of energy demonstrations, not only recorded by science, but so magnificently displayed in the heavenly pageantry, or the beauty of a spring day, or the force of thundering, mountainous surf, or of a lovely young human being, for any who will to read!

May we not dedicate that housing project to the scientific insulation of humanity and his so hard-earned civilization against further necessity of industrialized mass destruction of his commonwealth potentials and mass murder of his choicest young lives (albeit the revolting mayhem is statutorily legalized by declaration of war as prescribed by the protocols of the frequently bilious normal monopoly obsessions)?

May our housing not insulate us against this filthy periodic necessity, complicatedly endured, to effect the simple evolutionary adjustments which humanity's ignorantly self-imposed environment conditioning has hitherto failed so repeatedly and miserably to prepare man to peacefully effect for himself?

If man's amazing original spontaneity and speculative previewing imaginative faculties were growthfully nurtured (instead of ruthlessly strafed) by a comprehensive environment arrangement adequate to its necessities and to his creative impulses, practically maintained by scientific dwelling mechanisms, might he not prepare with glad and humble heart the appropriate and scientifically timed adoption of progressively efficient designs for future guarantee of his cooperative industrial welfaring?

Because such a progression constantly does more with less, must it not harvest an increasing raw material inventory, self-emanating from "scrap" for successfully and successively retooling-up man's commonwealth, amplifying a regenerative circuit from out the apparatus thus vacated by obsolescence—a regenerative circuit valved to sun-emanating energy in its many radiant materializations? Would there not thus emerge an automatic increment sufficient to account for the most lavish scientific piloting of the course? Could housing be that important? Can we afford to pass up the chance that it may be?

Naked man had only one advantage over environment which was sufficient to prolong his association with it. This was his cerebral advantage. Man running and bounding on his legs can manage to jump to a height about equal to his own six-foot stature. With cerebral articulation of observed mechanical principles in Nature he can, though seeming superficially to encumber himself with the additional weight of a pole, run forward and, with the same quota of energy employed in the six-foot jump, now vault over a barrier better than twice his own height. Thus he demonstrates the cerebrally combined mechanical advantages of angular acceleration with the fulcrum principle, a cerebrally detected compounding principle resulting in the principle of dynamic self-leverage.

The cerebral advantages are progressively pyramided upon the compounded and irrevocably cumulative basic-data-grid of technology and science. The web-interstices of the basic-data-grid, in which there are still many blank spaces, are, however, being ever more closely woven together with the memorial strands fashioned by mind, will and courage out of utter intellectual integrity.

Though the treasured basic data web is closely guarded by the increasing host of academic science and technology, both its original detections and ultimate domestications were and are solely articulated by that most precious of all characteristics of living man, the power of the selectively precomposing creative imagination, which, as Morley phrases it, is "The Holiest Ghost we shall ever know."

Deriving compound advantages out of the basic-data-grid, we have learned in astronomy, navigation and ballistics that the degree of accuracy of forecast is directly proportional to the degree of completeness both of inclusion and evaluation of the convergent force factors, the total resultant flow diagram of which unfailingly prescribes the tracking, time and station schedule of events for those who are faithful and industrious enough to survey scientifically the appropriate dynamic system.

Therefore, confident that the same reliable trend prognostication principles must adhere also to man's social affairs, I can now only apply myself with vigorous humility to the task of prognostication, a process which sincerely attempted might appropriately be designated as Total Thinking, a necessitous rather than a pretentious invention.

I figure[12]: that any planned postwar housing now in preparation by the components of the professional housing world as now and

12 The "original" typescript found in the Fuller Archive (Series 8 Box 5 Folder 4) appears to be a hand-bound carbon copy of the version submitted for publication by Fuller in 1942. In it he precedes the phrase "I figure" with a numeral 1—and similarly each subsequent "stanza," indicates the next number in sequence, and recants the phrase "I figure," the last stanza being 155. In a change from the original, for the version published in the first edition of *Ideas and Integrities* he deletes the numbers, as well as replacing each repeated "I figure" with an ellipsis "...".

hitherto constituted will get about as far as a ten-ton truck can be jerked by its self-starter before the battery goes dead.

...that this calculation includes every phase of housing from A.A.A. (for academic architectural aesthetics) through A.F.L., A.I.A., A.M.A., and so on down through the seventeen thousand possible combinations of nuances of human association describable by three initials, organized for intentionally better or unintentionally worse public or private purposes, and all fulcrumed upon the simple, exploitable fact that man requires shelter, sanitation, and privacy in varying degrees dictated by the larger factors of environment.

...that the stationary engines of the old world housing business are permanently stalled. This statement in no way refers to special engineering projects whose activities, having now sincerely adopted scientific method, are each hour turning in more amazing records.

...that old housing is stalled and its postwar planning invalid because its philosophy is obsolete. It is obsolete because its premise is essentially unscientific. Science has been interrogated falteringly about patchwork palliatives, but has never been asked whether the invention of housing as a whole was soundly conceived.

...that the invention of housing, as we have known it, provides no simple and practical means, economically or mechanically, for swiftly interpreting each scientific research gain in principle and precision into the everyday environment mechanics of man.

...that far from coinciding with contemporary scientific concept, the over-all housing thinking lapses backward at least three thousand five hundred years to pre-Greek conjecture for its major premise.

...that its truly ignorant premise derives from the superficially stationary aspect of housing structures. This illusory stationary aspect happened to coincide with the gravitational effect demonstrated by stones accidentally recumbent in a pile.

...that all postwar-wise housing plans as yet coming to light still start with sewer, water, and light arteries laboriously buried in the ground, a three-thousand-year-old invention, immediately immobilizing all subsequent design. However, willfully more ignorant than the designers of three thousand years ago, this start overlooks the fact that the original drains were led to a few of the better run stone temples and palaces as accessories after the fact, as corrective expediencies. The fact to which the buried arteries were accessory was that the house was usually built of the stones immediately at hand and therefore that the edifice was located on the spot as a measure of energy efficiency and not, as architecture would have it, because housing should aesthetically "arise from the bosom of mother earth," or "spring from the native soil."

...that site planning for postwar will take no consideration of the interim degrees of multiplied mobility developed for man by the war, which would make possible setting down a city of one hundred thousand well-equipped persons in twenty-four hours in the mountain reaches of Tibet, because postwar planning goes right ahead by-passing all scientific gains of the whole three thousand years' climb from the first emergency sewer systems, and limits the planning to the mechanical advantage rating of man three thousand years ago, when he had one-twenty-five-thousandth the physical augmentation modern mechanized man has—as he now considers most activities other than housing in the terms of around-the-world in flying-hour tons.

...that architecture starts the plan not only with every limitation known to the Egyptians, but also complicated a million-fold by three thousand years of clinging growths consisting of every possible scheme of parasitic exploitation of that original Stone Age immobility of the anchored victims of housing. So old are the vines now that most of them are heavy with the cultivated fruits of ethical and legal precedence, and are perfumed with the venerated aesthetic. And then, too, say the "good old housing" exploiters, "a rolling stone gathers no moss."

...that this stationary premise assumed in the formulating of housing concepts continues in utter denial of the scientific and now fortunately quite popular concept of an atomic universe totally in motion, in which one rolling stone can knock over ten pins again and again. Who wants to gather moss anyway, asks the around-the-world-flying man! Plenty of time to raise moss when you are dead.

...that just as communication and transportation have progressed from wire to wireless and track to trackless respectively, with concomitant, manifold increase of their time-space mastery per unit of expended energy, always developing in synchronization with the contemporary philosophical concept of essential motion, that just so will housing of scientific necessity finally progress from its vainly weighted-down footing, from a rooted to a frankly rootless art, with vast gains for man in the terms of environment control per unit of expended energy.

...that the change will come about as a potential motion-for-security's-sake, and not as a motion-for-motion's-sake innovation; that this mobility for security will be articulated whenever evolutionary necessity requires repositioning of dwelling locale for consolidation of the progressive interim gains in living, learning, working, and enjoyment standards, or when anticipation of obsolescence or public convenience indicates mutual advantage in change.

...that by thus synchronizing with the reality of motion, the major premise of a new housing industry will become scientifically tenable.

...that inasmuch as the word "economics" means the body of knowledge pertaining to household management, that the latter's mobilization will cause the whole economic prospect of man to come of scientific age.

...that with mobilization of high standard living equipment, that the age will not only have its new-grown wings, but also have powerfully energized talons to secure each freely-selected, graceful landing. The American eagle is an excellent symbol of industrial man's future. We are wont to depict the eagle alertly poised with intense potential mobility and therefore with well-demonstrated security, even upon the most precipitous advantage.

... that this derooting will thus actually control the new economics of man by freeing his dwelling from its parasitic subsistence on the back of an industrial jungle host of sewer, water, gas, and garbage systems, and by insinuation of man into individually powered and processing dwellings, unlimited in range of location of secure poise, on mountain top, in remote valley, or island, without time severance disadvantage and with ever-improving standards of living.

... that in the new economics resultant to flying and securely-poised dwelling, man will discard his treacherous misconceptions of wealth, which hold that it is comprised only of the items about him which stand still, and between which little things shuttle with strings tied to them, trolleys to wires, wires to centrals and centrals to mortgages, all reduced to "securities" that can be placed statically under lock and key. The sunlight has never been called "wealth" except by the poets or by laughing youths, who are wild poets. The lawyers have never been able to tie a monopoly string to the sunlight or to tie it back to some system of less refulgent sovereign deeds.

... that man will soon set up a new accounting system geared into the true wealth of power-potential truly accounting our dynamic mastery of environment by science-educated control of energy—that is of energy all external to man's integral pittance of that all-pervasive phenomenon which uniquely characterizes life as action (motion) or reaction (heat). This is the new concept, An Energy-Borne Commonwealth of Humanity, instead of monopoly and patronage affluence, pyramided on a bedrock acre base.

... that the mass of materials which the old building world so inefficiently employed will be expeditiously scrapped and run through the mills again. This applies to materials (1) directly frozen into structures and (2) indirectly employed in the concomitant inventory of employed materials to fabricate the heavy plant equipment and rolling stock which in turn process, transport, store, and handle the ill-conceptioned buildings' materials, all of which compound to astronomically inefficient or entirely superfluous tons.

... that these recaptured materials will eventually be reassigned with scientific discretion to efficiently conceived tasks in the industrial cycle.

... that if dancing one-and-a-half-ton automobiles and pounding ten-ton trucks, and thunderingly alighting twenty-five-ton airplanes can be initially supported on compressed air structures in pneumatically stressed tension skins with the additional advantage of locomotion, and that if sixty-ton airplanes can be supportingly hung from the sky by a pneumatic-lag vacuum, and if a hundred-thousand-ton ship with a relatively delicate steel skin can be supported on a liquid plastic foundation of water (because of the ship's pneumatic content being maintained in expanding pressure by the weight of the blanket of atmosphere above, whose specific gravity is sufficiently less than the water to permit of its supporting the otherwise sinkable steel by marrying it to the air in efficient comprehensive design), that human families of less than one half a ton total working load, who present no stress requirements of the magnitude germane to airplanes, trucks, and ships, should be easily structured in their miniscule dwelling requirements by a few atmospheres of compressed air confined within less than a ton of stressed skins.

... that all essential pneumatic and hydraulic compression components of structures are comprised of the locally available substances occurring in nature at or near almost any spot on earth as compound liquids or gases, as, for instance, water and air, or even dry "dirts," which have hitherto been used in buildings only as constituents of frozen plastic masonry, which cannot dynamically distribute its stresses to the enclosing tension components of the design, as can pneumatic and hydraulic systems of structural composition.

...that only the tension components of structure need be centrally fabricated for wide distribution to structural assembly locations, the compression components being always locally available if pneumatic and hydraulic conceptions of solution are employed by the designers.

...that because the stress-ability of modern, scientifically designed tension components has advantages varying from two up to ten to one over compression component abilities, that the production and shipment of only tension components will reduce the over-all industrial loads by as much as seventy-five percent.

...that in this war crisis it is technically treason to allow ourselves to be short sixty-five thousand freight cars weighing fifty tons of steel each, which shortage is equivalent to the number of cars required exclusively to transport the solid foundation and flooring materials unscientifically employed as frozen compression elements to structurally support the tiny weights of the one-tenth-of-a-ton load of men who comprise the negligible working loads of housing, or to support machinery from below that could better be suspended, etc.

...that we adhere to this unimaginative stupification of building concoction only because we are confined by a thousand codes to comply with essentially the same designing systems employed five thousand years ago when the compressive strength of masonry (fifty thousand pounds per square inch) of the post-Stone Age still had a great advantage over available tension components of grass or bark or wooden sections.

...that with eyes trained to appraisal standards of post-Stone Age lore, that industrial engineering, such as that of "gas tanks," and "good architecture" were bound to be incongruous, because the gas tank was in tension; and that because "good architecture" remains "good" because of race hypnosis, the unadorned engineering design seems monstrous and threatening.

...that the differences in efficiency of these new dynamic and the old inert structures can be readily discerned by noting that the tops of many public service gas tanks in large cities are each several times larger in horizontal plan than is, for instance, the waiting room floor of the Grand Central Station in New York City, the station mausoleum designed essentially in the inert classical manner appropriate to stones balanced on stones, though of necessity held together by an enormous hidden steel tension structure insinuated within (instead of efficiently containing) the design. As a deck, these gas tank tops would easily carry a load several times greater than the live load of people who fill Grand Central in a holiday crush. Despite this many times superior spanning and carrying capacity, the gas tank decks are structured of 1/1000th the weight of fabricated materials of the station, which had to be transported far in appropriately heavy transport units over appropriately heavy railway systems instead of directly by air as would be quite economical with gas tank components.

...that the materials–raw, partially processed, or sub-assembled–of old housing (which term includes all the latest prefabrication compromises), have weighed on an average of one hundred to one and have bulked on an average of ten to one in excess of the quantities necessary to accomplish the desired end result, and have fallen as proportionately short of satisfactory performance as they have of energy conversion efficiency.

...that the American people, who during the last century have produced their own weight in copper products and one hundred and twenty-six times that weight in steel products, were so production rich that they were product careless.

...that they have become technologically poor now (haven't enough to meet wants), because of the super-wastefulness of many of their designs, particularly of past housing design. Their assets are frozen in inexcusably inefficient design because those who have managed their affairs have been downright ignorant (no matter what other expedient characteristics they have possessed). The U.S. citizen has one hundred and forty pounds of copper per capita frozen into his product designs (mostly building) with only fourteen pounds per capita known to exist per world citizen, including all surfaced metal and all known geological reserves. U.S. man has nine-and-one-half steel tons per capita as his own share of the social mechanism, where less than one ton should suffice, were moderately good design (technically speaking) demonstrated.

... that the inefficient design is due to lack of over-all philosophical discernment of the managers, particularly regarding the vast step forward in civilization, which it was their historical opportunity to make, and lacking which they have instead invested their productivity in a metals imitation of the Old World, starting with cast iron or bronze replicas of Greek columns, friezes, and didos appropriate to extreme specialization of the Stone Age art, carrying this absurdity through to metal imitations of wood windows, steel coaches, bronze mass-production doughboys, all representative of an inferiority complex and mistaken identity in history.

... that the Old World (Europe and Asia), having waited long and seemingly in vain for our New World (American) contribution of a cerebrated design for creative living, is now showing us the new design pace, but perversely articulated in destructive instruments, as of a world species committing suicide, having nothing better to do, or rather being denied the right by its ignorant managers, to turn its potentials to creative extension.

... that the Old World is leading us the creative perversion pace in design by employing our own unique springboard and only special contribution to social history, mass production, which might, under comprehensive management less preoccupied in fighting for guarantees of high risk odds for no risk arrangements, have been applied to insure happiness and enlightened growth of man himself.

... that upon inspection of the metals' industries inventory record, the essentially unused copper and iron content of the obsolete and overweight buildings, whose contingent materials inventory accounts for more than one half of all of the metals produced in the last century, is alone sufficient to supply our complete production needs of these two major metals for five more years of war, though we were unthinkably to shut up every iron and copper mine.

... that practically all the metals produced in the last century remain on inventory in the equipment, rolling or stationary, of plant and structure, of which business management in general (including the banks and law firms) has been sole management custodian.

... that the minority, classified as "business executive, et al.," rather than the American public at large, must bear the blame for the lack of comprehension of the potential historical contribution of America and—worse—for debasing American man's otherwise great idealistic frontier objective into money-grubbing.

... that this grubbing is an economic result of the inert characteristic of architecture's environmental imposition on the viewpoint of the individual.

... that this perverted objective has made a static virtue out of grubbing the last kernel out of only the first productive setup of what might otherwise be recognized, if allowed to grow, as a regenerative and geometrically amplifying system of wealth circulation and living standard advance, a veritable golden-egg-laying goose, destined (eventually, why not now?) to spread its energy conversion service to all people on this tiny planet.

... that despite the seemingly large bulk of metals which might superficially be judged to have been distributed by end product sale into the personal custody of the individual citizens, that the proportion of all processed metal actually reaching them was very small and only seemed large because it was sliced so thin.

... that the small proportion of all the metals in private custody was revealed when the populace was recently called upon to support their fighting boys at the front with scrap badly needed by the steel industry; for then the American home folks, though fanatically combing attics, cellars, yards, pot cupboards, ornament dressers, and tool boxes, scraped together only twelve million tons of iron and iron alloy, which is only four-fifths of one percent of the surfaced, processed, and placed-in-use iron metal now on inventory in the U.S. economy. Extremists think that the citizen wasn't thorough enough in the first scrap drive and could go back and dig up another, final twelve million tons. If we add to this the twenty-four million tons total of excess metal in personal custody or about the premises of the public, the additional weight in metals contained in its national inventory of automobiles (basing computation upon the record 1941 registration of motor vehicles), the total figure of metals in popular custody as of Pearl Harbor date, prior to the first scrap drive, reached only fifty-four million tons as compared with the billion-and-a-quarter tons in corporate, industrial, or government custody at that eye-opening date. Of this latter huge tonnage, the government portion is negligible, as is typified by the small percentage involved in the unprecedented twelve-million ton Navy and twenty-six-million ton merchant marine goal now set for war's peak. The combined popular custody tonnage subject to the individual's or his government's mandate might be brought up, by inclusion of state, county, city, and regional authority bridges, dams, and equipment, to a sum total of two hundred million tons, in comparison to the one billion, one hundred million tons remaining solely in corporate or trust custody.

... that this proportion of relative mandate over the surfaced inventory of metals leads to some cogent political conjecture.

... that just as the tongue, as a mechanical invention, precedes the phenomenon "word" as a fact, and *ipso facto* the political consequences of the word's invention, that in exactly the same way *all* mechanics are to be appraised as causal rather than as resultant to political evolution.

... that in view of the fact that mechanics pace political evolution, the development of advancing industrialism in America provoked its political adventure in forthright democracy.

... that the advancing industrialism invisibly threw the complete determination of man's political fate, as dictated by mechanical evolution, to the prerogative in design advance of, first, the industrial financiers, and, subsequently, the self-perpetuating industrial management few—not at all to popular political mandate.

... that political fate rested entirely upon the limited technical wisdom and far more limited world development vision of the industrial management few.

... that it may be said in strict technical veracity that democratic management has not yet existed in America and that such weaknesses as have up to now been revealed in the social organization of American man are not limitations of democracy at all.

... that the democratic test in the U.S. has been in any realistic sense a trial of Charlie McCarthy for the whims of Bergen.

... that it is no wonder the industrial businessmen sprang to democracy's defense in its hour of need.

... that under the surface cloak of an entirely theoretical application of democracy, a money-minded few have pulled all the mechanical strings and that the manipulators, to play fair with them, are to be criticized for their utter inability to comprehend the broad meaning of such contributory facts as those we have just cited (and which have often been cited to them by their hired technologists), which ignorance explains, though it cannot condone, their consequent failure to act intelligently upon them.

... that, though one hundred percent "responsible," they are guiltless of any malevolent attitude towards society.

... that these leaders have been found wanting, and that the failure is at the center of the world storm, and that their cries for another chance for democracy are provoked only by the pattern of their ignorant association-of-ideas, and that their pleas for democracy and its rainbow-haloed free enterprise (the right of the best corporation lawyers they can hire to write new rules that give them new license), may be appraised only as their scheme for prolongation of their quite undemocratic custodianship of the works for the sake of relatively diminutive dollar dividends-preposterously diminutive by comparison to the net earnings in standard of living that will accrue if and when the democratic body politic is given the controlling voice over its industrially organized and mechanically implemented commonwealth.

...that the fifty-four million tons of obsolete end-product metal in direct personal or popular custody of American man is equivalent to only one-half a year's production of his steel mills.

...that you may think the individual has a lot more tonnage than that alone inventoried in his plumbing, heating, and hardware, but realistically exploring, we find that only two percent of the U.S. population own their own homes outright, which therefore places the essential custody of this "home" inventoried accessory and arterial system tonnage within the control of corporation trusts or government. Though holding ultimate title foreclosure powers, the government to date has laboriously supported rather than challenged the corporate and trust prerogative over this tonnage, in order to avoid the political disturbances threatened by realistic inspection of the deflated functional value to which this junk tonnage is collateral throughout the vast "securities" structure of the country.

...that of the billion-and-a-quarter tons of strategic metals in fabricated status now in custody of *others* than the individual, and therefore beyond his control to do anything about until he knows the facts and can support the initial moves of his representatives to remedy legislatively over seven hundred million tons were fashioned into their present inventory shape and function before World War I, and much of that tonnage even before the turn of the century.

...that, from the over-all service efficiency viewpoint, this inventory tonnage of seven hundred million, equivalent to eight years' complete production of our present steel mills' war capacity, is, with no important exception, obsolete as now formed.

...that the fact that the horsepower output per pound of engine metal has advanced two thousand five hundred percent in the interim, is ample substantiation of the typical cause of obsolescence obtaining in the older portion of the inventory, which, however, so long as it promises any dollar production, no matter how small, is "good," so far as the short range viewpoint of its custodians is concerned.

... that the custodians of the plant structure and equipment deem them to be potential of earning a pure, even if small, dollar profit, just so long as they are standing, no matter how empty or idle, because the amortization was long ago completed; and therefore as custodians they don't have to take any responsibility for the success of a better service use of the materials involved by a new imprint of energy and technology.

... that they are unwilling to part with the properties on the "headachey" basis (from their viewpoint) that its revamping might possibly amplify the effective striking power of America twenty-five-fold, as indicated by the technical gains in scientific service industries such as communications. Multiply any of our industrial or military figures by twenty-five and see what that would mean to the war winning.

... that this inefficient inventory, just by virtue of its existence in such preponderant size, puts a premium on suppression of efficiency increase from a prescheduled dollar income viewpoint of management.

... that the easy monopoly of average *laissez-faire* protects inefficiency by allowing only slow and controlled improvement by trial balloon introduction of innovations by the least successful divisions of the industry.

... that the no-risk premium on retarded growth is a real behind-the-scenes stumbling block if not an anti-war success motivating force, for, because of it, improvement in design is countenanced only for fighting equipment when our items are directly out-designed by the enemy—lest the war, with its wastes otherwise advantageous to monopoly maintenance, upset the seemingly good-enough system of preferred stagnation.

... that it was probably hoped by the huge, unwieldy, obsolete inventory custodians (if they were aware of it at all, which is doubtful), but at least by the legal tacticians for them, that the public scrap drive as such would satisfy the public demand for solution of the vaguely publicized scrap problem, hopeful that the war might be won without too serious design advance concession, though glad to have the public liquidate its own small tool, accessory, and improvising materials position by tossing in its scrap pittance (which is, incidentally, so inefficiently thin, being mostly light-gauge sheet product and plating, that as scrap it is used only by the metal producers as a last resort).

...that the custodians will, however, finally get the picture straight regarding the advantage in wealth gains accruing through accelerated velocity of scrap recycling, in which each cycle represents an impress of sun-free energy into the cumulative commonwealth standard of efficiency advance.

...that when the problem of its preferred introduction, because comprehended, happens to coincide with survival necessity, then the whole essential economic volition of the world will be converted from an inert to a dynamic asset system.

...that once the scrap is really recycling on an efficient basis, new design will be constantly in demand to warrant a new cycle and that the world-wide industrial wheels will turn as never before.

...that out of the starting phase of tonnage recirculation, industry should net better than a quarter of a billion new dwelling service units.

...that industry will thereafter not only continually provide more and better housing with its materials inventory, but will also trade tonnages of its inventory as scrap for other materials of greater advantage with the government's strategic materials stockpiling and priority control board, trading on a basis of weightstrength-efficiency formulas resolved to net foot-pound efficiencies.

...that this vital scrap problem had something vital to do, then, with both housing and war, and that scrap trend is one of the major force factors shaping our prognostication trajectory.

...that the traditional *attitude* of new ore producers and ore body reserve owners toward the scrap problem, i.e., that it is just a necessary evil to be classified as a "monger" activity and "the less said and the more exported, the better," even if it is to our enemies, is not to be considered seriously beyond noting that they have held it as a matter of policy that the less scrap getting back into re-circulation, the better market they theoretically could command. Because design advance would accelerate scrap recirculation potential, they were fundamentally against design advance and brought that attitude to bear throughout every intertwining directorate influence on the whole economy.

...that the basic metals producers have their faults but they are not particularly dumb and are certainly not afraid of major physical operations, as any who have reviewed far flung mining operations must admit.

...that their potential of efficient public service is now great because of a number of combinable circumstances which will eventually gear together; that these circumstances are, for instance, to be discovered in the fact that today their investment in processing and fabricating equipment is distinctly greater than their amortized investment in ore bodies, and that scrap processing is less costly than new mining processes.

...that a new world industry of housing, for instance, if well developed in its organization and on daring enough lines, will bring the metals refiners and initial-use-form fabricators into active forward motivation.

...that the successful maneuvering of this attitude change toward emphasis on design advance instead of on blind support of mass production of "or equal" products will spell the difference between democratic victory and defeat, which is all the difference there is.

...that realistically appraised in productive cost comparison to raw production, it is not unlikely that this unexpected scrap increment of the U.S. commonwealth could and would be accountingly arranged by legislative enactment to wipe out the national deficit.

...that before this World War fate is really over, we will witness an American Unbuilding Program which will exceed the highest rate of building activity ever attained in the past boom years by many-fold, and which will exceed even the rate of concurrent war bombing demolition, which latter accidentally releases materials for new uses, and is an unmartialled articulation of the inevitable trend. In the American case, forced by the materials and manpower emergency, the demolition will be premeditated because of the distinctly greater metallic content of the American structures as compared to European.

...that in either case of planned or bomb-wrought demolition, evolution will be demonstrating the large-scale incorporation into popularly comprehended industrial phenomena of the recycling of material elements into progressively more efficient use forms, a phenomenon which was becoming popularly evident in automobiles and ocean liners, but was not hitherto importantly evident in the housing world, whose end product the economic-supporting propaganda schematically inferred to be desirably permanent in arrangement.

...that so strong was this economic sentiment of "permanency" regarding housing in an otherwise dynamically developing world, people at first considered their purchase of an automobile in the light of a permanent family acquisition, wherefore a five-thousand-dollar investment in a well built, permanent Winton Limousine seemed cogent in 1910. Mankind went so far with its permanence whimsies as to consider its breeding complements not as free will partners but as permanent material possessions.

...that one of the major changes to be wrought in world thinking by this war is the acceptance of the concept of change itself, relative to which equilibrium is the word which describes controlled design arrangements of dynamically desirable complementary associations. This constant change and progressive equilibrium is the propagative key to the infinite vitality of the democratic principle, which, if never schematically allowed hitherto to take realized command of man's affairs, was always pumping along, dynamically active in his behalf, when his best interests seemed to be hopelessly frozen. Certainly, adaptability to constant change will be a characteristic of postwar housing, and dynamic equilibrium the key-note.

... that the erroneously titled "credit" system, that crude-fueled the now stalled old housing world, was constantly rediluted at a one-for-two mortgage equity rate, and that the credit-less credit system will be summarily abandoned by even the most powerfully conspiring secret forces of tide fighters.

... that inasmuch as the two hundred percent collateral forfeiture "credit" system is devoid of real substance in the scientific sense, nothing of its vacuum will be available for recirculation, and that with its vanishing will also disappear the whole legal fiction of real property and its extenuated nonsense of chattel mortgaging.

... that thus will exit deathage as a fulcrum of exploitation of an acceleratingly Live world which of necessity is learning to eliminate the vain fear of death from its cosmos.

... that if fixation on death preoccupies the manager, we had best get him out of the control seat. Practically the whole of the change in contemporary history is written in the natural substitution of the designation "pilot" for that of "driver" of our most special era transportation.

... that the economic issues of the now-stalled housing world were so snarled and entwined about that housing world's throat that its hungrily-gulped first prewar breakfast choked it to death instead of reviving it as many an interest had hoped.

... that housing's deathbed watching almost scared the official war effort to death, and that, after having inspected the deflated and pitifully inadequate legacy of that old housing world, the war effort has finally had to go ahead the hard way without the seemingly desirable advantage of a well-ordered housing organization to gear its manpower to general mobilization and essential decentralization of production and to a world flow system.

... that the possibility of a newly incepted scientific industry of housing to expedite and vastly facilitate the initial American war effort was sentenced to solitary internment by priority rulings comprehendingly issued six months before Pearl Harbor.

... that the infant scientific housing industry was mercilessly kicked around for a year previous to its "duration" sentence by a host of forces now useless to recall by name, but all of which were dominated in the last analysis by fear, by cerebral paralysis or selfish preoccupation that failed utterly to witness the accelerating evolution, preoccupations, be it well marked, that must be completely abandoned by those who will witness war's end. These are not ear-marked criticisms. The inseparable ramifications of the old housing world are as broad as the whole economic system built thereon.

... that you may say, "Why don't you cut out all this political-economic stuff and get along with the stark facts of description of precisely what you think the postwar housing is going to look like?" And I say to you it isn't going to look like anything until the war is over and that I can't envision its coming at all except in the terms of the meaning of the war. I say, and I have given realistic testimony to prove, that is why we have had to have a war: because we couldn't free ourselves for thinking without the detaching effects of war. Short of war, we just let well enough alone. We were swivel-moored to the rooted-down tonnage of our lugubrious past.

... that within the broad ramifications of the old housing world lie embalmed all the essential causes of the now-unleashed total war, and that therefore we cannot toss aside the question of housing until the war has been won, as we are urged to do by the unthinking and superficially patriotic in the phrases characterizing the shortening temper of busy-bodies who have long been frustrated in their attempt to revive yesterday in the midst of the upheavals and splintering of the scaffolding in the building dock as the ship of dynamic world commonwealth, its release interminably postponed, starts inexorably down the science-greased ways toward self-launching as the blockings of wooden structures give way to rot and termites. Soon she'll be majestically water-borne and riding the tide, capable of being maneuvered over every ocean and of weathering all storms.

... that this total war is a World Civil War amplifying into full cry the prototype local civil war of the United States of eighty years ago, which marked the first popular phase of transition of man's wealth-making from the anarchical, ignorance-limited and seasonally hazardous agricultural method of energy husbandry to the richly amplifying commonwealth method of industrial production piloted by science; employing vast, inanimate energy augmentations applied to ever more precise mechanical and chemical arrangement advantages.

... that the extent of this wealth is so unlimited, having reliably harnessed forces as lasting as the solar system as to allow of fabulous piracy so long as the new wealth source remained properly unaccounted for by any adequate, new, scientific bookkeeping system.

... that true audit would clearly reveal to popular comprehension that the solar system, rather than the "First National," or "The Federal Reserve," or "The Treasury," is the source of all physical wealth when released by science through technology.

... that, with sun energy wealth (in one of its many conversion phases) leaking in from a myriad of new sources from which, by any recognized feudal agricultural economic precedent, wealth was not supposed to gush, the astonished discoverer of each latest leak could stand in front of it and fill his back pockets without question of his legal proprietorship to that wealth, by any precedent of the obsolete accounting system's stewards.

... that this world-shocking impact of a meager realization of a potentially unlimited commonwealth upon the awareness of a civilization which had with superstitious ignorance struggled for an existence within the arbitrary and cruel limits of the system of "one against the many" and "survival of the fittest—only," detonated the one hundred years' civil war of man.

...that because the cause of his revolutionizing was too brilliant for him to face and believe, he listened with misgiving and resilient distrust to the sanctimonious inventions of the equally bewildered pocket-fillers who were afraid to be wise, lest they lose their newly-gained smart advantage.

...that this World Civil War is being waged, wittingly or unwittingly (and mostly the latter), for the total emancipation of man, not only from the swift ravages of ruthless war, but from the slow and far more painful ravages of a ruthless peace, with its unsung heroisms and its betrayed self-communion over its mutual survival problems.

...that social telepathetic self-communion over vital and mutual survival problems is betrayed because it is misbespoken by popularly published perversions of its mutual intent—the perversion being accomplished by omission by any special interest, Baptist, Communist, Episcopalian, or Democratic, of the required balancing components of any dynamic system of mutual volition.

...that this perversion of socially-generated volition is hard to detect, not alone because it is a vacuum instrument, but also because it is practiced by all "sides."

...that the ruthlessness of an unworthily arranged peace must ever be promulgated by the principle of might makes right, whether the kinetic monopoly be imposed by the few or the many, through vacuum stress or pincer pressure; and that man's insulation against the selfishness of monopoly of his commonwealth or common sense, and therefore his emancipation from that selfish fixation, will be provided only by scientific organization of his physical environment and wealth-making into a starkly mechanical reality, a reality the benefits of which politics can *at best* but promise the individual a chance to seek—a promise easily forgotten.

...that right here, in the cited difference between scientifically comprehensive engineering anticipations and political promises, is where our total Civil War thinking encounters the theory of the origin of the postwar housing. *What physical guarantee does man need of certain realization of his promised emancipation?* Obviously, scientific extension of his environmental control—not a political gesture.

...that from the curves of those trends which are apparently converging toward integration of the multiple of plus factors, i.e., those promising man's increased welfaring—that the particular phenomena, which will eventually be identified (probably years after the fact) as constituting origin and prototype of the true postwar housing, will occur only by critical emergence for causes as yet certainly unknown.

...that the virginally emergent, that is to say, unheralded postwar housing will appear in important volume during 1945 and will have attained enormous proportions by 1948, proportions that will dwarf into insignificance any previous historical performance of new housing on any per-capita-per-unit-of-environment cubage as yet put under a measure of successful control by man.

...that this enormous volume of postwar housing will range rapidly upward within a decade to an equilibrium level of production in the magnitude of two hundred million new units annually, grossing an annual rental income of approximately one hundred billion dollars, though computed at the fantastically low figure of five of today's American workman's hourly-wage-geared dollars per month per capita—including heat, light, and maintenance in private, individual quarters.

...that these individual quarters will be substantially proofed against fire, flood, pestilence, violent atmospheric disturbance, physical or psychological injuries or discomforts caused by inadequate design, scientific knowledge or technical performance.

...that this emergent postwar housing will be a mechanized human container service, purveying to you a controlled atmosphere of seventeen cubic feet of air per minute per person, free of toxic or disagreeable odors and dust, at a dry bulb temperature of 74° F, relative humidity forty-five percent, wet bulb temperature of 60.5° F, dew point 51.3° F, vapor pressure .01869 pounds per square inch, with reasonable plus or minus controls, with a noise level below the audible threshold, and with every essential refreshing and resting and sensing (illumination, etc.) device necessary to your happy well being ready to hand.

... that the mechanized containers will be but incidental apparatus of a World-Wide Dwelling Service—that is to say, the mechanized containers will be incidental in the same way that the telephone table hand set is an incidental (though obviously integral) mechanical item in the vast interconnected system of scientific apparatus which together makes up the world-wide communication system, a system which you voluntarily join up with by expressed subscription and in which you have no technical function except that of "user" and a system in which no mortgages, replevins, etc., occur.

... that if you don't play ball, the service is "shut off"—engineering simplicity replacing legal complexity.

... that by this latter, larger mechanical continuity, it is now physically possible for anyone near the earth's surface to speak to anyone else anywhere about the global premises, provided both have contact with at least a portable radio transceiver set.

... that it must be realized that this universal permeation of "self" completely obsoletes the old economic concept of things, immovably "in place," or absolutely "at rest," and of a few slowly shuttling, mobile gadgets that were ever a legal control headache to a system strictly predicated upon the proposition that wealth is "fixed property"—estate that is "real" only when "static."

... that the now-developing, scientific, world-girdling air transport and communication services, together with the new, scientific dwelling service, will all be part and parcel of an encompassing larger unit system, eventually complemented and insured of direction by world-girdling energy distribution services, sometimes beamed by radio, sometimes by wire, and sometimes transported in batches as fuel—a sort of "American plan" Living Service, a De Luxe Travel-or-Stop-Over-As-You-Please Service, ticket good for a life time, anywhere on earth, and available to all.

...that this total living service will reliably provide a complete set of ever-advancing standard-of-living conditions, whether you be speeding, poised, lingering or dwelling, upon the surface of the dry land, the high seas, in steaming tropic, on the fly-teeming Arctic tundra, on floating ice, high in the sky, on a mountain top, under the sea, or within the depths of the earth.

...that the duration of location occupancy will be proportional to proximity to strategical conditions and to population density, and that government land lease will be predicated in time limits upon reasonable pleas—socially beneficial custodianship, etc.

...that in the role of occupant you will have nothing to do personally with the mechanical process of moving, nor with the design and semi-automatic operation of the mechanized containers' energy processes as thermal, light, or work phases, any more than you have to do with the moving of your telephone or with the original design and upkeep of a suite on a liner.

...that you will notify the Service that you wish to move at such and such a time to this or that spot, and will be advised promptly whether the spot is already busy and, if not, for how long you may engage it and what the rate differential above local zone service will be, if any, as predicated on zoning distances from service centrals.

...that, dimensionally, the containers with all apparatus will average per occupant about fifteen hundred cubic feet and not over five hundred pounds when fully in use, including all machinery; or approximately three cubic feet of controlled environment per pound of scientifically arranged materials.

...that the mechanized dwelling containers will compact in service transit to less than fifty cubic feet per occupant, or one thirtieth of its in-use bulk.

...that these "living service" weights and volumes will include everything that the individual does not carry in his personal luggage, tool kit, files, and display miscellany.

...that the balance of the individual's possessions, outside of his customary reference requirements, will be expediently deposited in, or loaned or donated to, vaults or public collections without loss of access on the one hand and with increased public enjoyment on the other, while at the same time freeing the individual to enjoy his world-girdling freedom of motion and poise.

...that the dwelling containers will be fashioned out of the whole family of new alloys and chemical synthetics in increasing variety, as demonstrated by the scope of materials that enter into air transport fabrication.

...that the metals, broadly speaking, will be more generally found in the production and service phases of the industry than in the end product, with the notable exception of the latter's primary energy propagator and its mechanical equipment.

...that the synthetics (plastics) will predominate in the end product's visible surfaces, though probably skeletonized delicately within by metallic reinforcements.

...that the mechanized dwelling containers, considered as end product, will be constantly improved in design and that new models will be progressively fed into the broad service operation as the service organization progressively scraps and recycles the materials in improved efficiency of disposition, essentially unheeded as a process of change by the service user, exactly as does the telephone service evolute by scientific expediency, the user being a "party" to its evolution only as a potential or kinetic statistic.

...that the individual or single family mechanized dwelling service containers will constantly reflect the latest advantages of scientific knowledge gained through pure and applied research, thus affording man direct, cooperatively effected benefit of the environmental complements to his welfare, without conscious designing initiative or effort on the part of individual man as practiced in the past only through inspection of his own selfish immediate requirement, spotlighted exclusively for his consideration because, "No one is going to look after my best interests if I don't myself."

... that man has been working against his own welfare, because his unscientifically appraised, individual requirements were always so wasteful and inefficient as to keep the commonwealth bankrupt and innocent of increment which, if allowed to accumulate, might be scientifically diverted toward instrumenting the organization of his scientifically cooperative "living service."

... that the educational system enjoyed by the new life incubated in the evolving "living service" facilities will be a combination of radio, movie, television instruction,[13] industrially devised and recorded by vast mutual programs of service and the arts, and that this instruction, freely tapped by the occupants of the containers, wherever they may be, will be amplified by actual experience at the source as a practical proposition made possible by the energy work efficiency gains of the world-girdling living service.

... that, in reality, the whole globe will become every man's backyard.

... that any detailed discussion now of the mechanical "features" is petty and superfluous, other than to note that it is probable a world-wide scientific service of the magnitude now looming up will engage in such terrestrial development as that of utilization of the cold of the Arctic and Antarctic and of the upper reaches of the air, together with the constant winds and reciprocating tides which will all be gathered into the heat exchange system and energy-storing operations by production of liquid oxygen in vast

13 **"1936 About 200 hundred television sets are in use world-wide... 1939 Vladimir Zworkin and RCA conduct experimentally [*sic*] broadcasts from the Empire State Building. Television was demonstrated at the New York World's Fair and the San Francisco Golden Gate International Exposition."** From "The Invention of Television Timeline" by Mary Bellis, About.com, http://inventors.about.com/od/tstartinventions/a/Television_Time_3.htm (accessed July 9, 2009).

quantities in those cold polar and stratospheric regions and development of its controlled expansion uses in the energy cycle.

... that long before employment of these cosmic sources of energy, today's wastes of the sanitation cycle will be converted to energy work, providing as they do by natural process 110-octane methane gas; and that synthetic fuel for human bodily processes, together with other new food forms already developing, will sum-totally affect the mechanical apparatus requirements of the dwelling containers in a revolutionary manner.

... that it is possible that competition of these over-all services for annual contracts with the individual will become the new major political diversion of the world, as Imperial Dwellingways proselytes for voluntary contract constituents in competition with Pan-American Plan or Intercontinental Cooperatives.

... that these mechanical containers will serve as constant referendum voting booths, recording the temper of their vast intercommunicated population.

... that the new life incubated within these containers will be energy-conscious to an amazing degree, will think dynamically in foot-pounds of energy involvement (not by consciously mumbled calculation). The new life will know how to psychoanalyze itself and its social proclivities, learning how to do away with destructive war as a means of evolutionary growth.

... that unselfishness will be as practical a concept as the ability of a steel ship to float by the cooperatively arranged disposition of its atomic body politic, and that the individual will be guaranteed his inviolability, by the nature of mathematics, and that life will be essentially a lesson to be enjoyed.

... that in order merely to survive, when environment is comprised of unscientific structure, equipment, philosophy of concept, or environment represents an outright hodgepodge of ignorance, the human occupants must "rise above it" by exercising a strict schedule of self-limitation, together with an immaculate discipline of person and premises.

... that when the occupants of unscientifically conceived environment fail in sanitary self and environmental discipline, that then the standards of their lives rapidly degenerate.

... that when the environment is scientifically conceived and rendered, the human occupants can then divest themselves of the necessity of onerous and Puritanic hardship of conduct and yet accomplish successful and happy living in naturally engendered sanity.

... that because cleanliness is popularly accepted as next to Godliness, daily routines tallying by categories one and a half hours of dishwashing, one and a half hours of clothes, towel and bed linen washing, one hour of house cleaning, two hours of cleaning and preparation of food, one hour of self-cleaning, externally and internally, interspersed with an hour for back-resting, all add up to an eight-hour day devoted to yesterday's dirt, lest that dirt become today's filth and tomorrow's disease. And in all those eight hours devoted to the clean-up of yesterday, not one constructive act nor forward gain in the standard of living is accomplished.

... that it takes a seventh day, hallowed for resting, and considerable preaching, praying and psalm-singing, to keep a mother housekeeper in good humor as she progressively relinquishes her own potentials to the next generation.

... that in the sense that a child is pure, that all people of any age are also innately pure, and that they are not made better by practice of severe routines of religion or self-discipline, but that those routines, which have been pivoted for millenniums upon development of habits of effective sanitation of the body and physique, have been instituted out of survival necessity as a sort of fervent sing-song sanitation, akin to Negro slave spirituals, or Volga boatmen's chants, or even to sailor's charities, invented out of many psychological causes, not one of which today has any obvious relationship to the actual rhythm of exertion.

... that if people were synchronized and instrumented in mutual inter-services, designed *creatively* throughout, that is, anticipating tomorrow as one with yesterday; and these services were focused upon the most simply effective scientific control of our environment processes, that people could then continue to maintain the purity of spontaneous action and reaction with which they were born, and do so quite unconsciously, that is, without having to cite or recite a moral under which they were acting.

... that, granted a scientifically-designed interservice, people would be able to continue in the original purity and dignity of nativity without having to go through the innocent corruption, realized degradation and reform or perish cycles, heretofore inherent in the ignorant chaos of unscientifically encountered environment. And out of these cycles of initial purity, subsequent corruption, degradation, and reform, few, if any, whole beings are ever recreated in the flesh or even in spirit.

... that, sum-totally, the whole gamut of religious and moral codes of the past have been necessary to man as palliatives of environment rather than as improvements of his innate qualities; that the words sane and sanitary, which both derive from the Latin *sanus,* meaning healthy, sound or wholesome, originally intended to communicate that the integrity of original process or phenomena remained unblemished.

... that so old have the fundamental sanitary requirements become most of them have acquired a patina of aesthetic or religious tradition, which celebration of them in itself obscures the original cerebration, or whyfor, of the simple, sanitary requirements; until finally meaning has been obscured entirely by the dilettante vacuum accruing to all art for art's sake—or specialization pursued for special rather than comprehensive issue.

... that, in its broadest philosophic sense, this reasoning indicates the enduring superiority of benefit to man inherent in loving as compared to the temporary and miniscule advantages accruing to selfishness.

... that the degree of probability of preservation of inherent sanity in the individual is proportional to the degree of maintenance of inherent sanitation in environment; that beyond the inherently functioning sanitation there is no super-sanity to be attained by passion or formula—by mysticism or morality.

...that here man may actually help himself to a higher degree of living enrichment by scientific design, not to improve, but to protect the original radiant beauty of curious energetic life, of truthful process, of paradise never lost.

...that the modern disaffection from religious dependence decried by the sect proprietors springs from the release from sanitary precaution in its broader, necessitous sense, provided by modern mechanics and science, through which shower baths, sulfa compounds, steri-lamps, and radio-summoned air ambulances, and scientifically pooled cooperative blood banks, have retained people nearer to God than they have ever been returned by the moral sanitation of the sect proprietors, whose original founders gained their popular strength through effective admonition in these fundamental problems of sanitation and survival, and not by initiation of collection-plate routines, abracadabra, sage political moves or real estate investments.

...that I conclude our world-wide contemporaries are not less fervent, loving, trustworthy, and individually aware of the profound mysteries and universal omnipotence than were their forebears. In fact, I figure that quite the contrary is true.

...that the people are now more deeply conscious than ever before in history of the existence and functioning principles of universal, inexorable physical laws; of the pervading, quietly counseling truth within each and every one of us; of the power of love; and—each man by himself—of his own developing, dynamic relationship with his own conception of the Almightiness of the All-Knowing.

...that our contemporaries just don't wear their faith on their sleeves anymore.

...that people have removed faith from their sleeves because they found out for themselves that faith is much too important for careless display. Now they are willing to wait out the days and years for the truthful events, encouraged individually from within; and the more frequently the dramatic phrases advertising love, patriotism, fervent belief, morals, and good fellowship are plagiarized, appropriated and exhibited in the show windows of the world by the propaganda whips for indirect and ulterior motives, no matter how meager the compromise—the more do people withdraw within themselves and shun taking issue with the nauseating perversions, though externally exhibiting quiet indifference, nonchalance or even cultivating seemingly ignorant acceptance.

... that this wholesale and published exploitation of integrity and squandering of the meaning in words has come to such a pass that people the world over no longer trust any impersonal corporate statement and promise, although seemingly accepting the mandate of the moment in quiet resignation that might superficially appear as subscription to interpretive pronouncements of the limited liability oracles.

... that all these profound developments in the exterior and interior relationships of man and his privately intercommunicated intelligence are precisely bound up with the mechanics of his environment.

... that men know and have known for long of the relative security to be found, on the one hand, in values of the static system, as developed by proclamation and necessary acceptance, and, on the other hand, within the dynamic system, as discovered by reality of awareness. For I note that throughout history when men sought to punish one man, they first demoted him, that is, deprived him of degrees of his net motion privileges; on second offense they forthrightly arrested him; next they imprisoned, and if he still struggled, shackled him. As complete and final punishment, they killed him. Here indeed was complete demobilization of the individual.

... that that is why men spoke long ago of the "quick" and the "dead"—true freedom of articulating individualism must permeate the whole of environment. The only limitations must be those discovered sanely by the individual in the relationship of operation of universal physical principles.

... that "quickness" in sanitation—that is, in degree of spontaneity equivalent to unconscious and therefore natural act, making possible free action in every direction, accomplished through the complete integration of intelligent universal principles into cooperatively performed services, which we call industrialization—must find its broadest historical application in production and development of the scientific dwelling service.

... that mankind's prewar plight is similar to that of the fellow who painted himself into the middle of the floor because he was so preoccupied with the technique. Man has applied the benefits of industrialization—at least a priming coat—to everything except his most important spot, the worn-out place in the center where he most frequently treads, his habitat. Man is at last willing to apply industrialization to his home itself, now that its air conditioned brightness and efficiency have come so provokingly to his attention with the new war effort manifestations, but he doesn't know how to get out of his own way to effect that final application. Suddenly the air raid warning sounds and he streaks for the door, paint or no paint, only to find himself when the "all clear" sounds unexpectedly outside the situation and free at last to attack the problem objectively. There, outside of each of their houses, contemplating them with critical eye, stand each and all of his neighbors. That is where man and his housing are today.

Marine Corps heli-lift of a 42-foot Geodesic Dome from the U.S.S. *Leyte*, Hampton Roads, Virginia, 1957.

Geodesic Dome on the U.S.S. *Leyte*

The 100-foot Travillon in Winrock, Arkansas

Kaiser dome (150 ft. diameter) in Honolulu, Hawaii. It was assembled in less than one day.

Interior of the Kaiser dome. Erected in 1957, its acoustics are considered to be superb.

Twelve men and a boy perch on a 10-foot Playdome at Harvard University

The 40-foot Plydome Chapel with windows of colored plastic, constructed for the Columbian Fathers in Korea. Test erected in Hamford, Iowa.

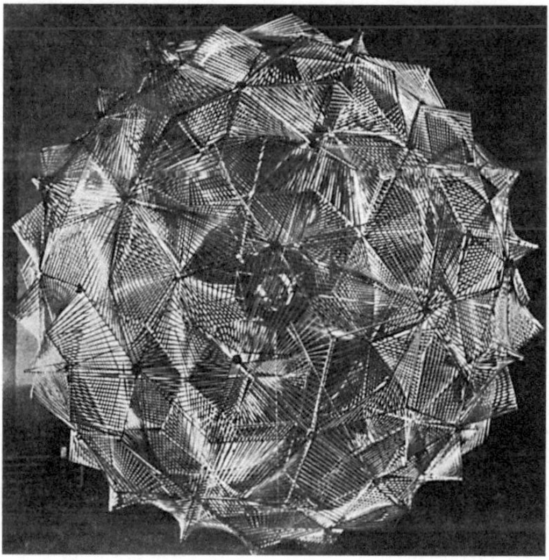

Roy Gussow's Geodesic symbol for USIS in Bangkok, Thailand

Steel Geodesic Dome of the Union Tank Car Company in Baton Rouge, Louisiana. The dome—384 feet in diameter, 116 feet high—was designed as a car rebuilding plant.

The Cornell University Pinecone Plydome

Radome on the Arctic DEW line

Radome Octetruss in the garden of The Museum of Modern Art, New York City

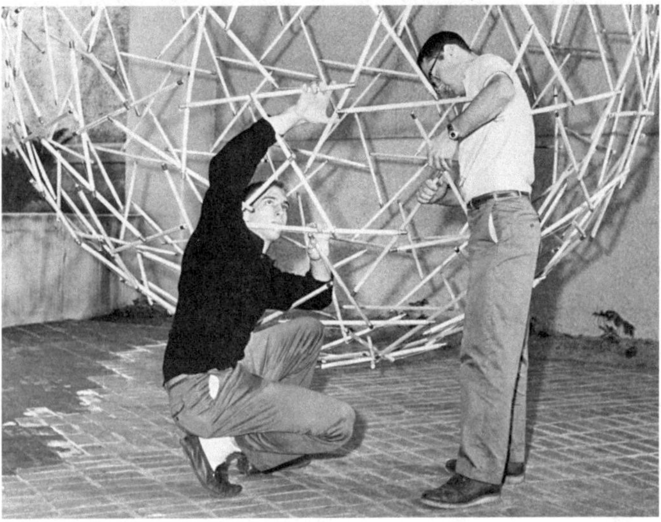

Tensegrity Sphere at Southern Illinois University

The author and the Kaiser Dome in Moscow, 1959

The Graham National Foundation in Pryor, Oklahoma. The dome was constructed by Kaiser Aluminum Company.

Anheuser-Busch Aviary built by Union Tank Car Company at Tampa, Florida

The author and Tom Moore inspect the latter's prestressed, lightweight, concrete "Dog-Bone."

Interior of the Miami Seaquarium

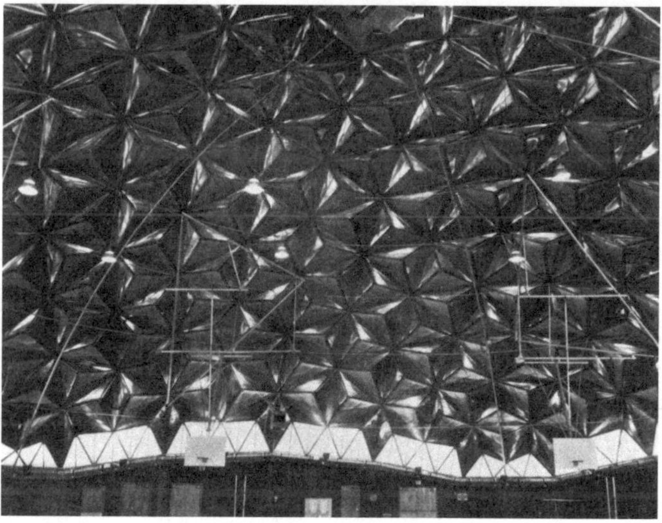

Palomar College gymnasium in San Marcos, California

Pease 39-foot hot weather pavilion

Exterior of Buckminster Fuller's 39-foot dome-residence in Carbondale, Illinois

Buckminster and Anne Fuller's living room in Carbondale, Illinois

Dining room-kitchen of author's home

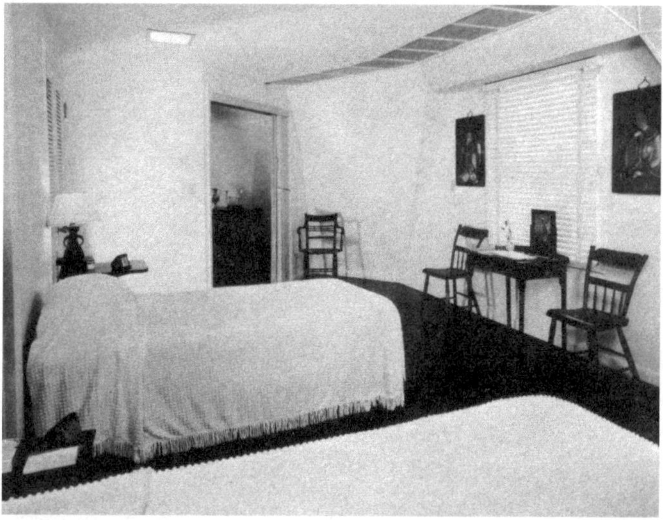

Bedroom of author's home

Kaiser dome over a Lutheran church in Florida

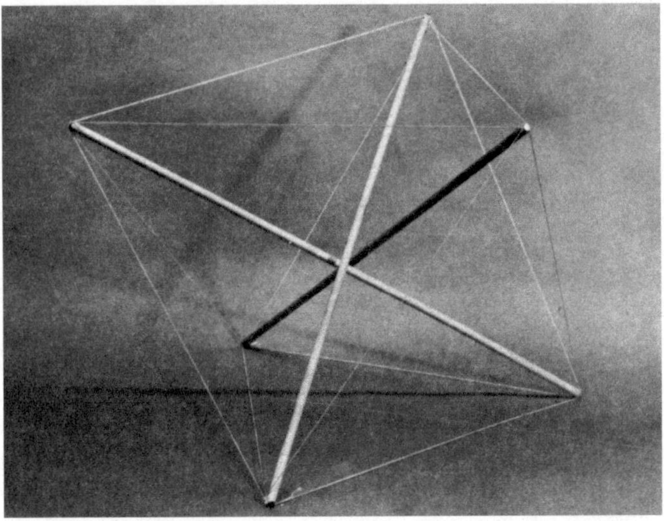

Tensegrity Octa (Ted Pope)

A four-foot Aspension Model in Tokyo

Bamboo dome assembled by the author with students of the Bengal College of Engineering, Calcutta, India

6 Fluid Geography

It is a sailorman's credo that there is a generic difference between himself and a landlubber. While admitting that sailor blood sometimes may be trapped inland for several generations, he believes that it never loses its dynamic proclivities. Though landlubbers may frequent the seas by political appointment, tourist urge or commercial necessity, conscientiously memorizing nautical language and techniques, the sailorman believes that landlubbers are fated to wear these acquisitions only as paraphernalia, distinctly superimposed upon their static roots. He reasons, therefore, that, while a Kansas Citian may get to have four stripes, unless he has inherited seagoing corpuscles, he must remain strictly corny, not salty.

Irrespective of the validity of this credo, there exist fundamental differences between the practical requirements of the sailorman's and the landlubber's lives. By exigencies, sailors have come to be the only men of commerce dealing directly and daily with the mechanics of the stars. Confronted with large quantities of unknowns intervening between identified ports, they came early to rely upon instruments and skills of the intellect, upon scientific imagining. In principle, "blind flying" has been employed at sea for centuries. Without thinking of themselves as cosmogonists, sailors naturally develop a spontaneous cosmic viewpoint. They view the world from outside; they "come upon" the land.

April 1944. Originally appeared in *American Neptune*, accompanied by Fuller's "World Map on Dymaxion Projection" (see pp. 170–71).

But not so the landlubber. Though half a millennium has passed since Copernicus and Galileo urged upon educated people that the heavens were not turning about the fixed earth, landsmen in general and even their rock-mounted astronomers persist in "seeing" the sun "set" and "rise" in their personal lives.

Intending to help their children to grasp the "very difficult" concept of total heavenly motion, the landlubber theoreticians have devised planetariums within their great cities. Instructed by this device, the children approach personal conviction of the ceaseless motion of the planetarium heavens, only to be thrown into life-long confusion at the critical moment as the closing landlubber phrases come to their stimulated attention: "Now the sun is rising again in the East, the lights are coming on, the machine stops, and we return you to New York (to the practical life in which the sun, as a handy gadget, still zooms around the contentedly static earth)."

To the landsman "the East" and "the West" are places, to the sailorman they are directions in which he may move. To the sailorman entered upon the great Pacific, it is final proof of the landlubber's nonsense that the sun is not only forced to do this rising and setting act, but perversely to do so on the wrong stage. Viewed from the Pacific, the sun rises from the Occident and sets in the Orient.

By exigency, too, sailors constantly exercise their inherent dynamic sensibilities. The ceaseless universal motion of the sailorman's life persists in his brain, even when he is landed on the beach. For hours and days after he has come in from the sea, his legs go on adjusting him to the slowly heaving motion of Fifth Avenue. It isn't hard to convince a sailor that the watery, gray-mist horizon toward which he may be sailing is rolling down to reveal the sun, or that his circular horizon segment of the moment is one little wet spot on a great sphere, ponderously rotating to obscure the sun to the westward. He sees everything in motion, from the slopping of the coffee in the pot to the peregrinations of the major magnitude stars. Amongst all these relative motions, the pole star alone seems to float motionless as the world's mooring buoy in the sky.

To the static-minded landsman, it is an insensible statistic that the moon is about 239,000 miles away from the earth. To the sailorman, it is a natural sensation that the moon-earth pull is so great as twice daily to be able to lift many feet aloft the thunderous tonnages of water upon which he sails. By measured reasoning he "sees" the moon lifting the water as it circles after its rotating and orbiting mother-ship Earth. So fast is the orbiting that the sailor knows it is difficult to obtain an accurate navigational sight from the moon. However, to the static landsman, that moon seems to hang motionless as a luminous flat medallion in the periodically glimpsed scene.

To the landsman, a trip around the world means the conversion of a bank account or an Irish Sweepstakes prize into a procession of hotels; to the sailorman, it is the logical fulfillment of his work, punctuated by visits to the beach.

While it seems that a preposterous case of rationality versus irrationality can be made in favor of the sailor, what is really being demonstrated here is a principle transcending identity with either the sailor or the landsman. One common observation of an effect of that principle is "Necessity is the mother of invention." The sailor is much better acquainted with that trying dame than is the landsman, if for no other reason than because land activities generally are based on eight-hour workdays, after which the office and factory are shut down; whereas the sea can never be shut down. While physical laws persist both on land and sea, their slow articulation on the dry, crystalline land could be disregarded for two-thirds of the day. The landsman stables the horse, garages the car, or merely walks into his house and sits down. Inertia, unchallenged, promotes careless philosophy. Every day the seafarer is exposed to three times the necessitous experience, for even when off watch he is still in a dynamic environment. Moreover, the mutability of the liquid state and the proportions of tonnage and velocity to which the sailor is continuously exposed are many times those encountered on the land. Thus by compounding of factors, technology advances far more rapidly at sea.

If we will remember that leverage, for instance, as a universal principle, may be abstracted from immediate identity with sea gear for reapplication on the land, we can readily understand how the technical advantages gained on the sea gradually come to satisfy land emergencies. In the light of this technical leadership, we can understand why rule of the world derived from rule of the sea.

Frequency of technical emergency is accelerated to an even greater extent in the gaseous state. Airmanship emergencies require the most exquisite of solutions. In short order, aeronautical engineering has reapplied to its needs all of maritime technology. While the air technology may not as yet have taken complete leadership away from the technology of the sea in the pacing of man's affairs, it hastens inexorably to such predominance.

With the land as the bottom of the new unbroken air ocean, as so brilliantly taught in the 1930s by George T. Renner[14] of the Civil Aeronautics Authority to elementary school America; with sailors, aviators, and landsmen all crossbreeding into a dynamic world citizenry; and with historical events accelerated from a frequency interval of centuries to intervals of hours, all men are, so to speak, now in the same boat and are necessitous, among other items, of a precise means for seeing the world from the dynamic, cosmic, and comprehensive viewpoint.

The map which is the primary exhibit of this chapter [Figure 1], was invented for this purpose, and while it is certain to be bettered by subsequent inventions (it is for the moment the most reliable comprehensive projection) it describes the earth's surface

14 George T. Renner was also the author of numerous books about geography, including *Human Geography in the Air Age (A Text for High School Students)* (New York, 1942).

with the minimum total score of distortions from the many well-known geometrical processes inherent in translation of the angle and scale information from a spherical to a flat surface.

Presently, we will discover why distortion is at a minimum. The mechanics of this projection, for those who enjoy inspecting the intricacies of the engine room, will be exposed toward the close of this article. The mathematics will be found to be as neat and stark as the buckets within a turbine casing. But for the moment what is important is that the trend forecaster can rely implicitly upon the impression of shapes and relative sizes and distances to be derived from this comprehensive device. We may, therefore, proceed at once to ascertain the inherent advantages and make trial of their ability to reveal major trends in world affairs.

This new projection is particularly successful because it makes possible the reassembly all on one plane of each and any of the continents without broken contours. Further, it makes possible the assembly of those whole continents in any of the arrangements in which they occur relative to one another on the globe, as one explores successively the infinite number of great circle continuities. This new map is unique in that the continental contours are transferable in unbroken integrity from their spherical disposition to the flat map representation without perceptible deformation or modulation of size and with uniform scale measured in great circle arc segments bounding each component section.

Unblemished by the peripheral sinuses necessary, first, to the scoring open and, secondly, to the peeling of any solid, this continental contour integrity is the joint result of a new mathematical discovery on the one hand and, on the other, of emancipation from the formal cartographic tyranny traditionally imposed by the Poles.*

* In the March 1, 1943, issue of *Life* I published a world map on the dymaxion projection, with thermal latitudes shown in color. The dymaxion grid was there oriented from the North Pole, placed symmetrically at the center of a square, and the Greenwich meridian cut across the square at 90°. This was irrespective of the

Figure 1
1944 "World Map on Dymaxion Projection"

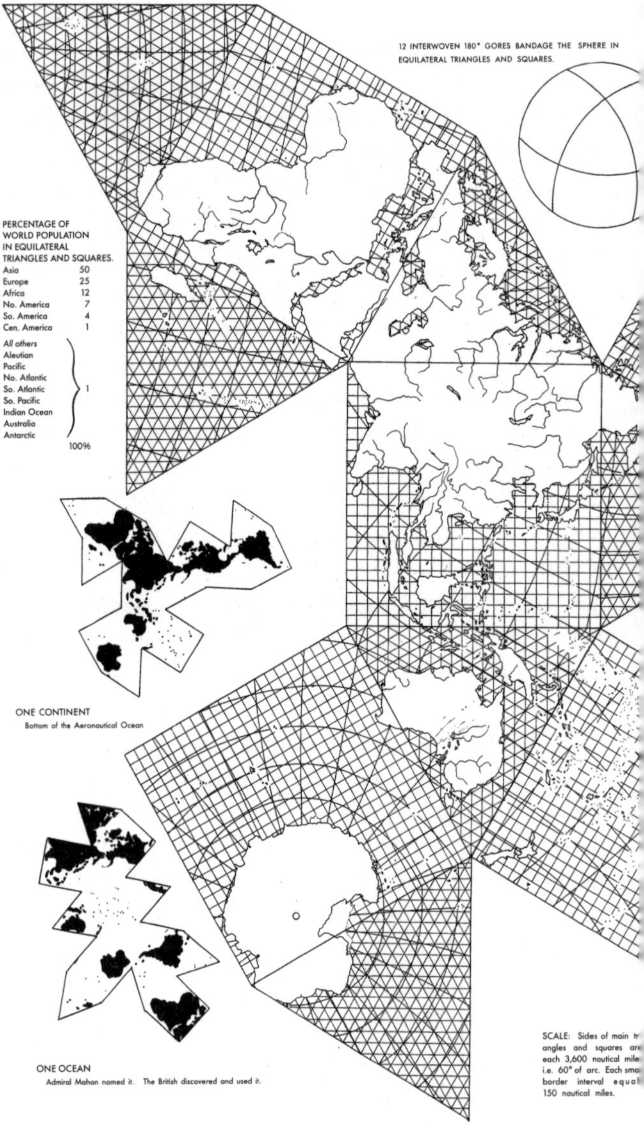

24 EQUIANGULAR TRIANGLES WITH COMMON INTERNAL AND EXTERNAL VERTEXES.

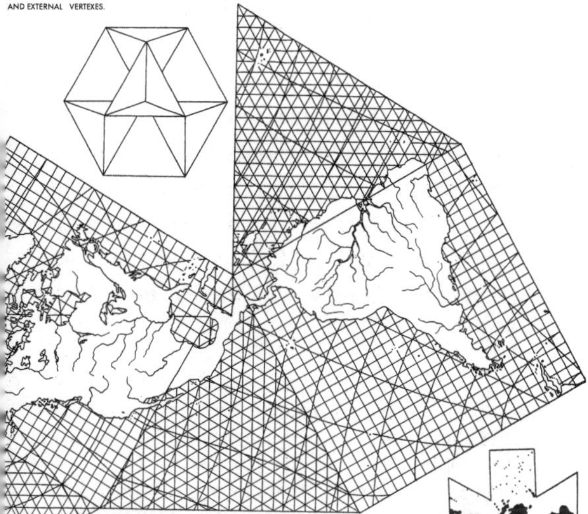

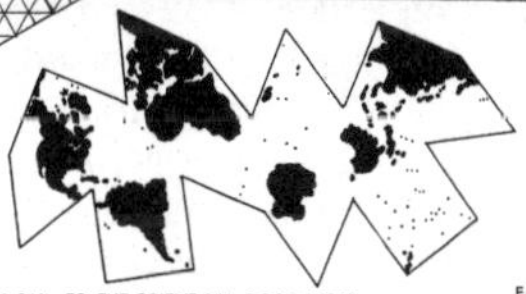

EAST BY SAIL—TO THE ORIENT VIA GOOD HOPE

From the Spanish Main via the Piratical Indian Waters. 12,000 mile great circle route from New York to Australia.

EAST BY STEAM
TO THE ORIENT VIA SUEZ

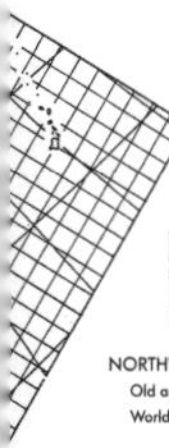

NORTHWARD TO THE ORIENT AND NORTHWARD TO EUROPE

Old and new worlds on either hand. Russia overhead and Mackinder's World Island trisected.

STRATOSPHERE STRATEGIC

European triangle controls the altitude merry-go-round.

WORLD MAP
ON DYMAXION PROJECTION

BY RICHARD BUCKMINSTER FULLER

Employing only great circle grid reference and comprising variable focus, uniform boundary scale of sections, and universal viewpoint, i.e., the Earth's center and the astronomical zenith are always perpendicularly above and below each point, wherefore corresponding terrestrial and celestial sections are always parallel and angularly congruent throughout.

 Patented 1946

As indicated in the miniature arrangements surrounding the large map Figure 1, there are many alternate assemblies, the components of which always total up as a complete map of the world. Each, by "picture psychology," focuses attention on the central portion of its mass, yet retains all other factors in appropriate contributory status. For instance, one of these pictures is the sailorman's One Ocean World, fringed by the shoreline fragments which are his particular concern. It discloses the relative vastness of the Pacific and emphasizes that ocean's longest axis, from Cape Horn to the Aleutians. Oriented about the Antarctic, the waters of the Indian and Atlantic Oceans open out directly from the Pacific as lesser gulfs of the one ocean.

favor to the land masses (obtained in the map published in the *Neptune* Figure 1), *Life* deeming it essential that its readers recognize the familiar polar landmark which none of them had ever seen.

My first world map, entitled "Dymaxion Traffic Chart" was published in 1927 in my book, *Time Lock* Figure 2. It is a perspective projection of the land hemisphere with the French Riviera at its center, and shows the North Pole a fifth of the way down top center, and the Aleutian Chain at the very top. Most of the Americas, Africa, Europe and Asia can be seen, though the southern half of South America, Southern California, Capetown and the Indo-China to Australia areas are missing. Numbers of little airplanes are shown, flying the logical world air routes—circling the Arctic as a major traffic turntable, as well as crossing through Europe to Dakar, over the Atlantic to Natal and up the chain of the Americas. Spotted all through the then-unpenetrated Arctic and tropics are shown a number of dwelling machines, modern environmental control devices which would make possible maintenance of service-conditions for the airports in these then-unlivable areas. To the best of my knowledge, this is the first world map which shows the comprehensive air traffic. It was republished in *The Architectural Record*, January 1934, p. 10.

My second world map Figure 3, copyrighted in 1934 and again published in 1938 as an end paper for my book *Nine Chains to the Moon*, was my first experiment with unique projection methods. It was a one-continent map in which all visible error was massaged into the ocean areas. It was done with an integrator and a series of center lines from centers of areas, a method impossible for popular duplication or for any navigational means. Its main purpose was to clarify the one-continent concept which joins the chain of continents together over the Aleutian route. It was subsequently used in the February 1940 issue of *Fortune* to demonstrate the relationship of world population and the world energy slaves, and has been hung in the Smithsonian Institution.

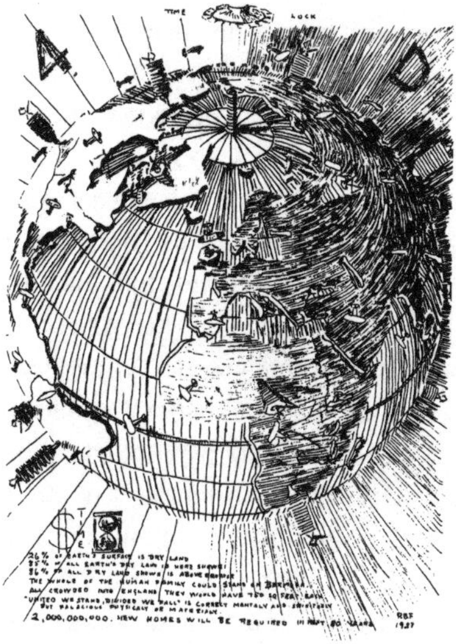

Figure 2
1927 "Dymaxion Traffic Chart"

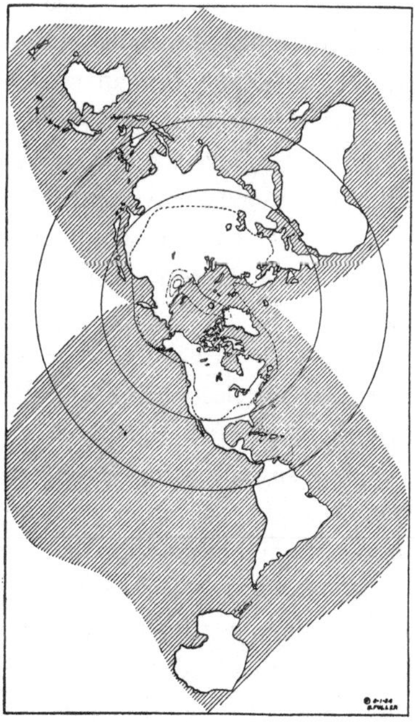

Figure 3
1934 "World Map"

To convince himself that picture psychology is not an esoteric mystery of painters, the reader has only to compare the impressions derived from looking first at the one-continent arrangement and then at the one-ocean assembly. Turning away and reporting his impressions, he would be inclined to testify that these maps were composed of different components; that the one-continent map was comprised of seventy-five percent dry land area, that the one-ocean map was comprised of ninety percent water area. The fact is that both maps are composed of the same pieces. Though less dramatic than the example presented, the many other possible arrangements are endowed with equally unique psychological differences. Each of the arrangements is as important as any other, depending upon the geographical location with which the individual has habitually been identified.

The sailor may ascertain by inspection the most advantageous courses to his many world ports from the tactical center of that watery workaday world. So far as he is concerned, the whole world is one ocean, one-quarter of whose uneven bottom crops up through the surface in peaks and plateaus. When he comes in to the shore, he is coming in to the peak of a mountain range about five miles high. To our modern cosmic sailorman, coming in to an airfield in Tibet over the Himalayas is approximately the same sensation as coming in to Puerto Rico over the Antilles ranges, rising abruptly 30,000 feet above the Nares Deep.

There are also many rearrangements of the map to emphasize whole continental masses. By means of these elective arrangements, our thinking may be realistically insinuated within the special geographical environment of the people of any one world area as predicated upon their own set of conditions of direction and proximity to all the rest of the surrounding world. It is in this feature that we discover the dynamic leverage afforded our world appraisal by this device. No longer need the American continents, for instance, with only twelve percent of the world population, occupy relentlessly the central and non-distorted portion of the world map, assigning fifty-two percent of the world's population to an insignificant, fragmented, and distorted Asiatic borderline position.

In the particular assembly chosen for the large display, one sees all the continents linked together without visible distortion, without a break in their contours, for the first time in history.

The sailorman's interest in world history relates only to the net difference in means of travel between component parts of his unit globe. All history "pays off" to him in total sustainable knots.[15] The shrinking dimensions of his world are computed in relative velocities.

We can see by experiment with this map why he laughs at the suggestion that *"East is East and West is West and never the twain shall meet,"* for he sees that men as individuals have not only moved in the total course of time in all directions over the face of the earth, but *that they emigrated essentially out of one major pool of civilization,* which was Indo-China,[16] Here East and West were originally one. From this one major pool there grew two main spearheads which we have come carelessly to identify as unrelated. This division into East and West occurred as the offshoots drew into diametric global positions in the course of their eventual encirclement of the earth. Growing out of the same unit mass of civilization, the eastbound and westbound spearheads progressively absorbed the lesser sources and their tendrils in Africa and South America, as well as the interweaving complex migrations.

---

15 One nautical mile per hour—a unit of speed used on ships and aircraft. One nautical mile is equal to 1.15 statute miles.

---

16 Fuller was long convinced humans evolved out of the "coral atolls" of the South Pacific and North Indian oceans, based particularly on his views about "ocean" people, derived from extensive research throughout his life. For example, decades after the date of this article, I recall his enthusiasm about a book by Austin Coates, with whom he corresponded and met in the 1970s, entitled *Islands of the South* (London, 1974). See also the chapter "Speculative Prehistory of Humanity" in Fuller's book *Critical Path* (New York, 1981). For current thinking on the evolution and migration of early humans, see *The Journey of Man: A Genetic Odyssey* (Princeton, NJ, 2002) by British geneticist Spencer Wells.

The differences between the two spearheads existed only in the effects of environmental changes upon their cumulative technologies. The spearheads attained extreme diametric east-west remoteness in the period approximately called the Dark Ages.

The sailorman, alert to currents, can see the flows of history as the static historian fails utterly to do. He sees how some people have turned adversities into technical advantages, how they have gradually reduced the limitations to their elected motions, and how they have in fact accelerated their movements.

Let us retrace on the new map the major civilization flows in order to see more clearly the historical significance of our present dynamic world conditions.

Both major migrations appear as the gradual extensions of the horizon by successive generations. Because everything flows in the direction of least resistance, and because the heat to the south was too great, as was the cold to the north, the least resistant directions were approximately east and west. The next extensions of the generations are directionally random because the geography is random, but they are extremely uniform in the unseen thermal latitudes.

Establishment of these two great world trendings was unplanned by any systematic organization of society. These divergent trends are the articulation of biological forces demonstrating progressive equilibrium everywhere throughout the universe. Their dynamic inter-relationship, as modified by the total geographic scene, determines our fate.

Springing jointly from the Indo-China area, the spearheads both start in an easterly direction, but split at the Malayan tip.

One main stem grows in a general northeasterly direction along the islands close to the Chinese and Siberian coast, along the Aleutians and eventually down the coast of the Americas, with myriads of subsidiary spearheads penetrating inland from all along the main tendril. The nearer to the beginning of the main stem, the larger and more plentiful were the branches.

As offshoots of this first major spearhead coasting northeasterly, many tribes penetrated the Mongolian hinterland, passaging westward to the north side of the enormous Himalayan ranges. The vastness of this region lost them for millenniums, even to the point of seeming extinction so far as the people still remaining in the land of their origin were concerned. Historically, these lost migrants are not heard of again in India until, as the Mongols, called Moguls, they come over the mountains in the days of Genghis Khan to rule their sedentary forebears. During the course of the thousands of miles and thousands of years of the many separate inland trekkings, the appearances of the individuals develop distinct and unique characteristics. Many demonstrate color evolution as a result of sustained changes in radiation conditions.

Many of these tribes reappear westward all the way from the Mediterranean to the Arctic Sea. They arrive in successive waves, for instance, as the Hellenes in Greece, and the Hungarians and Tartars along the Danube. Some of these tendrils double back toward the Pacific. Fragments of their more recent and vivid easterly motion have sometimes obscured from anthropologists the preponderantly westward pattern of the early Asiatic migrations.

Somewhat similar technical evolution characterized all of these people's wayfaring. They were constantly on the move because of the sharp changes of the northerly climate and vagaries of the sparse vegetation. Because of this mobility, they developed very sheer efficiency in their mobile living and hunting apparatus and in their survival routines. These wandering hordes, equipped for their inland migration with already-efficient technologies won from the sea, subsequently devised portage efficiencies which enabled them to overpower the more easy-going southerly peoples as they encountered them.

Despite this impressive inland migration, the greatest mass of the easterly spearhead's main stem stayed near the sea and fished and farmed along the fertile shores of the many river mouths of the China coast, where their progeny still exist as a teeming marginal life.

Reeling our continuity backward millenniums to the original ancient pool of civilization in Indo-China, let us inspect the coursings of the second major spearhead.

This second spearhead, which broke off from the first at the Malayan tip, drifted out into the myriad islands intervening between China and Australia. Though part of this seaward drifting was by accident, part of it must have been attempted by choice and, as such, constituted considerably more daring than that demonstrated by the people who hugged the coast. The separation of the spearheads constituted a first screening of psychological types. This psychological screening imposed by elective dealing with the dramatically presented problems of the unknown offshore deeps has been repeated constantly in subsequent history. For this reason sea history plays an important part in developing the psychological factors of modern problems.

Subsisting on the less fertile soil of the islands, and of necessity forced to wander from time to time, the people of the westerly spearhead learned to navigate or control their course of direction between the islands, to identify their chances with the favorable winds. Gradually they learned to make the passage even with less favorable winds, by quartering down wind, and, finally, by right-angling. In time they developed techniques for sailing better than abeam to the wind. From this broad reaching they learned to point up even closer toward the direction from which the force came.

Eventually they learned to turn the forces to their service, rather than to fight them or to give way to them. They discovered that they could challenge their fate successfully. Next they learned to translate this angular wind advantage into increased speeds. Out of this technical about-face, accomplished by the island sailors of the southwest Pacific, grew the second major world migration, tending to girdle the world in a northwesterly direction. This second migration got underway in its ultimate direction at an accelerating technical advantage over that of the northeasterly-bound or number-one spearhead.

Developing its technology at a slower pace, the major northeasterly spearhead came naturally and in due course to evolve the square-rigger out of its down-wind sailing junk. The fore-and-aft rigs of the northwesterly-bound spearhead evolved from the swift South Seas proa or double-ended outriggers and catamarans. This second spearhead, having completed its U-turn and was now westbound in the face of the prevailing winds, renegotiated the Malayan tip. It then worked westward along Indian Ocean shores until it reached the Persian Gulf.

How can we be so sure of all this? Because in marked contrast to the fragmentary character of man's land-evolved mechanics, dug up only from ruins, every one of the boats and sailing types evolved throughout these earliest historical motions of man are still in use and may be found in operation today under the very same rules of technical logic and thinking as characterized their slow invention in the very same environment and part of the world where they were created. It is not necessary to guess how these ancient technical developments were used and, therefore, what they implied. What is more, boats were able to carry larger cargoes of the components of civilization than could be carried overland by men or beasts. Boats may be found in every phase of transition. Choosing at random, we witness, for instance, the single log evoluting into the compound log-raft bearing a straw thatched hut, or the hollowed-out hulls replaced by ribbed and stretched skin kayak evolving into the canvas-decked outrigged rowing shell, or the half-raft-half-hull sampans, or the portable American Indian canoes, or the round basket boats rolling down the banks of the Tigris and Euphrates Rivers. The dhow, demonstrating a great advance in sailing technique, is today the work boat of the Persian Gulf. It is the same fore-and-aft rig with which man negotiated the westerly passage of the Indian Ocean.

In design, building technique and materials, the dhow follows the practices of Biblical and pre-Biblical times. It can point up into the wind more closely than the best of the America's Cup Defender sloops, though the handling of a dhow's spars is most crude and difficult by comparison.

Beating up the Red Sea and negotiating the Arabian Desert in the first overland navigation by caravans, the dhow builders again fashioned the same kind of ships in the Mediterranean, where they appear to have been the early vessels of the Phoenicians.

The major westerly spearhead is here wedded with the Hellenese tendril from the faraway northeasterly spearhead, as the peoples of the Peloponnesus and Phoenicia clash and integrate. This marks the first important phase of our intimate history of civilization. The conjunction of their respective advanced techniques, occurring under more favorable climatic conditions than those to which the Hellenes had been forced to accustom themselves, compounded to bring forth a civilization so distinctly in command of its environment as to provide the first large increments of time in which to demonstrate the arts, sports and philosophy. The two Asiatic migrations and the sea-borne spearheads are the mobile flanks to and the provision of leadership for the progressively settling-down population in their wake. The latter come to make up the great body of early Mediterranean population. This cross-breeding pool is what we call Western Civilization.

The fundamental difference between the Asiatic peoples and those of Western Europe and the Americas is intimately associated with these two fundamental histories of technical relationships to forces. While neither the major northeasterly nor the major northwesterly spearheads blindly opposed the forces, they respectively demonstrated diametric methods of using them. They demonstrated diametric attitudes toward life and death themselves—of ready commitment of self to death by the eastbound Asiatics, and stubborn refusal of it by the Westerners. To the Asiatic, riding serenely down-wind, often over the horizon never to return, it is logical and noble that life may be suddenly terminated. He does not question the forces, the omniscience of the deities. Any back-eddying on the down stream flow is ignoble. Hara-kiri will cancel the ignominy.

The western-bound spearhead people of Europe, and of the Americas in particular, were repeatedly shuttling to windward and back, working the adverse force. The challenge provided by death has invoked amongst them the advancement of technology in general but in particular in medicine, resulting in marked extension of the life span. The unnaturalness of death to these people has caused its threat to outweigh ignorance and tradition in the vital emergencies and to admit science at the eleventh hour in a popular application, the extent of which has not been equaled in any of science's other potentials.

It is sound scientific speculation that the Garden of Eden episode documents the first psychological difference between easterly- and westerly-faced peoples. Adoption unto himself by the individual of the deity's knowledge of good and evil as first exhibited in the legendary beginning of the westbound civilization, illustrates this fundamental difference between flowing with forces and turning them by rationalization into multi-direction advantage.

Both concepts are noble. One concept obtains immediate serenity by complete commitment to the sagacity of the Almighty, mysteriously bespoken by all events beyond the seeming control of His routine functions. The other concept wins serenity by faith in the ultimate over-all sagacity which therefore assumes welfare of the many to be implicit in every adversity. It gains its nobility, however, by assuming personal responsibility to discover and nurture into realization the universal benefits which, though tendered by the Almighty, must be earned by truthful labor.

Reaching the Americas by the uphill route, the northwesterly spiral had acquired a myriad of technical advantages proportional to the multitude of adversities. This technically enhanced spearhead of society we have appropriately identified as the industrial. The American industrial civilization has been likened to a salmon which insists upon climbing waterfalls in order to propagate. Now ages old, no logic could justify sudden cessation of that force-eating northwestly trend.

Of course, East was to meet West. They met first in Greece and thereafter repeatedly as Vandals, Huns, etc. But they met for the first time after having come completely around the world from opposite directions, when European voyagers met the American "Indians." Of course, the westerly-bound were certain to go into the psychologically strange encounter under adverse conditions. Of course, the westerly-working were ultimately certain to turn the impact of the major trend forces to advantage. Already the westbound have pushed the eastbound three-quarters of the way back.

These population and technology flows are implicit in the comprehensive concept of the world which the accompanying map dramatizes, and typify the big motions that the sailor comes naturally to comprehend and cogitate by realistic imagining faculties. He also sees the whole world, its waters and its atmospheres, its electrical properties, as a continuously and reliably operating dynamical system.

Long before the movies came along to provide Disney-like educationals, Rear Admiral Alfred Thayer Mahan, U.S.N.,[17] described for popular envisioning how the British sailormen had surreptitiously discovered that there was only "one ocean," near to whose center in the low-forty latitudes around the Antarctic, there roared a made-to-order, one-way merry-go-round to carry them swiftly eastward to the Orient, and from there swiftly eastward again into the Atlantic. Thus the English and Europeans logically spoke of China and India as the Far East.

17 Alfred T. Mahan (1840–1914) published numerous books on the subject, including *The Influence of Seapower Upon History, 1660–1783* (Boston, 1890).

Lieutenant Matthew Fontaine Maury, U.S.N.,[18] without any benefit of sympathy in his enterprise, but inspired by the cosmic eyes of the sailorman, made the preposterous proposal that the daily and regular log entries of the sea captains about weather conditions, wind directions, current drifts, etc., be methodically reported into a central record, despite the fact that the data might be years in reaching headquarters. Silly, impossible, impractical. But Maury, gradually accumulating information, began to advise sea captains that if in January they took one route and on the fifteenth of March another, they would reach their destination ahead of uninformed competitors. So impressively right did his predictions turn out to be that the United States then lent itself with vigor to his world-measuring program, adding this dynamic newcomer to the early universal language of green and red running lights, lighthouses, and bell buoys—all of them the common language of the world sailormen. The collection of data and scientific forecasting urged by Maury has developed directly into today's forecasting meteorology which guides successful world flight.

However, in Maury's time the down-wind sailing advantages, which could have been popularly employed, never appealed to adversity-embracing northwest spiralers in North America. The Americans wanted to do it the hard way. Noting that the English had monopolized the easterly and down-wind sailing below the continental tips, Americans forwarded their great sea-going tonnages right up onto and across their continent.

Thus, the American railroads developed out of the ocean steamer technology. Seagoing technology went up on the land onto steel rail canals. By principle, they brought up onto the land their ship masts, yardarms and lifting tackle, as cranes and winches to build bridges and great buildings. It was this ability, demonstrated most dramatically by the American transcontinental railways, to

18 Matthew Fontaine Maury (1806–1873) was the author of what is considered to be the first textbook of modern oceanography, *The Physical Geography of the Sea* (New York, 1855).

transport unprecedented tonnages, formerly carried only on the water, that was recognized by Sir Halford Mackinder, the English political geographer, and subsequently by Karl Haushofer, the German geopolitician, as tantamount to converting the dry lands to the functions of oceans. This concept formed the nucleus of the present mechanized warfare and automatically precipitated a reassortment of world economic and military factors.

As the industrial host of the northwest spiral populated the western American coast, it met direct flows of the easterly spearhead for the first time. Soon thereafter its into-the-wind sailing technology literally took the spearhead aloft to inaugurate the trans-oceanic service phases of the air age westward across the Pacific. The flying ships were heavier than air and therefore were borne aloft entirely by energy-control technology. Thus, once more, they discounted the easiest-way technology whose balloons appeared centuries earlier on the China coast. Abandoning even motorized and directable lighter-than-air craft, the northwestly spiral's airplane technology preferred to count upon obtaining its buoyancy, one hundred percent, on projections of the intellect. Now proven far swifter, safer, and higher flying, this modern stratospheric sailorizing is demonstrating dramatically to the static-minded landsman that he is indeed living in an all-motion dynamic universe.

Here the real principle of isolationism demonstrated its own fallacy. Isolationism was something deeper; it was staticism, blind inertia. When you have a whole continent to yourself, thousands of hours away from others, you can play ostrich or any other game, year in and year out, and you can falsely attribute your advantage to Santa Claus or any other cause and no one can deny the error. But if you want to play ostrich on Broadway, you are liable to get knocked over from behind.

Now, as land and air navies grow rapidly, while colliding in *cataclysmic* demonstrations, the sailorman's viewpoint becomes ever more popularly cogent. And that viewpoint, enhanced many-fold by new instruments and instantaneous, world-girdling communication, begins to see the spinning little world even more neatly. As yet somewhat ahead of popular comprehension, the modern sailor has investigated the higher reaches of the world's thin wrap of atmosphere. He now sees that not only does the Earth spin eastward, but that the water upon its surface, though displaying many a back-eddy, also spins eastward in net motion and at a greater velocity than the easterly spinning of the earth below it. Freer still of land obstacles, he finds that the atmosphere also spins in an easterly direction at an even faster rate, and that the atmosphere's main flows circle primarily around the Arctic and Antarctic Circles, while its back-eddies articulate stormbreeding counterspirals downward at the Poles, with a steadily flowing back undertow around the Earth's Equator known as the "trade winds."

Thus the sailorman discovered, to the surprise of the static-minded landsman, that the earth is not spinning in space under its own momentum at a slowly running-down speed, but that forces are pulling the Earth around, the elements in their more plastic condition pluming forward to reveal the pull.

Thus also the sailorman discovers, to the surprise of the landsman, that it is only one-third as far to go in the stratosphere from Kamchatka to Alaska as from Alaska to Kamchatka, provided one's plane can average two hundred miles per hour. He also discovers that a seventy-mile-an-hour dirigible could not make that stratosphere flight at all. He discovers that he was wiser than he knew in sticking to his intellect flying.

By flight in the stratosphere Arctic Circle, in present trans-oceanic equipment, it is much quicker to go to Russia from Alaska via Greenland, and to go from Norway to Minneapolis via Siberia and Alaska, than to back "uphill" via Greenland. This is information that yesterday's practical people would have said was of no importance. It will certainly not be many years before this is more important information to most people than the Pennsylvania Railroad timetable is now. Our new map has the ability to demonstrate relatively greater air distances by appropriate arrangement.

The sailorman knows that the library globe is mounted in an azimuthal circle, and its polar axis is tipped only to demonstrate the theory of the earth's motion relative to the sun. Observing how much complication is introduced to inadequately reveal a somewhat irrelevant fact, the twentieth-century sailor classifies this library globe as a pretty contraption, as beguiling and misleading as the planetarium in its ineffectiveness. Forced to deal more realistically with a spherical world, he found the globe was a miniature plaything, too small to provide him with important navigational data beyond the most sketchy plans of great voyages. A globe large enough to reveal working data on hazards and aids to navigation would lose any ship in its vast innards. Sailormen need both sectional charts and comprehensive maps.

Then, too, it became evident that one can never see the whole world at once by means of looking at the globe. One cannot see even half of it, due to the rapid increase of curvature tangential to the lines of perspective. The viewer, holding the picture in his brain, could spin the globe and piece together the imaginary continuity.

A typical landlubber invention designed to correct this shortcoming was once exhibited in a New York City museum. This globe was big enough to permit the viewer to stand inside. The usual exterior surface data was inverted to the interior. However, unless one could see through the back of his head, vision was limited as before to less than one half the surface. Though hailed by the intelligentsia, this item disgusted the sailor.

Preposterously distorted in its polar regions, Mercator's cylindrical map [Figure 4], tangential at the Equator, was none the less preferred by the sailor to the globe. He found Mercator's map could be unrolled to represent the whole world. So long as man's comings and goings were centered within the warm belt girdling the Earth at right angles to its axis, the Mercator map was a pretty satisfactory affair.

But as suddenly as cities have been wiped out by air bombings, there has come upon the people the necessity for seeing the

Figure 4
Mercator Projection World Map

world as vividly as the sailorman has. Suddenly, within months, people have come to realize that they can girdle the planet in an infinite number of directions. The world has been surprising itself by coming in its own back doors and down its own chimneys from every unlooked-for direction. This has called for a revolution in map making and in cartographical principles such as history has never seen. A need has risen for new methods of peeling data off the globe and for assembling the peelings in such a manner as to gain useful knowledge of the spherical coursings.

While still imbued with the static pictures and the traditional thinking, people viewed the first appearance of the new maps as a novelty. Any inclination to comprehension of the relative merit of the different maps as a result of comprehension of the principles by which they were constructed was thrown into utter confusion by the welter of pedagogic terms. Sinusoidal, conformal, azimuthal, gnomonic, orthographical systems, scared the layman away from making criticism of the appearance of Australia as a kidney bean three times the size of South America. Feeling the progressive urge to global comprehension, he produced a mass market for commercial globe manufacturing, but after a few swift inspections, these were relegated to decorative functions from their role as daily tools. Much more important to him were the newspaper maps of the daily war scenes.

Out of the newspapers and the novelties, people are beginning to see that there are some interesting new angles and proportions. Unfortunately, most landlubber cartographers prefer to impress people with the difficulties and aesthetics of their art rather than with implications of the dynamic geography of a world-industrializing people.

People are catching on that great circles constitute the spherical straight line and that there is an important continent at the Antarctic and not a jagged, icy fringe along the bottom of an east-west Mercator layout. This advance in popular awareness is despite the fact that during World War II the traditional suppliers of maps provided streamlined equatorial Mercator world maps for all the allied war offices and accessory bureaus, upon which maps the ocean distances between Greenland and England appear greater than those between Tokyo and San Francisco.

People are learning that "via the North Pole" is the shortest great-circle distance from America's midst to the center of population of the world. But when they were told during the war that Tarawa represented the first major gain in the direction of Tokyo, they were not well enough versed in their geography to realize that announcement that the Marines had taken the North Pole would have put the United States closer to Tokyo's center, and that the Marines were actually farther from Tokyo than Chicago is from London. And even those professional geographers and military tacticians who did know that these were the proportionate distances by great circle, have not, unless skilled in the dynamic sailorman's thinking, realized that in the terms of the air

Figure 5

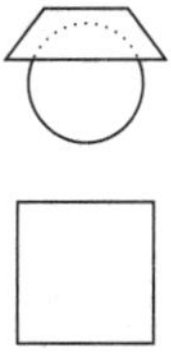

Azimuthal or Gnomonic
Projection Method

Figure 6

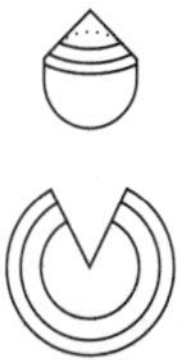

Conic
Projection Method

Figure 7

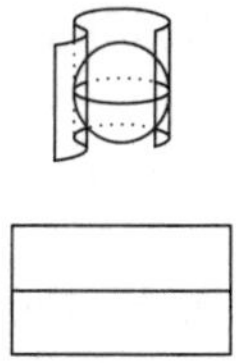

Mercator
Projection Method

motions which twist the great circle courses all out of shape, the north Pole is a third nearer to Tokyo than Tarawa, when full advantage is taken of atmospheric motions.

Because of this latter fact, it becomes obvious that the kind of map that static cartographers produce can only partially educate the people—that is, up to the realistic great-circle concept. All known traditional projection methods fall far short of providing a comprehensive, sectional cartographical device which may be mutably arranged in any direction in such a manner as to bring focus to bear on any of the dynamic inter-relationships of the world's surface affairs.

One such sailorman's mid-twentieth-century invention is the mutable map presented here. Appropriately, its faces represent the facets of the monometric construction shown in the accompanying drawing [Figure 1], which drawing represents the vector equilibrium of a sphere.

Unlike all known preceding projections, which represent transfers of spherical data to plane surfaces tangent to the sphere only at one point [Figure 5], as in the case of the azimuthal or gnomonic projection methods, or only along one central line [Figure 6], as in the case of the Mercator, or only along one or two segmental arc lines [Figure 7], as in the conics, this projection is one in which the coincidence with the projected sphere occurs all along the complete boundary of each section of the projection, thus retaining the unique cartographical feature of being the only projection in which uniform great-circle scale characterizes the logical terminal edge of each section to be projected, that scale being maintained intact after transfer from the sphere to the flat surface of the map.

Sailorwise, this new projection is made from the cosmic viewpoint—that is, the astronomical zenith and the center of the earth always remain, respectively, vertically above and below each and every point of the surface of the cartographic data. Not only is this true in its spherical arrangement but also in its planar projection into the sections of the comprehensive map.

Because the enclosing border scale cannot be elongated, distorted or contracted, and represents a great circle bent flat into a one-dimension line, the adjustment of the contained spherical surface segment to a plane surface segment must be satisfied by interior contraction of the data instead of by exterior stretching, as in all other methods of projection. Because of this feature the several pieces fit neatly together, being the mutual sides of adjacent polygons and being separated by the same great circle or straight line. Because the area of a circle increases as the square of its radius, the same error outwardly disposed must be distorted to four times greater extent than by inward disposition.

The segmentation of the earth's surface into eight triangles and six squares is not in any sense a matter of aesthetic choice. It represents one known subdivision possible by means of this universal-projection viewpoint, for the radial and chordal lengths must be identical in order to allow this symmetrically hinged opening of the sphere.

Having six axes and four dimensions, its parts may be rearranged to unpeel the globe continuously in all directions. Gnomonic projections through the surface facets of any of the regular polyhedrons will serve to provide a variety of sectional world surface maps. Striking an optimum between angular contraction and numbers and sizes of pieces, an icosahedron is the least distorted,[19] for these projection purposes, of any of the regular solids. However, the spherical vertexes of the icosahedron's twenty triangles must be reduced from 72° to plane triangular vertexes of 60°, a reduction of twenty percent, which percentage times the number of pieces gives the total distortion. On the other hand, the Dymaxion's fourteen pieces accomplish translation with a distortion of only sixteen percent, the Dymaxion's spherical triangles being only 70° and the vertexes of the square bearing the same percentage relationship between the spherical and the plane figure.

The Dymaxion projection method of transferring spherical data to the plane surface is extremely simple. Because of its universal viewpoint, it need deal only with the surface of the sphere and the plane surface of the map. A lattice of four great circles is formed about the sphere, each intersecting the other in such a manner as to subdivide each circle into six symmetrical arcs of 60°. This lattice provides fourteen spherical surface areas, eight of them triangular, six of them quadrangular. These spherical triangles and squares are equilateral. The surfaces of these triangles and squares are then interwoven with great circle grids, the triangles by a three-way grid of great circles and the squares by a two-way grid of great circles. These grid lines spring from uniform scale modular subdivisions of the 60° arc sections in as fine a degree as is desired.

The geographical data coinciding with these grids is then transferred to eight equilateral plane triangles and six plane surface squares. For purposes of this translation, the plane triangles and

---

19 In 1952, Fuller, working with Shoji Sadao, finally articulated and published an icosahedral version of his world map (fig. 8), which he concluded was optimal. It became the iconic version used in his work during the last thirty years of his life. Like the 1944 version, the pieces can be re-arranged in multiple configurations. He published this version with the name "Dymaxion Airocean World," often referring to it as revealing "a one world island in a one world ocean." This map projection is increasingly referred to by cartographers as the "Fuller Projection" world map, using the convention commonly used for world map projections such as the Mercator, Robinson, and Peters Projections. For more information, see: http://bfi.org/our_programs/who_is_buckminster_fuller/design_science/dymaxion_map/the_fuller_projection_map.

Figure 8
1952 Fuller Projection World Map

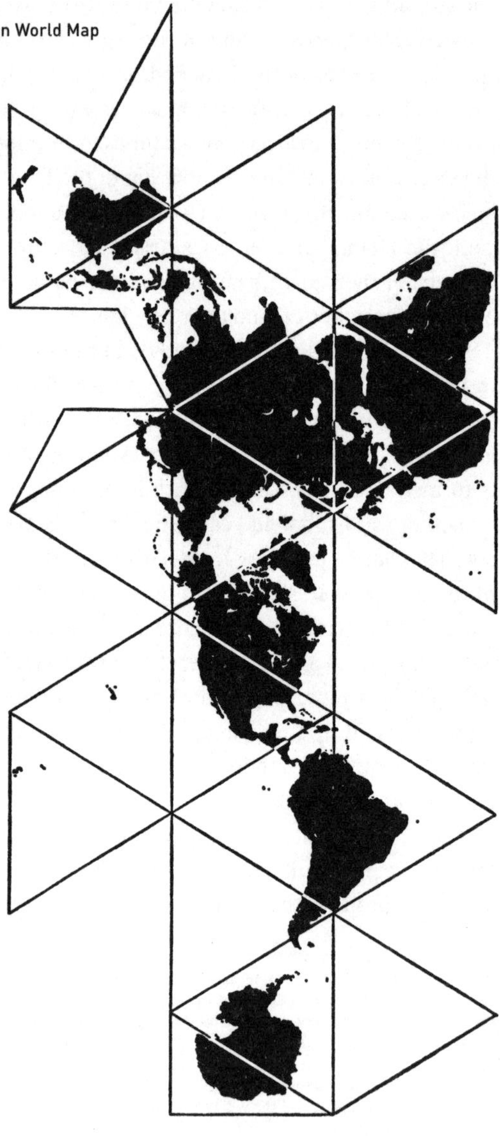

squares have been prepared as follows: Their surfaces are subdivided by respective three-way and two-way grids of straight lines. These straight lines spring from modular subdivisions of their boundaries which correspond in scale and number to the subdivisions of the original spherical arc segments of 60°. The spherical geographical data is then posted to corresponding positions in the appropriate plane grid spaces. The spherical great circle grids are thus treated as constituting straight lines in the plane geometrical surface. The principle of treating great circles and straight lines as constituting one and the same thing, effects the distribution of the angular contraction in a concentric disposition on the plane sections.

The key to understanding why this method accomplishes its translation with a minimum of distortion is that it treats the 180° spherical gores in two ways. The irreconcilable conditions of convergence and parallelism, characterizing the terminals and midpart of the 180° gores, are treated separately and symmetrically as triangles and squares respectively. All other projections impose the advantage of one feature against the advantage of the other by trying to solve both convergence and parallelism by one grid. These resolved gore parts of the Dymaxion map, by treating these conditions separately, allow four-dimensional unwrapping of the sphere.

7 The Cumulative Nature of Wealth

WEALTH. The measurable degree of forwardly organized environmental control, in terms of quickly convertible energy, capacities and performance ratioed system capabilities per capita, per diem.

Wealth is now without practical limit. All the constituents of wealth are now demonstrably inexhaustible and are all on inventory to man's immediate willing. Science has hooked up the everyday economic plumbing to the cosmic reservoir.

You can now have your cake and eat it. The more you eat, the more and the better the quality of the cakes to be had by further production.

Science continually does more with less each time it obsoletes and scraps old inventions. Scrap is resolved to some part of the inventory of the ninety-two regenerative chemical elements. Interim improvement in technical measurement of performance makes possible an ever higher magnitude of new performance by reuse of the same quantity of the original inventory of the chemical elements. Telephone messages per given cross section of copper wire increased from one to several conversations at the same

---

This is the only chapter in the book for which it was not possible to find conclusive information about its origins in the Fuller Archive at Stanford University. In the final manuscript delivered to the original publishers, Prentice Hall (found in M1090 Series 8 Box 30 Folder 4 [Ideas and Integrities 63.01.01 2 of 3]), the essay appears as a double-sided typeset and printed page, appearing to be a published article, though lacking any identification of title, date, nor publication (the only marks are page numbers, "15" and "16," and a note to "see appendix III"). The version published in *Ideas and Integrities* differs only in Fuller's addition of the first two paragraphs and minor copyediting.

time, then to scores, then to hundreds of messages taking place concurrently. So rapid is the rate of gain of telephone technology per given amount of copper that the telephone company has an almost inexhaustible mine of copper in its progressively obsolete equipment. The chief engineer of the Bell Telephone Company stated in 1936 that the stocks of copper owned by the telephone company, obtained from scrapping old equipment, would be sufficient for them to expand their service from the United States network to a world network without buying further quantities of new copper. This does not mean that they would always keep the wires. Part of the copper might go into the radio equipment between the long-distance centrals.

The formula for common wealth production is: Ever greater investment of now unlimited energy in redesigned tools and end product. The energy investments may be in the form of heat treatments, precision tolerances, metallurgical alloying, etc.—always contriving to afford greater tensile strength, finer edge, greater wear, etc.; and the degree of greater performance thus accomplished is always a net increment of common wealth. Because more has been done with less, the balance can go into new degrees of mastery by man of his given environment.

Ever greater reinvestments of cumulatively advancing technology. This is the regeneration of intellectual advantage.

Result: The provision of higher magnitudes of performance per pound of the ninety-two regenerative chemical elements, and per hour of man's time, and per unit of energetic expenditure, *ergo,*—again net increment, of reinvestible performance advantage, i.e., wealth.

We could progressively scrap the whole paraphernalia of civilization's present mechanical equipment, both production and end product, replacing these with improved mechanics and products of fractional dimension as compared to the scrapped mechanics, while netting not only a higher standard of living performance for ourselves, but enough raw materials and improved know-how to expand the physical apparatus of our standard of living to serve not just our U.S.A. seven percent but half the human family. The advantages gained by the latter would allow them in turn to develop new sources, sum-totally providing the new advances of science and industry to serve all the peoples of the world. What to do about war surpluses here and abroad is clearly indicated in these truths. Scrap them one hundred percent and reprocess the chemical elements into higher and more appropriate use forms, thus generating common world wealth. Spend ingenuity on brand new higher performance products rather than on makeshift application of obsolete gadgets.

Materials Equals energy as *mass;* physicists' law of conservation states that: energy can neither be created nor lost, *ergo,* there cannot be realistic energy depletion or debitor fundamental debt. Debt indicates depletion and borrowing from diminishing sources. There is no possibility of absolute debt* occurring in the new economics made available through the accomplishments of science. This is because the basic constituents of the wealth can no longer be depleted.

Know-how Technology (instrumented and documented intellect) improves with every re-employment because experience is consolidated in increasing degrees of precision, behavior and dimensional data.

Power Energy—larger and larger blocks of which, as inherent principles of an inexhaustible universe, become available to man's control account. The impoundment of ever greater blocks of energy within the arrangements of the ninety-two chemical elements to give higher degrees of performance of structure and mechanics constitutes the actual means of harvesting of universal wealth. It is as though the phenomena which we call raw materials, which are in fact our ninety-two chemical elements, were a fleet of cargo

* Because debt is a convention of traditional government, it will be increased to eventual absurdity. There is no other means of eliminating it in a democracy. Revolution could eliminate it only by democratic suicide.

vessels into which we load ever greater cargoes of energy, and as we load them they give higher degrees of controlled performance. As a result, we increase our control over our fate and that is the function of wealth.

Faith Inexhaustible faith of man in the validity of himself as an effective factor in the biological equation of the universe, to which latter the principle of essential priority of the commonweal is implicit—that is, that the individual is a product and servant of a plurality (but that his best service to the commonweal can be indicated only by admonition of the individual intellect, which can best integrate all factors of the creative equations).

In the principle of mass production industry, the significance of the individual as a machine of production continually diminishes and his importance as a consumer increases proportionally. The intellectual productive ability of science and technology which displaces the individual as a productive slave is cumulative to the whole history of intellect.

Through the new operating requirements of the transcendental industry, society must arrange a debtless system of increasing the availability of industrial services to all individuals and concurrently to an increasing number of their infinite needs in order to satisfy the science-industry-man equation. If not satisfied by creative ends, the forces now involved will be articulated to man's ultimate destruction because he lacked faith in his own validity—his validity as a never-ending, dynamic process of inclusion and refinement.

8 Domes—Their Long History and Recent Developments

Domes made by men have probably been used by man for hundreds of millenniums. Domes made by nature, as caves or as vaulted branches of trees, have probably been used by man throughout the million years we now, tentatively, concede that men may have been present somewhere around the earth.

Little, exquisite, bubble domes, too small for man-occupancy, are made by nature at possibly the highest mass production velocity anywhere manifest to man. Some are of split-second longevity. Some are of great longevity. Nature combines these miniscule domical structures in myriad varieties of complex structural arrangements occurring as both organic and inorganic compounds and as cellular agglomerates. Most of these complex domical structuring accomplishments by nature are realized at modular frequency magnitudes infra to man's sensorial tunability and apprehension.

In consequence of this invisibility man has ignorantly classified the whole gamut of non-sensorial module structuring by nature under the illusion-evoked designation of "solid" matter. Consistent with this illusion man traffics in various solid substances known as "materials."

Men do not, however, in reality build structures out of materials. Men build visible module structures out of sub-visible module

---

October 1959. The original manuscript begins with Fuller's words, "written at the request of the 'Consulting Engineer'," referring to a journal then published in St. Joseph, Michigan.

structures. There are generalized laws governing structure. The generalized laws of structure are oblivious to the special threshold existing between the man-tuned sensorial spectrum and the vast ranges of universe structuring infra and ultra sensorial to man's narrowly tuned conscious reception faculties.

Man has, however, through instrumentation, increased the spectrum ranges of his modularly tunable scanning of universal structuring. Wherever he succeeds in tuning in he discovers either orderly arrays or provoking indications of orderliness only mildly clouded by as-yet-non-tuned frequency phenomena. All these instrumental explorations into the infra-ultra sensorial spectrum ranges of Nature's universal structuring discover dynamic or potential events in mathematically regularized, complex interactions of omni-accommodative principles.

The mathematical patterning and inter-transformability of Nature's geometrical structurings are the only reality of universe. The infinitely regenerative dynamism, always potential in the fundamental relationships of the principles, in itself constitutes the intellectually tunable and ever inescapable reality.

The relative abundances of reciprocally patterning principles everywhere constitute the so far discovered inventory of minimally complex, *ergo* fundamentally differentiable structurally regenerative universal governance. The complex of interactively accommodating principles and their relative abundance accommodation are reality—the only reality. What man, in his sensorially preoccupied misapprehending, has termed "abstract," in contradistinction to sensorial, as well as that which man has designated as metaphysical in contra-distinction to physical, are altogether one reality. The fact of meagerness of the experience-generated knowledge of man in respect to the omni-regenerative structure of reality and the observational facts taken in the twilight zones between the meager known and the as-yet-unexperienced, in no way alters the unitary integrity of the utter inter-accommodation of complex structural interaction of the principles as so far sum-totally inventoried by the faithfully reported experiences of man.

In view of the foregoing, it is the working assumption of my present soliloquy that the principles of structure are universal constants, utterly independent of the phenomena “relative size” in any man-elected arbitrary modular terms.

So important have domes been throughout man’s total experience that the roots of the word for God, home and dome are the same—domus, domicile and dome. In the language of the sailors of Denmark and Iceland, the word is *dom.* Because of the age-long interactions of mysticism, with religions of hope and fear, in the daily lives of men, always centering in the home, the dome, ages ago, became symbolic of all the cosmic thoughts, hopes, supplications and glorious conceptions. From its comprehensive preeminence, the dome conception gave root to the words *dominate* and *dominion.* As a result of the slow process of communication casualties in the hearing and mimicking of sounds, prior to the written word, a great interchangeability of the consonants prefixing the syllable *om* took place. The D was interchanged with the 'T' in designation of the dome as a mortuary shrine and with a W as the gestation or pre-nativity shrine. Thus man went from W-OM-B to T-OM-B via the H-OM-E. Even the B-OM-B is a derivative of dome as the superaccelerated explosive nativity container. The Bikini bomb was dome-like in shape.

In ecological patterning, early man was the hunter and fisher, operating at extreme radius from his domicile center. His mate operated at the domicile. She became the dome-man, the homeman, the w-om-man; also, she was the man with the dome inside, the w-om-b man. Greater and lesser ecological circles, characterizing male and female peregrinations respectively, are still the ecological domains of the swift running wild mammalian life. Later the thought-hunting and recollection-researching male, hibernating in his domicile center, became H-OM-O sapiens, *domo sapiens.*

Some of my hypotheses regarding the evolutionary ramifications of the life-dominating word dome have been suggested by others, such as Baldwin Smith of Princeton University and Prof. Barry Bierman of the University of Natal, Durban, South Africa, but I will accept all negative reactions for the guessed-out significance of the OM root relationships in their widest historical-geographical patternings.

Early domes, made by men, fall into two important historical classes. One has a very long history, the other a very short history by comparison.

Class One of all history's domes is comprised of the hundreds of millenniums-old upside-down baskets which include the later evolution of baskets into boats and the re-upside-downing, once more, of boats to form the roofs of community meeting places and its later derivative *cathedral.* The nave (navy; Naga, the sea serpent god of the sea) is the upside-down boat. In Japan, the word for "ceiling" or "roof" means also "the bottom of the boat." In this oldest category of upside-down basket domes, there exists a word identification linking the earth's extreme territories which seems to tell us that men in their wooden basketry boats, rafts, catamarans and canoes had indeed conquered the whole dominion of earth. The once only oral words of South Africa and the Eskimo, designating their domical enclosures, are now spelled respectively INDLU and IGLOO. Only man's later invention of phonetic spelling and its interpretive application by geographically remote, different men, in the documentation of these extreme Northern and Southern Hemisphere sound-words, must alone have occasioned the difference in spelling.

Class Two of all history's domes consists only of the last four millenniums during which occurred the hard stone, crystalline "permanentizing" by man of the organic fiber domes. Here man sought for inventions which might bring the lasting quality of the non-man-made stone caves into the man-invented association of non-man-invented organic structures of Nature in the pattern of domical stability.

It is a good guess that Nature suggested this permanentizing to man when snow and ice amalgamated accidently, so far as man is concerned, with his domical basketry of bent saplings, reeds, thatching grass and skins. Realizing and testing the ice-augmented strength of this early version of fibrously reinforced crystalline aggregates (as prototypes of modern steel reinforced concrete or glass-fiber reinforced plastic) men ascribed the predominant improvement in structuring to the hard compressive ice component. They considered the preliminary basketry dome, upon which the heavy ice dome had been later formed, as now constituting a preliminary and removable scaffolding die, or form, which they later employed as centerings. Thus, a man's ice-cake igloos may have come into logical evolutionary development. From the ice igloo blocks, fashioned at the readily cuttable snow crust block phase, may have been derived the successively experimental information leading to the discovery of the structural strategy geometry consisting of horizontal rings of wedge-shaped stone blocks, rising in graduated concentricity, to an apex. Experiments with ice and snow would have been less dangerous than with blocks of stone.

The earliest domical structures of stone fashioned by men are those of the early sea-dominating people of the eastern Mediterranean Sea. The Greek historian Herodotus speaks of the Egyptians going through the Red Sea and into the Indian Ocean to the land of Punt. The mural records in the tomb of Queen Hat-Shep-Sut in the Valley of the Kings, inscribed four millenniums ago, report clearly on her Egyptian commercial fleet expeditions to what is now Somaliland on the northeast African shore of the Indian Ocean. I learned in southeast Africa that the name Punt in ancient language means the color *red*. The letter T is a feminine suffix. The Red Sea was once the Pun Sea. This is the same Punt root as the punt boat of the East Indian Ocean, the Malay Straits, Thailand, and Burma. The punt boat was the *pon*toon of the pontoon bridge. The people who bridged oceans by boat relays—first across the Indian Ocean—were the Puns, the redskinned peoples. These are the Punicians later alliterated into Phoenicians, and later alliterated into Venetians, Vekings (Vikings)—the Punicians of the Punic Wars, the Pun settlers of both the north and south shores of the Mediterranean Sea and, reaching out into the Atlantic,—the Punta La Garda in the Azores, of the Portuguese (probably Puntagese). These are the sailormen to whom the sea was the normal life and whose harbored, canalled and pontooned cities constituted their regenerative birthings at the sea's landed margin, as do the seals and sea lions go annually upon the land for their regenerative whelping and new launchings. These were *pun*dits of India: the wiseman, navigators, and astronomers.

Professor Thornton White of Cape Town, South Africa, architect of the town planning of the island of Mauritius, in the bosom of the Indian Ocean, was commissioned by the British Government, because of his great Indian Ocean knowledge, to conduct a survey of the total smuggling operations between the Orient and the East African countries. Thornton White met with his friends, the fleet captains of the myriad swift-sailing Indian dhows at Mombasa on the east coast of Africa. He was deeply impressed with the scientific elegance of the dhow captain's navigational art and with the profound simplicity of their reckoning and the integration of their total navigational experience. This lent credence to the dhow captain's confidence that their trans-Indian Ocean navigational success had been operative for no less than ten thousand years.

In appraising the statement, it is to be noted that Prof. Thornton White's status with the British Government is such that his opinion regarding the Indian Ocean smuggling governed the British Government's decision to discount, rather than to oppose, the smuggling. Professor White, an Oxford scholar and world traveler, a frequent visitor to America, stated, in dramatic contradiction to the legendary concept held in the western world of an uncouth, savage Indian Ocean sea pirate, that the captains of the dhow fleet, as a class, are the most cultured, intellectually gentle people he has ever known.

I have been studying the evolution of ship design throughout the ages and have traveled around the world to discover and strengthen my theoretical conviction that men have been successfully circumnavigating the earth, not just the Indian Ocean, for at least ten thousand years. The navigators, coming upon the land, became priests, and the priests effectively counseled, but did not teach, the kings. The priest-navigator conspiracy methodically buried in the ocean's depths the visible evidence gained through their mathematically calculated astronomical competence in navigation. Above all, the priest-navigator conspiracy kept, even from its sailors, their astronomically and geographically realized knowledge that they had circumnavigated the earth. The non-navigating sailors never knew where they were on the high sea. Though they returned to the same familiar places, they did not know by what routes they had come. All they saw was water.

In the comprehensive illiteracy of man and its preoccupation with the sensorially obvious, the conspiracy of a few scientifically operating men was easily accomplished. The conspiracy knew the earth was a sphere, a finite or closed system. Approximately all other men, including the kings, thought the earth to be a local plane surrounded by infinity, and each thought of his native region as the center of this infinite plane. World men lived in infinitely remote groups, each in its unique local pattern of relative abundance and scarcity of *a priori* resources. Only the conspiracy knew of the comprehensive and complimentary associability of the remotely distributed but finitely integratible world resources. The fabulous wealth-generating secrets of commerce-controllable resource integratibility lay wrapped in the invisible mathematical webs of spherical geometry and trigonometry, as applied both to the spheroidal ships and their off soundings, trans-ocean, trans-night, trans-fog, trans-fear, astronomical navigation and mathematical reckoning.

The early Aegean sailor's high-sea peregrinations inevitably took them into Arctic island hibernations, in man-made caves, under their ice and snow-covered boats. Closing in their boatroofed caves with rocks and ice cakes taught them of the ice fashioning of domes with horizontal rings of concentrically graduating wedge blocks. Nature's annealing of the ice to form a monolithic ice-dome provided a cohering hydraulic crystalline advantage countering the tendency of outward thrust disintegration occurring at the haunches of nontensionally cohered, domically piled up, compressional components without comprehensively finite tensional bonds.

Wedge-shaped blocks, like corks, have a polarized asymmetry in which one pole's shoulders have greater dimension than the other pole's shoulders. Wedges and corks may be piled up in oriented regularity so that the greater shoulders are always on one side and the smaller shoulders on the other. Horizontal extension of such piles eventually describes a circle which closes back upon itself at the base of the pile. Vertical extension of the pile curves upwardly and inwardly from the base circle, eventually closing at a domical apex. The outer shoulders of the individual components prevent any one component from slipping or sliding inwardly through its allotted radial domain space segments, toward the center of diminishing cordal dimensioning, within the finitely closed system of hemispheroidal pile-up.

Save for the friction between the dome's base and the earth's crust below it and between the progressively lessening frictions of the upwardly and inwardly tiered wedge layers, there is naught to restrain any of the wedge blocks from slipping or oozing outwardly from the finite aggregate. In the ice domes, the annealed hydraulic tension cohered the mass. To understand man's subsequently-arrived-at dome-building strategies, we must consider a plurality of factors which he differentiated intuitively, out of his hard-won sailor's experiences of masts, booms, long oars and rigging. These experiences generated a gradually generalized structural wisdom in professional sea masters.

A man may support a long column, say a fifteen-foot wooden pole, in a vertical position with the palm of his hand outstretched from his downwardly oriented arm. Small and continuous motions of the hand will keep the pole in vertical balance. In vertical balance, earth's gravity operates upon the pole only in a downward force, concentrated entirely within the neutral vertical axis of the pole, focusing all of gravity's force into the palm of the man's hand at the comfortably vertical arm-tension axis. An attempt by the same man to hold the same fifteen-foot pole horizontally with outstretched arm is frustrated by gravity operating perpendicularly—that is, at ninety degrees all along the pole as well as the length of his outstretched arm. The center of the gravitational force must be at center of gravity of the combined length of the pole and his arm—that is, at approximately eight feet outward horizontally from his shoulder. This means that gravity combines the total weight of the pole and the arm at the end of a horizontal lever eight feet (ninety-six inches) long from his shoulder fulcrum. This provides a force of twenty-five pounds at the lever's ninety-six-inch end, operating against a two-inch muscle tissue lever increment at the other—a forty-eight to one advantage, resulting in a twelve-hundred-pound loading of the muscle tissue.

The vertical and horizontal pole experience of man leads to his sensitive understanding of the effects of gravity on domes. Weather, quakes and fire are secondary to gravity as structural challenges, for these secondary challenges are variable factors which may only accelerate structural yielding to the constantly operative gravity by eroding the minimal structural section dimensions. Both the vertical and horizontal limits of the gravitational effects upon pole behavior are present in the dome and all the intermediary gradation effects between those limits.

It is in evidence that the horizontal vulnerability of structural components to gravitational effects requires the strongest answering stratagems. Columns are easy; beams are difficult. Ships' masts support their booms, not vice versa. The walls and columns of history's ruins stand the longest. Rarely are the horizontal beams, elevated floorings or roofs to be found intact, if at all, with the exception of domes which combine both horizontal and vertical behaviors progressively translated into mutual synergetical aid and integrated success. Domes of Istanbul, the Near East and India, which respectively comprehended these combined behaviors, have been standing for centuries—the Pantheon of Rome for two millenniums, and the tomb domes of Greece for three and one half millenniums—in better condition than their contemporary and much later column-and-wall neighbors of antiquity. Not so antique, but of sad significance, the Japanese have made an historical monument of the dimensionally unaltered dome framing of the only structure that remained at target zero of the first atomic bomb dropped upon Hiroshima in 1945.

The top half of a dome's circular arc is approximately horizontal and the bottom half's circle of the dome's total area is approximately vertical. The top half tends to operate as unit mass, yielding most readily to gravity, and the bottom half of the dome as a vertical ring reaching up to the dome's haunches, tends to resist gravity with greatest ease for the same reasons that govern man's experience with the vertical and horizontal pole-supporting. It is surprising news to the layman that the greatest compressive forces in wedge block domes occurs within the top twenty-degree are of the dome. The pressures are far greater than those caused only by the dome's dead weight around its bottom.

Domical pile-ups of wedge-shaped blocks, without any finitely cohering tensional bands, tend to yield to gravity in their top parts and oppose it in their bottoms by spewing the unopposed haunch height ring tiers outwardly—thus uncrowding the remainder of the top-tier wedges which now have ample room to fall individually inward and downward. If the spheroidal domical pile of wedge blocks is graduated upwardly and inwardly in almost vertical conformation in the form of an upended half cigar, the gravitational forces will induce such friction as to occasion structural stability and approximate elimination of the critical haunch area.

I have visited the earliest known stone-wedge navigator-priest designed domical structure of man, the tomb of Atreus, approximate contemporary of Agamemnon in the latter's kingdom of Mycenae in Greece. The Mycenaean Greeks are of the Cretan sea-master pre-Ionian people. This t-om-b d-om-e of Atreus is of elegantly modulated vertical cigar shape. The Greek name for the shape is *tholus,* which is the same name as the sailorman's vertical cigar shaped wooden thole pin, two of which, mounted in the boat's gunwale, formed an oar lock and one of which, mounted in the stern, formed a pivot for a sculling oar or rudder. Thole pins thrust through collar flanges around masts formed cleats on which were wound halyard ropes whose fastenings could be quickly loosed by pulling the thole pin not only out of the wound or belayed rope but also out of the collar hole to let the rope run free–(thole pin, tomplon, belaying thomplong, belaying pin). To keep the thole pins from sliding downward through the holes and to render them most graspable by the hand, their top thirds have a hand-filling bulbousness immediately below which a shoulder rim flares out.

This thole pin shoulder and cigar head gives its nautical conformation name to man's first stone dome. The Mycenae tholus dome is not only the oldest stone dome, but it is the most perfect in its preservation and dimensional elegance of any dome I have seen anywhere around the world. To insure its structural stability against outward thrusting of its wedge blocks by later vandals, ramming outward from inside the dome, the Greeks concealed this dome under a naturally appearing mountain of earth. The gravitational effect of the mountain of earth continually thrust the wedged blocks into the tightest possible self-crowding and successfully hid the tomb for three and one half millenniums.

The Roman arch, developing a thousand years later, was, of course, a far less intellectual borrowing of a simple curvature section taken through this Greek sailorman's stone adaptation of his arctic ice-dome prototype. The Roman arch employed this domical plane section in parallel series, holding down the outwardly slippable wedge by superimposed masonry and earth. Because parallel planes do not aid one another, nor cohere, the whole parallel set had to be held together like vertically standing books by "book-ends" in the form of buttresses impinging perpendicularly upon the cylindrical arch's terminal faces.

All stone, ceramic or concrete block dome buildings are covered by the principles outlined above. When men developed the capability to produce iron chain in quantities sufficient to make wrought iron anchor chains for ships, as a practical, feasible and economical commodity, closed circles of the chain were employed to gird the dome bases and haunches as safety factors against their outward thrusting. Because the domes were laid in vertically diminishing diameters of horizontal rings, if the chain were lifted upwardly it would be too large for congruence with the lessening circles, and its binding effectiveness eliminated. The vertical wedge-contoured section of the domes themselves tended to thrust such chains upward and their safety-factor function was rendered so dubious that many chain-bottomed stone domes fell in, throughout domical history. Stone, wedge, block componented domes, which have survived through time, have been characterized by one form or another of haunch height buttressing of inertial restraints in a variety of ingenious and sometimes visually illusive structural inventions. Some of these involve a plurality of domes around domes, as in the great dome complexes of Istanbul in the whole Byzantine cathedral complex.

I am not at all suggesting that all dome-builders consciously followed the Mycenaean prototype or were even aware of it and its possible, if not probable, arctic laboratory prototyping. However, both geometry and gravity are universal and their interactive behaviors are so fundamental that no matter how experiment begins, if its lessons are heeded, they must lead inevitably to the universal relationships, only mildly modified by the local environmental arrays of pneumatics, hydraulics, and crystalline constellations of nature's constructional inventory. Little boys, wherever there have been snow falls, have learned to heap and roll the snow into plastically cohering masses. Thereafter, with their relentless experimental appetite, many children learn, through intuitive initiative, that they can dig a hole into the side of their miniature snow mountain, which can be entered by them and progressively enlarged until they have hollowed out the mountain—thus more or less inadvertently arriving at a dome. The dome's end result of a coalesced crystalline aggregate is characterized by high tensional coherence re-employing the molecular surface tensions in highest geometrical advantage.

All this was inadvertent and entirely fortunate—as without engineering training, the child remembered, and probably later reconsidered the fact, that the structural integrity of his snow mountain was provided entirely by the outer zone of the snow mountain because he had removed its innards. Six millenniums ago, the Egyptians, with an even earlier boat-implemented background, wherein the ship's hull provided the same force-patterning structural stability as a tensionally banded dome structure, demonstrated their knowledge that they could tunnel and hollow out both their man-made pyramidal mountains, as well as nature's formulated mountains, when they riddled the Theban ranges with their tomb chambers.

The Egyptian mountain-chambering was an historical structural invention in marked contrast to the entirely solid formalized mountain-building of the Oriental temples, ghats and wats. However the Egyptian mountain-chambering, as well as the Sicilian domical tomb-chambering of mountains, were all in gross contradistinction to the performance per pound of involved physical resources employed by world sailormen in the designing and crafting of their ships. Ships represented a stabilized structural invention, thrusting their *holl*owness (hull) by displacement into the far more difficult hydraulic instability of the sea's water mass.

Inspired by nature's nut, mollusk, egg and vegetable shells, men learned, hundreds of millenniums ago, how to hollow out or build up and bind together hydraulic containers or vessels. Learning gradually how to expand the vessel-making art, men finally hollowed out large logs and then later shaped and tied together tree planks, later bent around stout frames. They pitch-sealed the seams between planks to exclude, rather than include, the hydraulic element, as had their earlier water-holding vessel, the vase—*ves,* short for vessel.

Vessels represent man's discovery, not only of the generalized principles governing stabilized separations of liquids and gases anywhere locally in the universe, but also of the generalized solution of local environmental pattern-controlling by man within the otherwise frequently hostile, if not lethal, environmental event patterning of total energetic universe. Vessels embrace the fundamental principle of finite local system mathematics. Vessels, as systems, divide the universe into two main parts—the withinness and the withoutness.

The concavity within tends to regenerative reconcentrations of the withinness by angular convergence of vectors impinging or echoing from its surface. The convex outer surface separates, diffuses and thins the energies impinging upon it or echoing from it by angular divergence. The convex-concave surfaces of systems are the prime energy pattern differentializers of universe. They occasion energy patternings either as local regenerative atomic masses or as universally divergent radiation.

Vessels are specialized realizations by man of finite local system theory, itself the realest of the real. The theoretically most effective vessels are the symmetrical and spherical (combined positive-negative hemisphere domes). The inseparably occurring positive (convex) and negative (concave) surfaces represent the most effective angular valving or shunting by man of the operative energy events of his environment, purposefully including this, excluding that. Vessels tentatively divide energetic universe into two fundamental domains, the macrocosm without and the microcosm within. Vessels constitute omni-directional spherical dams (domes). Physical experiments discovered and identified entropy as demonstrating the law of the increase of the random element which shows that locally confined energies will ultimately escape their local restraints.

Local perpetual motion systems are not permitted by a universe which, however, is itself the minimal, and always most efficiently and perpetually integrating system of comprehensive motions. Anti-entropy[20] shows that local systems also continually inhibit energies, but at rates inherently slower than their entropic rates. Both entropics therefore demonstrate that all spherical dams are inherently porous. Any spherical dam dome, described in the terms of atoms, consists only of a swarm of points contoured as the spherical zone occurring between concentric spheres. The spherical zone swarm of points are the non-intercontacting crowds of individual atoms and their respective individual nuclear components, all occurring only as different magnitudes of separate energy-event constellations.

Entropic and anti-entropic energy traffic between macrocosm and microcosm is only retarded by the frequency of angular pattern modulations occasioned by the successive, precessive shoulderings experienced by inward or outward bound energies passing through the primary atomic and secondary nuclear constellation crowds of the spherical dam.

Vessel design is concerned with the rate-valving and angular direction-shunting of the undeniable energy transactions between the dammed-apart macrocosm and the microcosm. As the traffic pattern of inward and outward energies are altered, inevitable energy pile-ups as differentials of potential energy-event directions are concentrated on either the inside or the outside of the micro-macro dam. These pile-up differentials result because

20 Fuller later adopted the word *syntropy* as a complementary principle to *entropy*.

vessel structuring and valving design inherently occasion frequency and angle modulations which can only decelerate the otherwise non-impeded energy traffic velocities of non-dome-dammed universe.

Vessels as local environment controlling structures are only challenged by four categories of force patterning:

1. Internal energy pile-up differential, beyond the critical limit of the dome dam structures' containment capability.
2. External energy pile-up differential beyond the critical limit of the dome dam structures' exclusion capability.
3. (Either #1 or #2) Differentials articulated as *exquisitely concentrated* energy actions.
4. (Either #1 or #2) Differentials articulated as approximately *evenly distributed* energy actions.

In the earliest known record of the land dome vessel, upside-downed and launched into the water, we find the probably earlier round pitch sealed basket vessel of the rivers, ovalled and axially elongated to form a round bottom, keel and rib-stiffened, sea-capable vessel with directionally favored low-resistance shape (ship) with (hollowed-holed) hulls which had already reached a scientifically sophisticated maturity of differentiated tension and compression functions in a multiplicity of highly specialized energy-structure tasks as spars, halyards, sails, rudders, oars and anchors. This earliest known picture of a ship, circa 2500 B.C., is inscribed in color upon the walls of that period's most advanced dry land structural innovating. This most advanced land building art of that time, consisting of the Egyptians' chiseled out cave-tombs, and of their gargantuanly cumbersome stone columns (improvised in a treeless land) and their enormous, yet short-spanning, horizontal stone block lintels, or beams. These historically novel and then most advanced land structures were in marked physical contrast to the exquisite performing efficiency, per unit of weight to function ratio, of the upside-down dome vessel ship-designing.

The Egyptians used their structurally innovated stone post and beam courts above grade for their living kings' pageantry and their below grade, man or nature-made, mountain-chambering for the "bon voyage" advantage of dead kings. The bon voyage equipment was frequently implemented with either drawings or full-scale, fully equipped real ships. The ships and their equipment were intended to take them into cosmic dominion. They were symbolized, in the mural drawings, as around a great sphere. The sphere has been interpreted as meaning "around the sun" or "traveling around the earth," as the sun appeared to do. These priest-authorized symbols disclosed both the priests' fundamental knowledge of earth's sphericity and their purposefully deceptive legend duplicity.

Some of the so-called sun ships of the Egyptian kings have been so well preserved in their tomb vaults that it is now possible to witness that their hull lines, overall dimensions, structural techniques, floorings, thwartings, plank lacings, prow and stern rudder-designing were approximately the same as the Viking (pronounced Veeking) ships of the North Atlantic—one of which also was in recent years unearthed in Norway from its burial ceremony grave. The Norseman's (North man's) ship and ceremonial equipment of tools and foods corresponded so intimately, by either a ship-designer's viewpoint, or a mechanic's viewpoint, that, despite the centuries, miles and skin-pigmentation differences between the Norsemen and the Egyptians, it is clear that the same maritime engineering and its concomitant philosophies and superstitions and economic tasks governed their contriving and use—as with one mind in one time upon one sea. In Scandinavia there are still traces of the upside-downing of these boats upon the land and their elevation as a nave in a subsequently evolved religious meeting building. The keel and ribbed ships inaugurated ridge poles (rigid pole keel) and rafters.

In Egypt, the living kings, when not enjoying their royal quarters upon the decks or within the cabins of their Nile River traffic-ruling ships, dwelt upon the land, not in their stone-columned courts, nor in their mountain-chambering, but in mud hutments (hut, hat, hus, bans, house, head, helmet, another epistemological transformation of the dome concept).

The only virtue of the stone-structuring innovations as a permanentizing of the wood and other organic products of nature, employed in building, was the expediency of finding a substitute for diminishing supplies of trees brought about by deforestation and failure to stem erosion and wind-blown desert growth. Because the permanentizing substitution of stone for wood took place in the Eastern Mediterranean, Asia Minor and the Orient and in the Americas, we do have records of structural conceptioning of the ages as previously realized only in perishable woods and theretofore utterly obliterated from the historical scene. The quality of durability is extraordinarily useful to us as an historical information relay system, but the virtue of durability, as a cosmic, infinity-seeking, security of the ego, is of dubious validity.

The anonymous millions of constructors of the pyramids and the techniques of their labors pique our curiosity and often provoke our admiration in greater measure than that spontaneously accorded by us to the name-identified kings. Certainly, the conflagrations of history that have taken place within stone walls have been equally devastating to those occurring in stone-free wooden structures. Fires burn more hotly inside furnaces than in the open. Today we witness would-be permanent wave after would-be permanent wave of progressively obsolete skyscrapers and lesser masonry buildings being expensively demolished and once more replaced with theoretically satisfactory "permanent buildings," emulating many of the permanentizing masonry techniques and sanitary theories inherited from the only-six-thousand-millenniums-long era of statical fallacy governing the misconception of building or aught else as desirably "permanent."

In diametric conceptioning, air and sea ships of steel and aluminum evolute economically as we progressively scrap, recover, reprocess, realloy and structurally reinvest the utterly indestructible elemental metal atoms in the swiftly evoluting series of accelerating safety and velocity capabilities of man's universe, interlinking and probing and resource-transporting vessels.

Separation of the whole history of domes into the two main classes of technology provides enlightenment upon the swiftly evoluting contemporary domical structures scene. While there are some borderline exceptions, the two classes have remained essentially distinct due to economic factors prevailing to mid-twentieth century, which have been suddenly changed due to the sudden maturing of world industrialization. The two main classes persist. The age-old Class One has evolved from grass basketry and wooden boats, through steel and aluminum shipbuilding, into the aero-astro air-frame power plant instrumentation and its production technologies. Class One is now entering the astronautical structuring era of remotely controlled environments.

The only six-thousand-years-long secondary Class Two is still clinging, interiorily and exteriorily, to the crudely upended, crudely borrowed and translated, steel ship skeleton skyscrapers. Class Two embraces the whole of public and private building construction arts.

Class One's original spherical symmetries have been, in many cases, spheroidally elongated to accommodate the swift directional functioning of their domical enclosures as transport environmental controls. Generally speaking, Class One embraces all curvilinear environment-controlling structures wherein the prime objectives are high performance per units of invested energies, weights, hours; successfully anticipated violent stressability; swiftly evolving, initially strong transitorial, specific longevity structuring; high priority access to intellectual, mathematical and industrial resource supremacies; extreme degree of functional differentiation with concomitant elimination of irrelevant fat and piggy-back alternate functions occasioning, for instance, fifty-thousand types of unique, non-fat parts and multimillions of pieces per each intercontinental bomber; world-around resources, world-around usage.

Class Two's structures, from the very outset of their permanentizing attempt, demonstrated a fundamental geometrical deterioration of the original dome's spherical competency of conceptioning and structuring. Curvilinear structures could be readily accomplished through bending of organic components without any important mathematical computation. The components, themselves, yielded in extraordinarily efficient c-curves. Catenaries draped themselves in mathematically elegant progression of changing inclination rates. When non-binding stone masonry was adopted, primarily for its fortification virtues, lack of mathematical capability imposed the straight line of sight technique and its simplest possible closure by a two-line parallel cross grid. The whole of Class Two's six-thousand-year history has been characterized by retreat from the curvilinear dome to the square cut domes or rectilinearity built upon rectilinear plans of unnatural square grid town planning, subdividing an unbounded plane, vanishing tangentially from a circular horizon of reality. Class Two, in contemporary youthful vernacular, is a "square."

Class Two structures are characterized by non-consideration of weight performance ratios in their conceptioning; inertia as premium stability; hopeful permanency; non-functional differentiation; non-functional fat; local craft production; safety factors ratioed by politicians; evolution flaunting; increasingly deferred payment occasioning long-term debt, socially underwritten, whose increasing hundreds of billions of dollars represent the relative inefficiency of Class Two's domical arts in competence, as ratioed to Class One's domical science competence.

Despite its obvious advantage over Class Two, Class One's domical science competence has much to learn and is possibly entering upon the most accelerated evolutionary phase in its whole history. This statement is predicated upon the following facts. Throughout all history, up to now, high scientific domical competence was so scarce a resource as to be made available only to the most exquisite high-seas and high-skies tasks of empire-building and empire survival. This forced relinquishment of the everyday environment-controlling tasks to the residually ignorant expediencies. Between its invention in 1904, and 1954, the airplane's long-distance-striking premiership brought it the combined subsidies of the nations of the earth, amounting to over two and a half trillion dollars of capital. As a result, the greatest industrial tooling and scientific competence of all history has been built into a gargantuan productive capacity for Class One's environment-controlling domical science.

When the first *Sputnik* accomplished orbit, it knocked the airplane out of the sky, as a weapon, as the airplane had knocked the battleship off the seas.

This has left derelict approximately the whole of the historically unprecedented industrial capability operative at Class One level of high scientific competence.

Because airplane-designing teams know nothing whatsoever about man's fundamental ecological evolution from a local cave man to an around-the-world air man and its inexorable requirement for competent living and working facility solution, the airplane design teams, charged by their business administration with tackling the problem of employing aircraft technology to everyday building arts, revert spontaneously to substituting, brick and shingle emulating, aluminum sheet stampings for wall components within the unchallenged, unconsidered over-all rectilinear inertness of Class Two's building arts ignorance. A myriad of other kept-mistress hangovers of the aircraft industry, from its golden subsidy days, will, for long, frustrate aircraft industries organization man's attempt to exploit the obvious potential replacement of the ignorant building arts of Class Two hangover by Class One's now available capabilities and capacities.

Unfortunately for the American and Western economies in general, the Communist bloc countries are unhobbled by vast dollar-powerful lobbies concerned primarily with permanentizing all the inefficiencies of Class Two environment-controlling arts, and their economics and negative financing. Russia gives every indication of converting its Class One technologies into the direct solution of its own and its allied world's environment-controlling and standard of living synchronization with world oriented air-astro age living-pattern requirements. Missile, satellite and jet transport production requirements of the combined world powers can and will use but a minor fraction of the total capacity and capability of the now-boiling-over Class One technology of the world. Russia and China may establish so swift a pace in application of the Class One technology directly to the living needs of the air-astro man that the western world will be forced by survival competition to junk its whole gamut of would-be-permanent, inert Class Two technological economics, and, sweeping the board clear, take advantage of its fortunately geared up tool and instrument capability to accommodate the whole new philosophy of preoccupation with Class One conceptioning and realizations. A complete revolution in the educational system and business philosophy is obviously involved.

As a preview of surprising technical vistas already opening to early phases of the major reorientation of Class One priority occupation in weapons development to prior occupation with air-ocean-world high standard of living requirements, I am submitting unembarrassed explorations, already undertaken, under generalized Class One domical strategy postulations. Reducing the generalized postulates to special case solution and practice discovers diametric reversal of the age-old engineering concept, which held that the law of diminishing return characterized the logistics and economics of progressively larger dimensioned building enterprises in any one schematic class. We discover in our special case exploration of unembarrassed Class One reduction to practice at the larger the clear span structure, the more efficient it becomes both in resource investments and in industrial logistics economics.

Problem

With minimum overall investment of technical-advantage-resources—that is, of controlled energy, either as chemical "materials" or as "work," the problem is to develop a universal and integral structural system:

a. capable of sustained enclosure and controlled isolation of conditions favorable to man's activities ranging in magnitude from single-family dwellings to major industries housed on the moon;
b. capable of inheriting all probable stresses' receipts and providing all positional advantage requirements;
c. capable of supporting appropriate mechanisms for valving all locally impinging random or periodic energy environment receipts into preferred patterns complementary to man and machine processes;
d. capable of elective omnidirectional penetrations.

The Generalized Structural Logic Resource

The tetrahedron (four-faceted structure) is minimum—prime divisor of omnidirectional universe into two fundamental domains—the withinness and the withoutness, the included and excluded, the microcosm and macrocosm. Tetrahedron is therefore basic structural system; all structure is a transformative phase or complex of tetrahedronal transformations.

All polyhedra may be subdivided into component tetrahedra, but no tetrahedron may be subdivided into component polyhedra of less than four faces.

The regular six-chord-edged tetrahedron encloses (defines) the minimum volume with the most surface of all "geometric" polyhedra or structural systems, whereas the sphere encloses (define) most volume with least surface.

As there may be no absolute division of energetic universe into "isolated" or non-communicable parts, there is no absolute enclosed surface or absolutely enclosed volume; therefore no true or absolutely defined simultaneous surface "sphere" integrity.

Figure 9

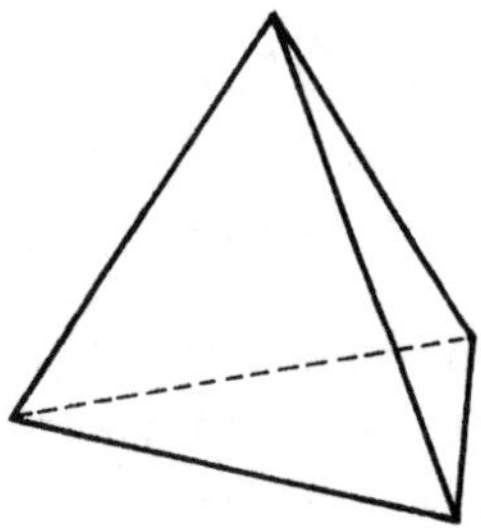

Tetrahedron

Therefore, a sphere is a polyhedron of invisible plurality of trussed facets—trussed because all polygons are reduceable to triangles or trusses and are further irreduceable. (Trusses are, therefore, basic polygons.) An infinite polyhedron is infinitely faceted by basic trusses.

When stressed with high relative internal pressure all polyhedra tend to define the maximum volume with the minimum surface—that is, toward the spherical convex-arc edged tetrahedra (the basketball and baseball are tetra-structured).

When stressed by high relative external pressure, structures tend to enclose the minimum volume with the most surface—that is, toward the chordal or concave tetrahedron (the symmetric collapsed baseball). The "regular" planar-bound tetrahedron is the zerophase between the convex tetrahedron (that is, the spherical tetrahedron) and the concave tetrahedron (that is, the four-webbed interaction between the six exterior edges of the tetrahedron and its center of gravity).

Great circle arcs represent the shortest lines between points on the surface of a sphere, and great circle segment chords represent the shortest distance between two surface points on the surface of a sphere. Therefore, the great circle arcs represent the limit structural transformative tendency of outward surface tensing by internal pressures; and great circle segment chords represent the limit structural optimum for axes of compression-resisting columns opposing external pressure by surface spreading.

We are seeking a structure impervious not only to extreme differential between internal and external pressure dominances, but also to highly concentrated internal or external loads or impact forces—yet permitting omni-directionally effective controlled penetrability.

Chordal-edged tetrahedronal structures best resist external forces and their vertexes best resist concentrated loads, while arc-edged tetrahedra best resist internal pressures, and their surface arc vertexes best resist concentrated internal pressures and impact forces, yet both permit omni-directionally valved penetrations. However, as the number of trussed faces of symmetric polyhedra are increased from the chordal and arc structural tetrahedra, through the hierarchy of great circle arc and chord trussed "solids"—that is, the octahedron (eight) and the icosahedron (twenty), the number of vertexes and edges increase providing more and dispersed structural interactions for resisting concentrated loads from more directions and also more and shorter chords, thus providing increasingly favorable slenderness ratios for the component compression columns. As the number of external truss facets of polyhedra are increased, the more nearly does the chordal (or compression) structure approach congruence with the arc or tension-structured sphere. The icosahedron has the highest number of identical and symmetric surface truss facets of all great circle defined polyhedra, providing twenty faces, twelve vertexes and thirty edges.

It is seen that if a further approach to the congruence of all-trussed chordal polyhedra with arc-structured spheres can be accomplished, not only will the vertexes and trussed facets (or penetration points) multiply, providing increased advantage in more directions against concentrated loads and more directions of penetration, as well as greater numbers of shorter compression columns to share the load—to be realized progressively with more economical slenderness ratios and sections, but also will the condition be rapidly approached when both the chord and arc lengths and spherical surface angles and their chordal facet angles become "practically" indistinguishable, and the polyhedron's surface becomes indistinguishable from the sphere.

It was discovered that a three-way great-circle grid may symmetrically subdivide the trussed facets of the icosahedron. This is what is designated as a three-way grid geodesic structure. Its frequency of modular subdivision of edge of the icosahedron's facets may be multiplied at will, once the spherical trigonometry rates of change of central and surface angle subdivisions have been solved.

This is the essence of the geodesic structures. At an edge frequency of sixteen modules, the arc and chord tend to "indistinguishable" differences of dimension. However, as the number of truss facets increase, the convex vertexial interactions approach a zero altitude condition, which, though ideal for tension or internal pressure, tends to allow concentrated external loads to push the convex chordal vertexes inside out—that is, to a dimpled or concave condition, whereafter the continuing concentrated external pressure will be resisted by tension increase in omnisurface direction (as a rubber ball draws on its skin as it resists punching in and gains reaction and spring back, causing bounce).

If we make microscopic inspection of a pneumatic balloon, we will find that the balloon skin is full of holes between its molecular chains, with a secondary and far smaller space continuity of "all holes" or "continuous space" between the remotely islanded energetic components of each molecule's respective atomic nuclear constellations. All these humanly invisible balloon "holes" are too small for molecules of gas to escape through. Because the balloon skin is full of holes it is really a subvisible spherical netting rather than a "flexibly solid film" within which the gaseous element molecules are crowded into lesser volume than required by their respective energetic, ecological domains, as fish might be within a seiner's net.

The resultants of forces of all these net-frustrated molecular actions are angularly outward of the balloon's geometrical center. Each surface molecule of the interior group of pressured gas has a vectorial action and reaction pattern identical to a spherical chord. In such enclosure-pressured gas, random sizes of molecules, each and all too large for the spherical molecular netting's holes, impinge randomly upon the interior webbing of the spherically tensioned net. There are, therefore, more outwardly pressing molecules and more inwardly restraining net components than are necessary to the structurally resultant balloon pattern integrity. However, in the geodesic, tensional integrity, spherical nets, the islands of interior compressional chordal struts impinge in discreet order at the exact vertices of the enclosing finite tensional network. My independent satellite or moon structures are then the most economical, frequency modulated, dynamic balances between outward-bound resultants of force and inward-bound resultants of force. The exterior tensional net is a finite system successfully binding the otherwise randomly entropic infinity of outbound, self-disassociative forces.

As already noted, a tensionally finite system has no inherent limit of length to section—that is, no inherent slenderness ratio, as do the explicitly limited slenderness ratios of compression members, wherefore we have in the Geodesic Tensegrity (my name for the discontinuous-compression, continuous-tension structures) the ability to assemble unprecedentedly large, clearspan structures, whose over-all diameter dimensions are limited only by the relative alloyed coherence of the associated metallic atoms therein involved, whose improving coherences are in swiftly multiplying metallurgical evolution augmentation. We can go, therefore, into the same magnitudes of clear-spanning dimensions as our largest suspension bridges. As suspension bridges demonstrate the continually improving tensile capabilities of constantly improving alloys, a suspension bridge could now be made twice the size of the Golden Gate Bridge. We may, therefore, consider clear-span, geodesic, tensegrity spheres in the magnitudes of two miles diameter as now realizable for use as satellite environmental controls or as hemispherical, or other spherical segment, earth-contacting enclosures (in which the earth completes the sphere)—for example, for arctic city environmental controls or as water floatable enclosures.

Whereas suspension bridge cables are parallel to one another and therefore give one another no more anti-rhombic structural stability aid than do the parallel tension wires of a barrel—in the case of the geodesic tensegrities, all the tension members cross one another in great-circle-chorded triangulations, thus providing the highest possible dimensional stability.

The progression of technical events above described alters all old engineering concepts regarding the relative increase in the over-all weights of structures. The now-obsoleted concepts heretofore provided early limits of practicality in the relative increase of weights of structures which occur when the linear dimensions are proportionally increased. In Egyptian pyramid buildings, doubling of the linear base dimensions brought about a four-fold increase in the surface and an eight-fold increase in the weight of the pyramid—that is, a linear dimension increase of two brings about a second power surface dimension increase of four and a concomitant third power volumetric dimension increase of eight.

When men later learned that the highest capability in strength of structures existed in their surfaces, due to the greater action-reaction, leverage distance that opposite sides of the systems provided, they hollowed out their buildings, which they had theretofore thought of only as formalized, solid compression warts on solid earth, such as the solid wats of Angkor Wat, or the ghats of Burma and India and the pyramids of Babylon and Egypt. But it is probable that men had first hollowed out their food and water vessels; later their log boats; centuries later, their buildings and, millenniums later, their sailing crafts' racing spars.

Later, when men learned that the structural strength at the surface was not provided by the "solid" quality of the exterior shell, but by triangularly interstabilized lines of force operative within that shell, they perforated the shell with holes between the force lines. The minimum holes were triangular. The pattern of triangulated force lines peppered with triangular holes in the hollowed-out structural shell became what we call a truss. We can say then, firstly, that the hollowing-out automatically reduced the third power volumetric multiplication of relative weight increase of structures as they increase in respect to their primary linear dimension increases. We can also say, secondly, that the piercing of the shells with triangular holes reduced the solid or continuous surface of second power increase of the shells and brought the rate of structures' growth into something nearer an over-all first power or linear rate of gain, for the force lines are only linear. When we introduce the tensegrity structure and its many surprises already accounted, we see that we have broken through to a structural knowledge and technique, which permits a progressively decreasing relative weight of structure as proportioned to the linear gain. This is to say, the gain of weight in structures, as ratioed to basic linear dimensions, is as one is to one minus $\frac{1}{x}$ weight ratio, as the same structure is multiplied in relative size.

In the above progression, as geodesic tensegrity frequencies increase, the sizes of the islands of compression diminish. Islands of compression are the only residual "solids" and their diminishing size diminishes their relative weights at a cube root progression of advantage. Halving the size of a solid spar reduces its relative weight by eight. Halving the size of a hollow spar reduces weight by a factor of approximately four.

When we combine the ability to introduce the above orderly mathematics into the electronic computers, permitting practical calculation and engineering "feasibility" nonexistent prior to that fact, with the fact that the higher the frequency the smaller the tensional sectional area (yet the higher the tensional sectional capability and the smaller the local islands of compression), it is statable that the higher the frequency, the more ephemeral the tensegrity complex and lesser the total weight of structure per given level of performance, and the less vulnerable the whole structure, by total violations by any or many inwardly or outwardly originating impinging forces, will be.

9 Comprehensive Designing

The Comprehensive Designer emerges as the answer to the greatest problem ever addressed by mankind: The Human Family now numbering three billion is increasing at an annual rate of three percent and is trending toward seven billion expected by the end of the second half of this century.[21] Of this number, sixty-five percent are chronically undernourished, and one third are doomed to early demise due to conditions which could be altered or eliminated within the present scope of technology; specifically, that area of technology comprising the full ramifications of the building arts, which now contains the negatives or blanks which match the lethal factors. Relative to this premise, Jawaharlal Nehru once said in Chicago: "It is folly to attribute the disquietude of the Orient to ideological pressures." Nehru went on to point out that the de-energized and doomed are prey to any political shift of the wind that might promise arrest of their fate.

At present all the world's industrial, or surfaced, processed and reprocessed functional tonnage (the *Industrial Logistics*) is preoccupied in the service of four tenths of the world's population, though one hundred percent are directly or indirectly involved in its procurement, processing and transportation.

January 1950. From a talk given by Fuller to the Faculty Club of the Massachusetts Institute of Technology. An amended version was published in *Trans/Formation: Arts, Communication, Environment* (1950), edited by Harry Holtzman and Martin James.

---

21 See note 9, p. 104.

All the politician can do regarding the problem is to take a fraction of that inadequate ratio of supply from one group and apply it to another without changing the over-all ratio. The politician can, of course, recognize and accept the trend rather than oppose it, but this does not accelerate it in adequate degree to arrive at a solution in our day and generation, and, more importantly, before the deadline of the doomed.

All that money can do is shower paper bills of digits on the conflagration. Relative denominations neither decrease nor increase the velocity of combustion.

How and by whom, if at all, may the problem be solved? Scientists are often charged with the task, but scientists as a class (irrespective of their proclivities as individuals) do not function in the *comprehensive* capacity, they function as specialists in taking the universe apart to isolate and inventory its simplest behavior relationships. Engineers function as invoked specialists in reproducing satisfactory interactions of factors ascertained as "satisfactory" by past experience and a wealth of behavior measurement. Both engineers and politicians would lose their credit from society if they incorporated the unprecedented in wholesale manner.

We hear and read frequently in scientific and philosophical journals of the desirability of ways in which problems of the universe may once more be approached by comprehensive and scientific principles.

A New Social Initiative

There emerges the need for a new social initiative which is not another function or specialization but is an integral of the sum of the product of all specializations, that is, the Comprehensive Designer.

The Comprehensive Designer is preoccupied with anticipation of all men's needs by translation of the latest inventory of their potentials. Thus he may quickly effect the upping of the performance-per-pound of the world's industrial logistics in fourfold magnitude through the institution of comprehensive redesign, incorporating all of the present scientific potentials that would otherwise be tapped only for purposes of warfaring, defensively or offensively.

In view of our myriad of performance-per-pound-advances of multifold degree (in contrast to percentage degrees) typified by pounds of rubber tire upped in performance from one thousand miles to thirty thousand miles expectancy without poundage increase (yet with complete chemical, though invisible, transformation), or of communication advance from one message to two-hundred-fifty concurrent messages per unit of cross section of copper wire (and both of these multifold advances have been accomplished within a quarter of a century), it is seen as a meager technical problem to consider advancing the over-all efficiency of worldwide industrial and service logistics fourfold (to serve one hundred percent of the population).

Some may tend to underestimate the comprehensive nature of the problem, saying the people are thus starving and we have the land capacity to raise the food. This conception voiced by the theoretical specialist or casual observer is without benefit of logistic experience. It is not just a matter of raising food but getting food to people, anywhere from zero to twenty-five thousand miles distant. And then it is not just a matter of getting food to people zero to twenty-five thousand miles away—it is a matter of getting it there at certain velocities; and it is not just a matter of getting it there at certain velocities, but it is a matter of getting it there on schedules in certain conditions, conditions of nourishing content, palatability and vital preservation.

And even then it is not a matter of success concerning all the preceding conditions, for the dumping of a year's food supply in front of a helpless family huddled on the street-curb is but an unthinkable tragedy. The maggots appear in hours. And once again the continuing energy controls providing progressive freezes, heatings, etc. cannot be effected by refrigerators and stoves dumped in the street along with a year's tonnage of food. Obviously, a world continuity of scientific-industrial controls resultant from comprehensive and technical redesign is spelled out as the irreducible minimum of solution.

For those who think that this minimum can be obtained through legislative enactment by the politician or by the establishment of new dollar credits, and who are forgetful that the total world tonnage is already preoccupied with service of only forty-four percent of the world-people, it is to be noted that the economic-statistical approach has been voiced by the press in conjunction with water shortages in the great American cities, such as New York and Los Angeles.

These are not problems unique to those cities, but symptomatic of the trend of the great industrial interactions. The economic-statistical solution, voiced by the politicians and the news, proposes further encroachments of the watershed origins through the rerouting of waters otherwise destined to lesser centers.

A typical question asked by the Comprehensive Designer is: What do people want the water for? They are using two hundred gallons per day per capita, consuming only one gallon for their vital processes while employing one hundred ninety-nine gallons to dunk themselves, and gadgets, and to act as a liquid conveyor system of specks of dirt to the sea. We note that scientists do not need water to dunk their instruments in, nor industrialists water to soak their machinery in. Are there not superior ways to effect many of the end purposes involving no water at all, and where water is found to be essential, can it not be separated out after its combining functions and systematically recirculated as chemically pure, sterilized, "sweet" and clear, and with low energy expense or even an improved energy balance sheet as a result of comprehensive redesign?

The specialist in comprehensive design is an emerging synthesis of artist, inventor, mechanic, objective economist and evolutionary strategist. He bears the same relationship to society in the new interactive continuities of world-wide industrialization that the architect bore to the respective remote independencies of feudal society.

The architect of four hundred years ago was the comprehensive harvester of the potentials of the realm. The last four hundred years have witnessed the gradual fade-out of feudalism and the gradual looming of what will eventually be full of world-industrialization—when all people will produce for all people in an infinity of interacting specialized continuities. The more people served by industrialization, the more efficient it becomes.

Positive Constituents of Industry

In contrast to the many negative factors inherent in feudalism (such as debt, fear, ignorance and an infinite variety of breakdowns and failures inevitable to dependence on the vagaries of Nature), industrialization trends to "accentuate the positive and eliminate the negative," first by measuring Nature and converting the principles discovered in the measurements to mastery and anticipation of the vagaries. Day and night, winter and summer, fair weather or bad, time and distance are mastered. Productive continuities may be maintained and forwardly scheduled. There are three fundamental constituents of industry; all are positive.

The first consists of the aspect of energy as *mass,* inventoried as the ninety-two regenerative chemical elements which constitute earth and its enclosing film of alternating liquid-gaseous sequence.

The second fundamental component of industry consists of energy but in a second and two-fold aspect—that is: (a) energy as *radiation* and (b) energy as *gravitation,* both of which we are in constant receipt of from the infinite cosmic fund. The third and most important component of the industrial equation is the intellect factor, which secrets a continually amplifying advantage in experience-won knowledge.

Complex-component No. 1 cannot wear out. The original chaotic disposition of its ninety-two regenerative chemical elements is gradually being converted by the industrial principle to orderly separation and systematic distribution over the face of earth in structural or mechanical arrangements of active or potential leverage-augmentation. Component No. 2, cosmic energy, cannot be exhausted.

Constituent No. 3 not only improves with use but is interactively self-augmenting.

Summarizing, components No. 1 and No. 2 cannot be lost or diminished and No. 3 increases, with the net result inherent gain. Inherent gain is realized in physical advantage of forward potential (it cannot be articulated backwards; it is mathematically irreversible). Thus, industrial potential is schematically directional and not randomly omni-directional. Thus, the "life" activity, as especially demonstrated by man, represents an anti-entropic phase of the transformations of non-losable universal energy.

The all-positive principle of industry paradoxically is being assimilated by man only through emergent expedients, and only in emergency because of his preponderant fixation in the direction of tradition. Backing up into his future, man romantically appraises the emergent dorsal sensations in the negatively parroted terms of his ancestors' misadventures.

The essence of the principle of industry is the principle of synergy, which I have explained in an earlier chapter. This principle is manifested both in the inorganic and organic. The alloying of chrome and nickel and steel provides greater tensile strength than that possessed by any of its constituents or by the constituents in proportional addition. Three or more persons by specialized teamwork can do work far in excess of that of three independently operating men. Surprisingly, and most contradictory to the concept of feudal ignorance, the industrial chain's strength is not predicated on its weakest link. So strong is the principle that it grows despite a myriad of superficially failing links! In fact, there are no continuous "links" in industry or elsewhere in the universe because the atomic components are, interiorly, spatially discontinuous.

The strength of "industry" as with the strength of the "alloy" occurs through the concentric enmeshment of the respective atoms. It is as if two non-identical constellations of approximately the same number of stars each were inserted into the same space, making approximately twice as many stars, but none touching due to the difference in patterns. The distances between stars would be approximately halved. It is the same with alloyed atoms whose combined energetic cohesion increases as the second power of the relative linear proximities of the component parts. Though the parts do not "touch," their mass cohesive dynamic attraction follows the gravitational law of proportionment to second power of the distance apart of centers. Therefore, alloying strength is not additive arithmetically but is advantaged by gravity, which, as Newton discovered, is inversely proportional to the "square" of the distance apart.

Man has now completed the plumbing and has installed all the valves to turn on infinite cosmic wealth. Looking to the past he wails, "How can I afford to turn on the valve? If I turn it on, somebody's going to have to pay for it!" He forgets that the bill has been prepaid by men through all time, especially by their faithfully productive investments of initiative. The plumbing could not have been realized except through absolute prepayment of intellectually organized physical work, invested in the inherent potentials of Nature.

Epochal Transformations

Not only is man continually doing more with less—which is a principle of trend which we will call ephemeralization, a corollary of the principle of synergy—but he is also demonstrating certain other visible trends of an epochal nature. Not only does he continue to increase in literacy but he affords more years of more advanced study to more people. As man becomes master of the machine—and machines are introduced to carry on every kind of physical work with increased precision, effectiveness and velocity—his skilled crafts, formerly intermittently patronized, graduate from labor status to continuity of employment as research and development technicians. As man is progressively disemployed as a quantity-production muscle-and-reflex machine, he becomes progressively re-employed in the rapidly increasing army of research and development—or of production-inaugurating engineering—or of educational and recreational extension, as a plowed-back increment of industrialization.

Product and service production of any one item of industry trends to manipulation by one man for the many through push-button and dial systems. While man trends to increasing specialized function in anticipatory and positive occupations of production, he also trends to comprehensive function as consumer. Because the principle of industry improves as the number of people it serves is increased, it also improves in terms of the increase of the number of functions of the individual to which it is applied. It also improves in terms of its accelerated use.

Throughout the whole history of industrialization to date, man has taken with alacrity to the preoccupation of the specialist on the production side of the ledger; but the amplifications of the functions of the individual as a comprehensive consumer have been wrenched and jerked and suffered into tentative and awkward adoption in the mumbo-jumbo and failure complex of obsolete feudal economics. Up to yesterday man was unaware of his legacy of infinite cosmic wealth. Somewhere along the line society was convinced that wealth was emanating from especially ordained mortals, to whom it should be returned periodically for mystical amplification. Also with feudal fixation man has looked to the leaders of the commercial or political states for their socioeconomic readjustments—to the increasingly frequent "emergencies."

Throughout these centuries of predominant ignorance and vanity, the inherently comprehensive-thinking artist has been so competent as to realize that his comprehensive thoughts would only alienate him from the economic patronage of those who successfully exploited each backing up into the future. The exploiters, successively successful, have attempted in vain to anchor or freeze the dynamic expansion at the particular phase of wealth generation which they had come to monopolize.

The foolhardy inventors and the forthright prospectors in humble tappings of greater potentials have been accounted the notable failures. Every industrial success of man has been built on a foundation of vindictive denouncement of the founders.

Thus the comprehending artist has learned to sublimate his comprehensive proclivities and his heretic forward-looking, toward engagement of the obviously ripening potentials on behalf of the commonwealth. The most successful among the artists are those who have effected their comprehensive ends by indirection and progressive disassociations. So skillful have the artists of the last centuries been that even their aspiring apprentices have been constrained to celebrate only the non-utilitarian aspects of the obvious vehicles adroitly employed by the effective artists to convey their not-so-obvious but all-important burden.

Thus the legend and tradition of a pure art or a pure science as accredited preoccupations have grown to generally accepted proportion. The seemingly irrelevant doings of the pure scientist of recent decades exploded in the face of the tradition of pure mathematical abstraction at Alamogordo. No one could have been more surprised than the rank and file of professional pure scientists. The results were implicit in the undertakings of artist-scientists whose names are in the dim forefront or are anonymous in the limbo of real beginnings. How great and exultant their secret conceptioning must have been!

The Time Has Come

The time has arrived for the artist to come out from behind his protective coloring of adopted abstractions and indirections. World society, frustrated in its reliance upon the leaders of might, is ready to be about-faced to step wide-eyed into the obvious advantages of its trending. We will soon see the emergence of comprehensive training for specialists in the husbandry of specialists and the harvesting of the infinite commonwealth.

Will the Comprehensive Designer, forthrightly emergent, be as forthrightly accepted by the authorities of industrialization and state? If they are accepted, what are the first-things-first to which they must attend?

The answer to the first question is yes. They will be accepted by the industrial authority because the latter has recently shifted from major preoccupation with exploiting original resource to preoccupation with keeping the "wheels," which they manage turning, now that the original inventory of wheels, or tools in general, has been realized from original resource. Though original resource-exploiters still have great power, that power will diminish as the mines now existing above grade, in highly concentrated use forms (yet in rapidly obsoleting original design), become the preponderant source of the annual need. Severe acceleration in the trend to increase of performance per pound of invested material now characterizes all world-industry. With no important increase in the rate of annual receipt from original mines, the full array of mechanics and structure requisite to amplifying the industrial complex, from its present service to approximately one-fourth the world's population to serve all the world's population, may be accomplished by the scrap "mined" from the progressively obsoleting structures and mechanics.

World-industrial management will be progressively dependent upon the Comprehensive Designer to accelerate the turning of his wheels by design acceleration. Each time the wheels go round, the infinite energy wealth of cosmos is impounded within the greater receptive capacities of the ninety-two regenerative-element inventory of earth, and those who manage the wheels can make original entry on their books of the new and expanding wealth increments even as the farmer gains cosmic energy wealth in his seasoned cycles.

An answer as to whether the designer will be accredited by political leadership has been made. Political leadership in both world camps has announced to the world of potential consumers their respective intents to up the standard of living of all world peoples by "converting the high technical potential to account through design."

Only the designer can accomplish this objective. Legislative mandate and dollar diplomacy cannot buy the realization.

As first of the first things, the designer must provide new and advanced standards of living for all peoples of the world. He must progressively house and re-house three billion people in establishments of advanced physical control. The mechanically serviced sheltering must be a continuity of roofs, stationary and mobile, sufficient to allow for man's increasing convergent-divergent interactions of transciency or residence, of work, play or development, interconnecting every center of the world and penetrating to autonomous dwelling facility of the most advanced standard, even in the remotest of geography. The logistics of this greatest phase of industrialization must impound cosmic-energy wealth, within the inventory of ninety-two chemical elements, to magnitudes, not only undreamed of, but far more importantly, adequate to the advancing needs of all men. Implicit is man's emancipation from indebtedness to all else but intellect.

10 Design for Survival—Plus

In substantiation of the assumption that the problem must be adequately stated at the outset, it is noted that many plausible prefabricated house designs have been tendered to the public through the press as allegedly suitable for mass production. The public credit has been repeatedly short-circuited and the new fuse of design initiative blown out. It is seen that the original presentations included but meager or no means at all for the distribution, erection, movability, maintenance and minimum economic occupancy as inherent components of the design and as direct responsibility of the producers.

Every time the total logistic involvement of the prefabricated house designs have been put to economic test appropriate to the respective prototypes, the original design concept of these houses has been found to be inadequate. Deficit financing has been required in afterthought or as an emergency measure to offset original inadequacy of concept (for instance, the significant scope, magnitude and nature of the project in the historical scheme of events).

To avoid bankruptcy of the projects, the deficit financing had either to be provided by the original private backers, a diminishing

---

January 1949. The original was a talk delivered by Fuller to the first formal meeting of the Illinois Institute of Technology to deliberate on the founding of a program "to assemble the abilities of science, engineering, and design in the realization of single-family dwelling units." Fuller goes on to add to this notation in the manuscript (Fuller Archive Series 8 Box 8 Fol. 9 [Design for Survival Plus 49.01.02]), "... through augmented advantage to industrial complex." And in a later version of the same, adds "—an advantage heretofore uniquely avoided by the proclivities of the housing tradition."

credit resource, or, most recently, by a federalized angel, that is, government financing by reconstruction loans.

When government finance is invoked, the vital factors affecting survival of the project pass into the realm of politics and out of the area of scientific measurement. Application of the vast social credit to prenatal design of industrial embryos constitutes short circuit just as thoroughly as if there had been "private failure."

Political hedging of "social" finance requires the administration of the funds by compromises inherent in bureaucracy reflecting the enactor's re-election dependence upon the favorable probabilities in the direction of preponderant incredulity, boredom, ignorance, inertia and mediocrity.

First flight by man could not have been the product of socialized development. Would-be flying devices suitable for political credit prior to first flight by man must of necessity exploit irrelevant monopolies in inertia—too heavy for flight. So important an evolutionary event (as successful flight by man) may only be won in principle from the potentials of universe through a complex interaction of a plurality of initiatives daringly taken by individuals. Self-sustained directional control of air-borne man represents the integrated product of a fabulous history of personal investment by innumerable individuals in daring sequences of single-handed and necessary failures, attendant upon undertakings only warrantable to the individual himself.

Integration of a complex of series of failures represents the only means of attaining from nature the original data essential to realization of evolutionarily tactical events. Not even the most benevolently motivated private or public accrediting can circumvent the vital events of acquisition of knowledge by man regarding critical factors and limits of variables governing his self-determinable evolutionary mutations.

In retrospect, it is easy for all to see how the myriad historical events of individual initiative in mathematics, chemistry, physics, mechanics, semantics, good faith, etc., have led up to realization of all the components of that complex invention, the airplane. Historians and parents teach children as though it had always been obvious that yesterday would lead to today. But we, the living, are always in tomorrow's yesterday, and in our tomorrow's yesterday percolate remotely all the vital undertakings of individual initiative destined to series of failures out of which will emerge the vital data on critical limits and variables, the which trickling, then running to many confluences, must flow ultimately to merge with the ocean of obvious environment into which the new life, continuously taking all that has gone before for granted, is born. It is a corollary that the tendency of man to invest only in seemingly "sure" things constitutes economic suicide. *Sure* is the prohibited direction of the return to yesterday. Compoundingly, it is evidenced that social reinvestment of earned evolutionary advantage in only "sure" things brings systematic suicide of whole socio-economic systems.

Prefabricated-house undertakings have to date been analogous to the designing of a telephone as constituting only a toy accessory independent of a communication network, wired or wireless, and the network's generating and maintenance services. The "toy" concept expanded into industrial economics reveals irresponsibility and incompetence at the research and design level.

Housing is inherently the last and largest physical preoccupation of industrial development, because it represents the sum of all historical advantages integrated into a new magnitude of extension of the ecological dimensions of man. Why have the prefabricated designs been irresponsible and incompetent? It is because consideration of the total logistic involvement was initially deferred or ignored, or ignorantly missed in the "gold rush" attempts to exploit rather than to process scientifically the potentials of the greatest historical realization of the principles of the industrial advantage—conversion of world *weaponry* to *livingry* systems.

Logistics is concerned with the total energy involvements. In the language of the most eminent spokesman for the pure science aspects of logistics, total energy involvement is stated as $E=mc^2$. $E=mc^2$ reads: The physical universe is energy, and total energy is disposed in inseparable, yet reciprocal transformations of principle—as, for instance, *mass* and *velocity* (of light). The reciprocals of velocity are further interpolated by man into time and space and matter interactions. The science of logistics converts all its energy formulas to ultimate range and frequency of hitting power at earth crust or immediate vicinity. Pure science as represented by Dr. Einstein, although dealing in the identical components of an all-energy universe as applied to astronomy, did not originally contemplate the conversion of the formula to "hitting power."

Now the same original data regarding transformation of all-energy universe may be translated into a third equation, that of human ecology. We are familiar with this potential in the language of capital and income investment in the myriad economic factors of man hours, kilowatts, tonnage and machines. But it should be an obvious requirement of scientific integrity that the formula cannot be effectively applied except in the terms of a comprehensive design which holds all reciprocal factors in continuous review and organizes them as a total system.

The original Einstein formula, expanded into its everyday industrial-social applications, must of necessity involve breakdown into a multiplicity of reciprocal components. Of course businessmen and industrialists have not thought of their undertakings as attempts to "expand the Einstein formula into everyday economics" and would vehemently deny the possibility. But translated expansion of the fundamental Formula of Physical Universe is nonetheless involved in the scientific pacing of industrial evolution.

It is common fallacy to attempt simplification of the total formula by dropping out seemingly minor components of the expanded expressions. It is a theory of management to thin out the comprehensive into seeming discontinuities, where isolation breeds quick familiarity by simplified occupation. It is an inevitable hazard inherent in the advantage of industrial specialization that the specialists in remote components tend to offset the over-all advantage by appraising the function of one another as irrelevant. The challenge which we are taking up is that of competent reintegration in design of the expanded fundamental energy equation. If technologists now lack confidence in scientific method as applied to man's housing, that too is a component of the original adequate statement of the problem.

After original statement of *a priori* general principles of industrialization comes the establishment of a comprehensive family of working assumptions unique to the specific problem. For example, we may assume as a most comprehensive statement of the negative aspect of the problem housing, the assertion of Edward Stettinius, written immediately after he served as Secretary of State of the United States, and as Chief of the U.S. Delegation to the charter convention of the United Nations, and contained in a letter to the author—to wit: *One third of the human family is now doomed to premature death due to causes arising directly from inadequate solution of the housing problem.* This statement is pointed up by a 1948 U.N. report stating, there was a net catastrophic war loss of fourteen million homes, the families for which still exist. There were additional millions of homes demolished by war but the families were lost with them.

This catastrophic loss is in addition to the evaporation of housing capacity in Europe as a result of a rate of population increase greater than new building velocity, aggravated by obsolescence and deterioration of pre-industrial crafts, etc. It is authoritatively stated that there is no means of solving this catastrophic problem within the life span of the people involved. This one European category of "unsolvable" housing problems alone accounts for one hundred million of the eight hundred doomed millions of the world as indicated by Stettinius. When this and other appropriate comprehensive assumptions of controlling factors and objectives of the program have been adopted, we next define the governing principles, as for instance the functions of: (1) The Industrial Complex, (2) Science, (3) Engineering, and (4) Design, each predicated on measured behavior and not upon wishful theory.

Functions of Industry

The following is typical of the family of definitions of principles which together comprise the Industrial Complex: Industry means tooled-up organization of effort into teamwork of specialized functions, which interact to provide total survival means and values for man superior to the sum derivable from individual effort. For example, if each of the sixty-nine million employed citizens of the U.S. attempted to budget his time in such a manner as to singlehandedly produce his family's total needs in foods, bolts, clothing, education, news, transportation and communication, etc., without lowering the performance standards of their living conditions, he couldn't do it in the ultrasplit second apportioned any item. It is seen that if the individual found it necessary to support his family singlehandedly, he would be forced to lower the standards of required performance to a minimum, so as to allow continuity of effort within any one category adequate to fulfillment of the natural processes of each category. This obviously precludes the availability of the higher standards of survival performance that accrue to the coordinated patterns of more deeply penetrating special knowledge and continuity of experimentation and production in the complexedly tooled industrial advance.

It is quickly seen that industrialization is not to be considered only as a form of prosaic commercial exploitation but also as a mathematical principle inherent in the universe. This principle, which is most typical of industry, I have identified as the principle of synergy. The functionings of industry are inclusive.

Function of Science

Typical of our working definitions as applied to science is: the function of science is to prospect for total society by taking the universe apart, that is, resolve it into primary factors and elements by progressive isolation and subsequently to obtain precise measurements of the behavior characteristics of the isolated events or components.

For example, science isolated the phenomenon fire from extraneous factors, and by isolating the constituent events and the product of events discovered that fire is not in itself an element but an accelerated combining process of a newly recognized primary element, that is, oxygen, combining with carbohydrates in ever-constant arithmetical proportion. Thus the isolation of the fire caused the subsequent isolation, recognition and naming of the new elements oxygen and hydrogen, and provided behavior measurements of the latter, by which man could predict events of combustion in such a way as to make combustion an accurate tool of technical advantage. As water and water vapor are H_2O events, the comprehensive event was a precise mathematical process. This was the beginning of purposefully produced steam as a tool. The steam engine was a victory of chemical science, not of mechanics as we have popularly supposed. However the functions of science ended with the separating out of the newly discovered elements from the universal matrix and with the measurement of the unique behavior characteristics of the respective elements (it being the unique behavior that constitutes elementality). It is readily seen that the present invocation of science to put together again the world it has taken apart, is futile in principle. Summarizing, it is the essential function of science to take the universe apart and measure the parts and sort them into usable categories. The functioning of science is *exclusive.*

Functions of Design

It has been demonstrated that the function of design in society is to make original assumptions for the schematic employment of the appropriate behavior characteristics of selected items of the by-science-separated constituents of the universe and to apply the new degrees of potential advantage to the evolutionary problems of the process broadly defined as "man." This combining of the potential and the problem by design is possible because the many events of the process "man" have also been separated out and measured by science. Though man's ego claimed a permanence exempt from all natural processes of his environment, he has come to an embryonic realization of the inter-penetrating extent of the psycho-physiological processes with the dynamics of the organic and inorganic environment. Rather than being a purposeful static thing, he is now a purposeful dynamic process. In summary, design puts together combinations of special behavior elements to arrive at special advantages for the special "process man." It is through design that man has evoluted to his present extended manipulation of environment. The functioning of design is *comprehensive.*

For example, in design synergism we discover that while chromium has one set of behavior characteristics, and nickel and iron still others, the association of the three in unique mathematical proportions provides a combined behavior pattern of superior performance in resistance to tension and impact in contrast to the behavior of any of its constituent parts (while also preventing oxidization of the iron, that is, its combustion). It can be seen that the principle of association of special categories of behavior to effectuate desirable synergisms is indicated not only in the definition of our principle, industry, as human teamwork, but also as a principle in itself governing both organic and inorganic factors. This is why we define synergy as a generalized principle. Design must imagine and discern, assume, purpose and attempt articulation, in as synergetic a manner as possible. Design, however, cannot guarantee its results. Borderline or failure-point activity provides pivotal data for the exploratory designer.

Failure in design is honorable; in science and engineering it is found to be a mark of incompetence, and failure in politics and finance is ruinous. It can be seen that when finance and politics have authority with the management of design, they continually want to terminate progress because in applying self-perpetuating traditional standards they disqualify the designer in the very practice of the qualifying phenomena that might measurably increase total human wealth. In short, design represents the point where man sticks his neck out and first attempts to use his scientific potential.

In connection with the concept of the designer's sticking his neck out on behalf of society to increase commonwealth, we are in need of a clear definition of *wealth,* for we do not mean that the designer should stick his neck out by issuing his own coinage. We define wealth as the organized degree of accountably tooled-up of forward controlling of environment and metabolic process requirements of men by man. Livingry considered as a multiple-purpose tool embodies the major wealth factors. As livingry is comprehensive to wealth, the deterioration of systematic means of livingry constitutes deterioration of wealth and signals termination of predictable controls of forwardly necessary circumstance livingry events—*ergo,* chaos. Design-improved livingry increases wealth.

Functions of Engineering

The behavior pattern of engineering indicates that it functions not at the original design level, but as an inverted phase of science. Engineering is the judicial authority that never assumes the initiative but decides and proves the assertions of science and design. Engineering thus establishes reliable data on the failure limits of complex associations and also measures the new synergetic behavior characteristics discovered by design initiative. Thus, engineering rapidly places on inventory comprehensive data pertaining to the known behavior characteristics of complex associations previously undertaken by design. These complex associations may be broadly defined as alloys, structures, mechanics, processes and services. It is a function of engineering to provide society with reliable predictions as to the behavior characteristics of complex designs predicated on competent experience. Engineering, then, consolidates the net gains of science and design in the industrial complex. Gains are design intuited synergies.

The Psychological Weather Is Favorable

It must be emphasized that there need not be any inferiority complex in tackling livingry in highest principles—that is, inferiority regarding popular, financial or political support. In fact, there ought not be any inferiority at all. We might go further and say: "If any inferiority is in evidence, failure is certain." Only the most daring elevation of the sights can possibly hit the vastly ranging target.

The target is vast in range because it involves upping the standards of living for people all over the world with such acceleration as to avoid world disaster inherent in the general, self-eroding chaos to effect a premature death for one third of the human family. As with controlled missiles, it is better to launch the projectile vertically until it gains enough altitude to be directed with minimum effort and maximum precision to its omni-directional target.

In support I wrote in 1949, "It is to be noted that the next war will be the first in all history in which there will be no front. It will be total, controlled from anywhere, and missiles may be remotely launched and guided to any target. The man controlling the missile will be located alongside the man making the missile and alongside the men who are feeding and housing the men making and guiding the missiles. Front, home, factory unify as *livingry,* a dynamically expanding, improving human ecology.

"Because science is universally permeative, the probability indicates offensive parity in a total war of controlled long-distance missiles. Therefore, it is mathematically probable that the winner will be that side which has the most effective defense. Effective defense is spelled out in terms of superior degrees of deployment ability—from vulnerable magnitudes of population concentrations.

(For instance, as stated February 9, 1949, by the U.S. National Resources Planning Commission, cities of fifty thousand and under are too small for economic expenditure of enemyhitting power.)

"When the population concentrations of animate and inanimate components of the industrial complex are reduced below 'payoff' magnitudes in offensive strategy, the battle is won (temporarily, for we now know life to be dynamic and progressive), that is, 'checkmate' is called. At this tactical event, the checkmated, while racing to uncheck through adequate degrees of decentralization, may cover with a counter-offensive by calling out: 'I have a new missile available in far larger numbers, which may be expended economically on hitherto invulnerable population concentrations.' Obviously, the progression, checkmating and counter-checkmating, will be one of increased technical ability to fire economically at smaller and smaller population concentrations. And, inasmuch as the *defensive* tactics represent the upper hand to be maintained in the dynamic equilibrium of ever-impending shooting totality, the winning technique must devolve upon superior deployment of higher standards of living facility-*livingry*.

"These principles of the strategy are well known to both sides. For the first time in history, livingry has been tacitly advanced to the front ranks of logistic priorities. In all past wars, housing has been the one item with no priorities. Housing has never had priority even in the peacetime offensives of exploitation of the land.

"Housing has always been bulked up from the residual and unwanted surpluses, that is, of low performance residues. For example, farm housing was built of the wood and stone first cleared from the land for the priority event of planting of seed to impound the sun wealth increment as food energy for the annual needs. The agricultural sun energy increments constituted the essential wealth augmentation of man in the past with frequent excesses to be traded for participation in the industrial complex. In every instance, war or peace, housing involved making the best of a poor deal. The wood, though valuable as a chemical resource for high performance constituents, such as alcohol, pulp or rayon, made a poor housing material in its performance against fire, termites, bacterial rot, etc. The uses for which wood was specifically needed in housing represented wood's performance characteristics at the lowest order of magnitude.

"In America, it is evident that as a result of the entirely new emphasis on defensive supremacy inherent in housing, the latter has been advanced to higher priority brackets. Accelerated production of housing is, of course, needed for an obvious peacetime function, to augment the population increase and to replace annual losses (in addition to floods, earthquakes, fire, tornadoes, etc.), the total velocities of which known practices have now proven inadequate to solve. However, beyond its historical function, housing is now required to deploy the whole of the population and instantly; not just to the outskirts of present cities but in deep decentralization upon the unbroken land, far beyond the practical limits of extension of the grouped, piped and wired supply systems. World rehousing or a new service industry of livingry for the peoples of the world, is implicit in the trends to accommodate accelerating range and frequency of oscillations by man between the interacting functions of deployment and concentration characterizing the evoluting industrial complex. This means new livingry for three billion persons within decades. Yet before World War II the largest production of single-family or deployed dwellings ever produced in one year by the U.S. was two hundred eighty thousand houses in 1925.

"Obviously, an entirely new use of the scientific potential must be made by the designers to amplify at least one-hundred-fold the velocity of the cubage to be put under livingry control annually.

This advance of housing to military priority is augmented by its concomitant advance in political strategy. The unique result of the first four postwar years during which man has given himself realistically to total thinking is that the political will of the majority, as expressed by the United States, has been resolved into one paragraph and surfaced through the political mechanics to eventual announcement by former President Harry S. Truman under the slogan of 'a fair deal for all the world' and specifically to be realized by 'converting the scientific potential to upping the living standards of the world through technology.' The significance of its intent may be detected by the fact of its announcement in the face of the epochal reorientation of approximately one third of the human family to alignment with Communism in China.

"This epochal event was a result of the expiration of the theory of the absolute power of money. In the total scene, with a third of the human family doomed through the inadequacies of housing, it was discovered that it is senseless to dump billions of dollars into Europe or China. These sums of money are merely digits stripped of immediate survival reality. The fact that thousands have died in China from exposure alone, not counting those dying of starvation, neutralizes any help sent in the form of food or money. They needed a shield from the ravages of the elements. People are corrupt only when no emergency threatens. They will not dive for gold or jewels when the ship is sinking in mid-ocean.

"They abandon intrinsics for functionals in the supreme test. They will only dive for buoyant objects. In the present world emergency the advantages of the industrial complex represent the only buoyant object which the people of the world know may effect their rescue within their durable limits. They know there exist accelerating factors of technical advantage within the present potential of the industrial complex that are adequate to cope with their plight. But, they know the industrial complex must be harnessed to world-wide advancement of living standards and at the logistic magnitude and velocity of total war—if their rescue is to be effected.

"The military reconnaissance party has taught the peoples of the world how the vast potential of the industrial complex may be explored to effectuate specific advantages and also how dramatically effective its logistics can be under emergency requirements. As, for instance, it clambered out of the sea as giant metallic monsters to climb the beaches of the amazed inhabitants of Pacific Islands, laying flat the trees and lands of those unconsulted world citizens, and putting out magic, mile-long carpets in the jungle upon which descended metal birds larger than whales in unending flow, from all of which emerged simple human beings who took the little jungle boy for a ride and gave him a Coke and sandwich. This, said the jungle boy and the people of the world, is the way to handle affairs.

"Through the Truman proclamation 'fair deal for all the world,' democracy then put the world on notice that it was reorienting individual initiative and enterprise as well as the sum-total industrial complex toward fulfillment of the doctrine of universal right to survive. This constituted a complete reorientation of democratic precedent. It removed primary survival from the *laissez-faire* doctrine of 'survival only for the fittest.'

"Russia has in the past, in conformity with broad historic precedent, continued its housing in the non-priority category and has focused priority on industrial requirements of the offensive. Russian engineers, interested as early as 1929 in potential commonwealth gains of the Dymaxion House, could not utilize its benefits because housing had no priority in any of Russia's first five of the successive five-year plans. Everything pertaining to industrial supremacy was on high priority and the upping of housing standards was continually deferred until the completion of the expected 'next' military conflict.

"It was reasoned by them that sixteen million people were in excess of any food or work accommodation and were unavoidably scheduled to die. 'We have an overabundance of people and trees.' Therefore, the people were doomed and treated as national heroes. If they willed, they could live out their lives in contrivances of the surplus wood designed in the most ignorantly satisfying traditional architecture, despite the latter's incongruity to modern engineering and science which pervaded Russia's industrial frontiering. In the race for world-wide industrial supremacy, which moved education by necessity to top priority, Russia upped the literate percentage of its total population from the world's lowest in 1917 to the world's highest by 1940. But, to do so, it also wiped out sixteen million aged or hopeless illiterates.

"Russia has now put the world on notice that it, too, intends to apply the industrial complex to upping the standards of living. However, seeking to avoid inference of luxury, Russian official newspapers demand that Soviet industry produce more household gadgets for the housewife in order to free her time, energy and intellectual initiative for augmented factory output. There had always been a need for this greater efficiency in Russia, but, political priority had once focused such efficiency only upon the direct needs of "the next war" and its immediately supporting heavy industry.

"Thus the cold war swung to popular persuasion by propaganda of world peoples that: the practical objectives of the warring factions each holds greater promise of realization of economic salvation and subsequent advancement because the principle of industrialization is uniquely fostered by their respective political systems. The biggest guns of this cold war exchange eventually must be a barrage of production of scientific dwelling machines, as constituting the comprehensive package of higher livingry standards. Thus there would be world economic preoccupation with competitive fostering of the new phase of worldwide industry—livingry. The upshot of this new preoccupation is progressive reduction of probability of further shooting wars.

"During World War II, the entire Russian industrial organization moved twice eastward over great distances. Since World War II, it has been moved once more. The exact location of Russia is no longer known. Without precise knowledge of geographical location, the expenditure of long-distance controlled missiles cannot be afforded. This works both ways.

"As Russia has already incepted the third deployment of industry, it will have to deploy its population to serve this industry, while at the same time eliminating its vulnerable population densities. Russia will need high-standard housing and housing mechanics on a vast scale to effect this deployment. Therefore, for the first time in history it is evidenced that housing has been advanced from a non-priority status either in war or peace to high priority position in both. Our sights for scientific research and livingry cannot be set too high. We need one quarter of a billion autonomous dwellings of high-standard mechanics at once!

"Walter Reuther, president of the United Auto Workers, once urged the Congress and the nation in general to inaugurate the production of twenty million houses within the country's aircraft plants. Though an enormous advance of the target magnitude in housing production (from the then-annual craft record of two hundred eighty thousand), Reuther's figure represented but eight percent of the total world re-housing program implicit in the now visible trend. The realization of these facilities from the universal potential involves a magnitude of wealth-making not only hitherto undreamed of, but one adequate to the total world commonwealth needs for centuries to come.

"To many, such an acceleration in building velocity would seem impractical, incredible. However, during the first week of March 1949, the following were among the technical accelerations which had occurred: our children's toy auto speed record had been upped from one hundred and forty-eight miles per hour to three hundred and ten miles per hour; and as a six-year-old child with a walkie-talkie relayed his commands by remote control to his mechanically propelled airplane model, the grown-ups circumnavigated the globe in non-stop flight in ninety-four hours. And the species, man, jumped twice as high. We do not mean that he increased his high-jump record from the six-foot range to the twelve-foot range, but that he jumped his advanced vehicle, the rocket, from a one hundred and twenty mile height to a two hundred and fifty mile height. In keeping with the new stride, the astronomers announced that the inspectable range of universe had been doubled, that is, to a distance of one billion light years–an eight-fold volumetric increase.[22]

"Only those research and development activities which can effectively employ billions of dollars can possibly engage the public credit. Q. E. D."

22 **In April 2009, the Harvard Smithsonian Center for Astrophysics issued a press release stating that their astronomers, "along with colleagues elsewhere in the United States and the United Kingdom, have discovered the most distant object in the universe—a spectacular stellar explosion known as a gamma-ray burst located about 13 billion light years away." The object, named GRB 090423, was found by NASA's Swift satellite on April 23.** Center for Astrophysics, Press Release No. 2009-11, http://www.cfa.harvard.edu/news/2009/pr200911.html (accessed July 14, 2009).

Model of the Dymaxion 4-D House in Chicago, Illinois, 1927

Buckminster Fuller's Dymaxion 4-D Automobile was featured at the 1934 Chicago World's Fair.

Dymaxion bathroom (420 lbs.)

Dymaxion Deployment unit (DDU), (4,000 lbs.) built in 1940–41. It was planned as a major housing facility in the United States, but military metal priorities caused it to be abandoned. The DDU was actually used on the Persian Gulf as radar shacks and desert dormitories for American personnel.

Fuller house (6,000 lbs.) in Wichita, Kansas

Parts used to build the Fuller house in 1945. They were designed to rest together and no one part weighed more than ten pounds.

Supine Geodesic Structure, Black Mountain College.
It was constructed from Venetian blind ribbon.

Necklace Geodesic Structure (14 ft., 50 lbs.), on exhibit in the garden of the Pentagon

Interior of paperboard Geodesic Dome at Yale University

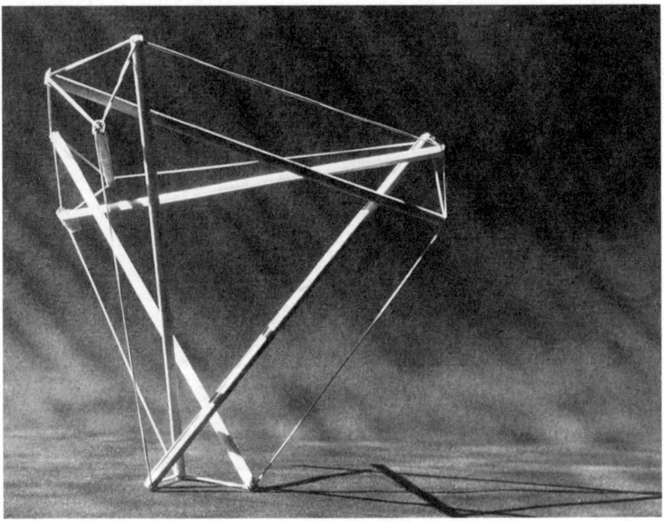

Tensegrity Integrity Tetrahedron, built by Francisco della Sala

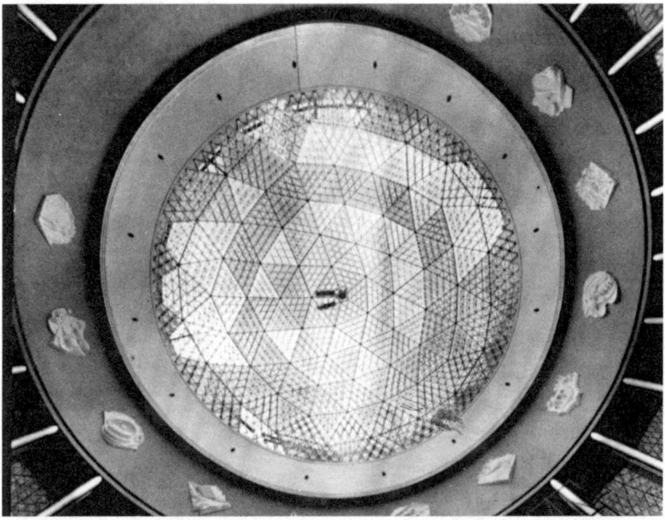

Looking up at the Geodesic Dome in the Ford Motor Company Rotunda Building, Dearborn, Michigan

Tension Integrity Sphere (40 ft., 1,000 lbs.), Princeton University

First airlift of a Geodesic Dome, Orphan's Hill, North Carolina, 1954. It was flown at 50 knots without yaws.

The author's proposed air-conditioned Geodesic Dome, two miles in diameter, that would cover midtown Manhattan.

Sky Eye 300-foot Geodesic Dome harboring a radio telescope

Exterior skin of Geodesic Dome (36 ft., 450 lbs.), University of Minnesota project at Woods Hole, Massachusetts

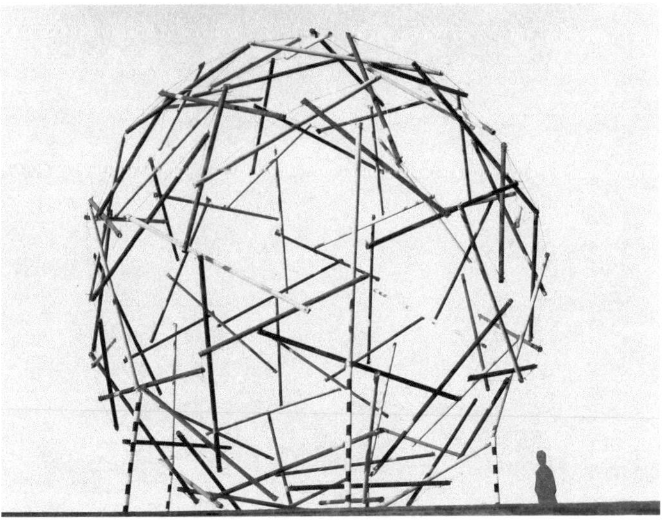

A 90-Strut Miniature Tension Integrity Sphere, Princeton University

Paperboard Geodesic Dome (36 ft. diameter), North Carolina State College

This 31-foot Geodesic Sphere (3,000 lbs.) was atop Mt. Washington, New Hampshire. It withstood 182 mph winds and did not ice up during a two-year test.

True rational volumes where tetrahedron is unity	Synergetically Symmetric: Locally symmetrical omni-triangulated	Synergetically Symmetric: Locally mixed sym—asym, omni-triangulated	Synergetically Symmetric: Locally asymmetrical omni-triangulated	Synergetically Symmetric: Space fillers	Synergetically Symmetric: complementary space fillers	System	Euler Formula V + F = E + 2	Fuller synergetic treatment extracts 2 vertices for neutral axis V – Θ Θ = 2 V + F = E	Fuller synergetic treatment divides by Fundamental *Withinness & Withoutness* *Convex—Concave* Twoness : 2 : Φ
1	 1 : 1				•	Vector edge tetra	4 + 4 = 6 + 2	2 + 4 = 6	1
4	 1 : 2				• •	Vector edge octa	6 + 8 = 12 + 2	4 + 8 = 12	2
3				•		Alternating + to—tetra vector diagonal	8 + 12 = 18 + 2	6 + 12 = 18	3 Frequency of modular subdivision of exterior edges of system
20					•	Vector equilibrium	12 + 20 = 30 + 2	10 + 20 = 30	5 (1 + 2 = 3) V^2 Φ + Θ
18.510	 1 : 4.63					Vector edge icosahedron	12 + 20 = 30 + 2	10 + 20 = 30	5 Topological Abundance constant *1 Vertex or* *2 Faces or* *3 Edges*
8.490	27.000 Area : Volume ration			•		Vector edge cube	14 + 24 = 36 + 2	Φ + 12 + 24 = 36	3 · 2
6				•		Vector diagonal rhombic dodecahedron	14 + 24 = 36 + 2	12 + 24 = 36	3 · 2
25.986				•		Vector edge rhombic dodecahedron	14 + 24 = 36 + 2	12 + 24 = 36	3 · 2
65.018	91.004					Vector edge dodecahedron	32 + 60 = 90 + 2	30 + 60 = 90	3 · 5
96			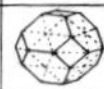	•		Vector edge tetraxidecahedron	32 + 60 = 90 + 2	30 + 60 = 90	3 · 5
						Vector edge triacontahedron	32 + 60 = 90 + 2	30 + 60 = 90	3 · 5
			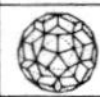			Vector edge enenicontahedron	92 + 180 = 270 + 2	90 + 180 = 270	3^2 · 5

The author's comprehensively finite topology chart

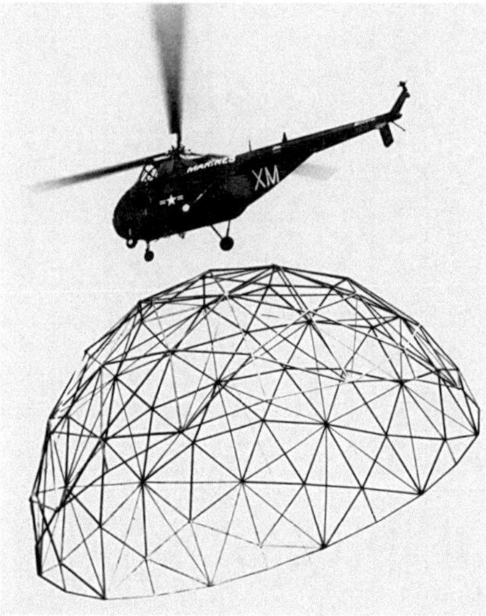

A Marine Corps Helicopter flies away with its own hangar.

A 42-foot covering for a swimming pool in Aspen, Colorado

Interior of a dome in Kabul, Afghanistan. The Afghans compared Fuller's dome to a Mongolian yurt and claimed it as indigenous architecture.

Exterior of United States Pavilion in Kabul, Afghanistan. It was assembled by native Afghan labor in forty-eight hours.

United States Exhibition at the Canadian Universal and International Exhibition, Expo '67. R. Buckminster Fuller/Fuller and Sadao, Inc./Geometrics, Inc. Associated Architects. The United States Pavilion was a Geodesic Skybreak bubble, 250 feet in spherical diameter and 137 feet high. The bubble encloses a volume of 6,700,000 cubic feet and has a surface area of 141,000 square feet. The space frame configuration is the result of a sustained program of testing and refinement in order to produce a lightweight frame of minimum visual obstruction. The structure is a prototype "environmental valve" enclosing sufficient space for whole communities to live in a benign physical microcosm. Montreal, Canada, 1967.

36-foot Paperboard Geodesic Dome, exhibited at the 1954 Triennale, Milan, Italy.

11 Preview of Building

I have listened with great interest to discussions regarding decentralization and centralization and I have thought that the question of whether it is valid to decentralize or centralize is unanswerable because it deals with *one* one-way sign in two-way traffic. It is a static question in a dynamic universe.

Man was invented a mobile device and process. He has survived through his ability to advance or retreat as his mortal requirements have dictated. Of his two primary faculties, quickness is of great importance but intellect is first.

He recognizes that vital quickness may be momentary reflex, but that satisfactory continuities are proportional to his degree of comprehension of the consequence of his initiative. Degree of comprehension he measures in the terms of the complex integration of all individuals' all-time experience, as processed by intellectual integrity. His quickness would be a spontaneous servant to that integrity.

Despite intermittent submissiveness to runaway momentums of residual ignorance, man guards most dearly and secretly his freedom of thought and initiative. Therefrom emanates the social-industrial relay, from self-starter to group starters.

Out of this freedom alone understanding may be generated. Man recognizes understanding as an activated circuit of mutual comprehension by individual minds. Understanding must be

---

April 1949. Originally a lecture by Fuller on geodesic structural strategy delivered to the "Mid-Century Conference on Housing" at the University of Michigan.

plural. However, because individual experience is unique, understanding can be developed only in principle out of the compounding significance of plurality of experience. Thus, man knows that the voluntary interactions of understanding dealing in fundamental principles will always master involuntary mass actions, and that individual freedom ever anticipates and ultimately masters mutual emergency.

As man has become knowledgeful, he has translated the principles discovered in universe into abetting his quickness and mobility. The physical effect of this translation has been demonstrated in important degree only within this past half century. Born with legs and not with roots, man is in principle mobile. Prior to World War I, man's locomotion was primarily accomplished by his legs. He rode in vehicles only about three hundred miles per year. Oft-repeated Army surveys show that man has always walked an average of thirteen hundred miles per year, and probably always will.

In 1919, it was evidenced that the species "man" had changed. *Man had become an invention which moved about primarily by mechanical means*. In the United States, he to and fro-ed in 1919 about sixteen hundred miles mechanically. He continued walking thirteen hundred miles per year, but instead of sitting in rocking chairs, he was sitting in moving automobiles. Thus he totaled twenty-nine hundred miles in 1919. At the beginning of World War II, the average man was moving mechanically six thousand miles per annum; however, he continued walking an additional thirteen hundred miles per annum, for a total of seventy-three hundred miles per year. The U.S. behavior curve in this respect is a pilot or "tendril" curve of the "world" curve to accomplishment of equivalent mechanical acceleration per capita. The world-man curve is now visibly rising toward ultimate coincidence with U.S. man's curve.

Up to World War I, man's primary economic ideas and social viewpoints were those developed within the visible horizon. Those who went beyond the horizons were rated as escapists—"irresponsibility" was thought to increase with motion. But as of 1940 the average U.S. housewife was clocking up an annual ten thousand mechanical miles and thirteen hundred foot miles, a total of eleven thousand three hundred, or a seven-fold step-up from her pre-1914 sixteen hundred miles. The average salesman was clocking thirty-five thousand mechanical miles, the average air hostess one hundred thousand miles, while continuing her pedestrian thirteen hundred miles. Our young people were about to accelerate *en masse* their annual comings-and-goings by world encirclement. Clearly, we could no longer insist that motion indicated irresponsibility—quite the reverse! Those who were masters of the greatest motion and velocity were the top members of society. Responsible participation of all workers involved accelerating mobilization synchronous to the evolving needs of the world deploying industrial complex.

We have come to the realization that we are in an all-dynamic universe, that the old concept of "at rest" is not normal. When we lie down to go to sleep, we do not shut off the valves and freeze into rigid statues. Our billions of atoms take on a myriad of constellation activities in lieu of a few galaxy motions of the day's routine regimentation of the body's sub-assemblies.

All our curves of measurement of man's earthly doings show an acceleration "upward," that is, with "at rest" regarded as normal, the curves of man's doings have taken the shape of a ski (reading from heel to toe). The curves have ascended now into almost vertical abnormality. Is this race schizophrenia? No! It is just that our standards of reference are cockeyed.

Obviously, we must now abandon the unrealistic "at rest" and refer all our affairs to the realistic yardstick of energy and its velocity aspect, as recently and universally adopted by science from Albert Einstein's work. To do so we need only revolve our charts to ninety degrees of angle, so that we may see the curves descending precipitously from the old heights of ignorance and abnormality and tending to level off into dynamic equilibrium with the all-motion universe, infinitely normal about us. Thus quickness displaces static death as the normal of both life and universe. Life is no longer exceptional-to but inherent-in the universe.

To Einstein's C^2, which is the symbol of speed of omni-directional growth of the surface of a light wave which is one hundred and eighty-six thousand miles per second "squared," the speed of sight (our personal eyesight) is normal, for it too operates at the speed of light, and not "instantly," which is an obsolete word of yesterday's magic. One hundred and eighty-six thousand miles per second is only relatively fast, compared to the velocities of man's invented vehicles. One hundred and eighty-six thousand miles per second is relatively very slow compared to the man-invented nonsense called "instantaneous," that is, infinite-super-billions-of-miles-in-no-time-at-all. Instantaneous is one of those out-of-this-universe concepts which we are now abandoning.

One of the most important contributions of science to society is its development of the ability to consider all of the wonders of the physical universe as measurable and rational and of immediate practical significance. The paradise of nature is for now and not for never-never.

Man's voice travels the telephone circuit, wired or wireless, at one hundred and eighty-six thousand miles per second. Sunbathing, he "sees" heat waves with his skin, received at one hundred and eighty-six thousand miles per second which is distinctly normal to his reality. Man spontaneously relegates his other sensorial faculties to secondary consideration. He can only hear by air-waves arriving at the tawdry velocity of one fifth of a mile per second. He can rarely smell events occurring at a mile's distance, but, aided by a hurricane, may receive his "whiffed" report at one fiftieth of a mile per second. Man can acquire tactile report at ranges no greater than that of his fingertip. He can grope no faster than one thousandth of a mile per second. Held to apprehension of the phenomena of universe by his groping tactile faculty alone, the velocity factor becomes approximately nil.

The world seems at rest. Relative only to the apparent inertia of universe, as apprehended by this lowest-order faculty—the tactile—could the velocity of visual apprehension be rated as "instantaneous."

Fortunately for man, he has always subconsciously asked to see the vital phenomena. Thus he "witnesses."

Solely within the paltry dimensions of life as serviced preponderantly by hearsay, smellsay and touchsay have the blinders of habit persuaded man to accept the ignorant "reality," which excitedly refers experience only to the negligible velocity of "at rest." Static brains will apprehend as radical and revolutionary every discovery and intellectually informed reorientation of the individual as won through progressive augmentation of the faculties of highest order—instrumented science.

Man sees only by omni-dimensional images illuminated within the experience-inventoried brain after images regeneratively fedback by the energy of momentary sensorial scannings. It is significant that he gets direct or nondelayed visual report only from the actively radiant energetic centers of light, notably the stars. All other visual reports wait upon indirect routing by their superficial *reflection* from passive structures of energetic impasse, the planetary mass phenomena.

With this coming of the realization of the normal velocity of energy—in the all-energy physical universe—we have to recognize that man is increasing magnificently his range and frequency of informed activity. Manifesting intellect as well as energy, man is taking progressive measure of the universe, and through intellect is slowly mastering degrees of its infinite energy.

Obviously, man now has to think beyond the limits of yesterday's politics, beyond the limits of yesterday's personal ambitions. By "personal" we mean the limited dimensions of the lower order senses. We will have to look at the problem of discovering the trends to tomorrow's building in a delimited manner, else we will have a poor preview of that building.

Do not assume that delimited thought is now easy. We all say we know that it is five hundred years since Copernicus postulated and four hundred years since Galileo demonstrated that the earth was not the static center of a universe revolving about it. The latter idea we now declare silly. But listen to your most advanced astronomer, when professionally off-guard at, for instance, a seashore picnic on a summer evening say to his daughter, "Look at the beautiful sunset, darling,"—and worse; he "sees" the sun setting—and so do you.

You are, practically speaking, five hundred years behind your own assertions of fact. You still say "up" and "down" when there are no such directions in universe. You mean "in" and "out" from the center of the spinning, cosmos-zooming earth ball. If you will say, "I am going out to the attic and into the ground level," you will accelerate your reliable reality. In that fast-moving "advanced" scientific activity to which man proudly refers us for updated thinking—the aeronautical world—the professional meteorologist reports to us of "winds blowing from the northwest," just as though the wing-headed little zephyrs drawn upon ancient maps were yet puffing from a place—the northwest, wherever that is! Whereas we know that the air is being "drafted" southeastward by the thermals and their low pressure centers, for you can't blow wind more than a few hundred feet—it turns around on itself. Every ring-puffing smoker knows that. However, air may be sucked over vast circuits. Then, too, we all speak and think of things when no things exist—all is dynamic interaction. So don't let's feel too smart. Let us humbly seek to put our reality into dynamic and intellectually disciplined order.

While the atomic space-ship may become the dramatic headliner in nearby decades, in the structure, mechanics and life of tomorrow's single family livingry, we will witness by far the greatest evolutionary change from the traditionally familiar. The traditional *house,* embodying the residue of personable ignorance, has, by its "at rest" fixations, contrived to stem the dynamic flows of emergent reality to a greater degree than any other category of life's fixed preoccupations. Thus, dwelling inertia has, in effect, stretched the delicate flexible tension structure of comprehensive evolution flowing by, until, as a pellet tensed in the critical vertex of universal distortion, it must be impelled violently toward our dynamic life needs, eventually to take equilibrious and synchronization after the severe reverberations have subsided. This greatest single evolutionary change in men's ways of solving their living problems will be witnessed before this century is over.

Stated in a less literary manner, the single family dwelling represents the very last major item of the whole of man's contrived environmental paraphernalia to come under his scientific scrutiny and subsequent transformation through astronomically augmented interactions of the world-embracing dynamic principles of industry.

All large buildings are processed by an army of engineers, economic experts, social scientists and the combined tactical thinking of our day's financial and labor leaders. In this respect of processing-by-combined-scientific-expertness, big buildings are almost on a par with the complex end products of industrial society, such as the ocean steamship, the automobile, the steel mill and the telephone system, organizationally, but not conceptually.

In contrast to the circumstances of conception of scientific industrial end products, less than four percent of this country's single family dwellings were erected by union labor; less than two percent were designed by architects and almost none engaged the services of the engineer in their primary complex designing. Engineers have only had a part in the original design of the mass produced household equipment, which is secondary.

The scientist, physical or sociological, has had an absolute zero relationship to the structuring of the single family dwelling, which latter nonetheless clearly persists as the major physical ecological contrivance of the human species. In it are gestated the first and all-important phases of the individual's group life. Here the individual learns that he is not only the product of union, but its infinite servant.

The lack of application of the historically accumulated intellectual advantage of mankind (as realized through the prototyping activities of the industrial complex) to the conceptioning of the family habitat is not because the single family dwelling trends to obsolescence as a way of life. It is because:

1. an *a priori* theory of life's trends and purposes has not been evolved,
2. an *a priori* theory of dwelling has not been evolved, and
3. the priority of full industrial-advantage has hitherto never been applied to the problem of the single family dwelling!

Where relative scarcities exist in the over-all scheme of satisfaction of man's needs, and emergencies develop therein, priorities are established.

The general principles of industrialization may be looked upon as comprising one great big complex and still-scarce tool which wraps up all the latest technical advantage in realizing predictable performance.

It is obvious that up to now man could not justify assigning priority of technical advantage to housing in wartime. He would not raise his home standard of living while the boys were in tent, trench or barrack, and required no upped standards for these shifting purposes.

In peacetime, priority of scientific and technical knowledge and effort has gone either to home industry or field occupations, or to outright emergency services.

In peacetime, home industry priority has gone to the fashioning of the simple universal tools, with which to consolidate the gains of his intellectual and technical experience, e. g., the screwdriver.

In the superficial evolution taking place in home industry, the houses of the commerce-expediters were essentially instruments of propaganda, persuasively proclaiming the physical wealth-increments exploitable in the industrial principle. Each propaganda-mansioning represented the natural coloring of a short-lived fashionable phase. Houses of the workers were the meagerest of knocked-up contrivances and hovels, designed only to bring their efforts into proximity with the evolving industrial complex. No priority of scientific acumen was involved in the conceptioning of either type of establishment.

In the field-preoccupations of hunting, animal husbandry and agriculture, the first two obviously did not require scientific and industrial conceptioning in the realization of dwelling or permanent abode. Hunting was an inherently swift, dangerous, single-handed activity of a man sleeping under the stars. Animal husbandry, though seasonally mobile, involved the most scientific and technical preconceptioning of the mobile habitat for the shepherd family, but the realizations of the scientific principles of his tenting were entirely remote from industrial rendition. *Ships* of the industrial commerce embodied the only industrial rendering of mobile habitats—habitats, however, designed with approximately no direct concern with family gestation.

In his original agricultural frontiering or field industry, man gave all priority of effort and of technical advantage, to affairs of the soil because not only his own family's survival needs could thereby be supplied, but, if nature were bountiful, his excess increments could be converted to increasing the technical advantage over nature feed specialists who were developing industrialization. For this he conceived omni-purpose wealth articulators, in the form of money or credit, with which to participate in the growing advantages generated by the industrial complexities simplifying personal work.

His housing was, therefore, contrived in an expedient manner out of salvage materials culled from the land, incidental to the clearing of the soil for agricultural purposes. He attended to his building in the "off" periods and after regular priority work. His housing was contrived as fortress and shelter against marauders and element. As noted, it was contrived out of the salvage—trees and stones—on a hopeful basis and not upon scientific and industrial predetermination of its behavior and stress capacities. He hoped that fire, tornado, termite, flood, pestilence and rot would not come—for he could not design these salvage materials into competence by making them look like a castellated fortress. Housing was never designed upon a scientifically predetermined schedule of comprehensive performance requirements, rendered in knowledgeful techniques by a vast orchestra of tools out of world-garnered and industrially evolved substances, which would not only assure predictable standards of performance in each category of structural and mechanical requirement, but would make possible complete logistic advance planning regarding the involvement.

Historically speaking, the important eras of technical advance have been precipitously introduced through the obvious wartime emergency which articulates the between-wars scientific accumulation of new degrees of potential advantage over the energetic properties of nature. The magnitudes of the between-war scientific accumulation represent a geometric progression. At the termination of each war phase the "ins" level off their economy to exploit the new degree of technical advantage. Deprived of participation in the technical advantage at this proven level, the "outs" take advantage of the geometric progression of the scientific potential and introduce once more degrees of technical advantage which, though of seemingly lesser physical investment, threaten supremacy over the economics of the previous technical level because of the imponderable yet enormous knowledge-gains in means of impounding larger blocks of cosmic energy within given pounds of terrestrial matter—thereby disposed in more power-full arrangement. The incompatibility of the two levels of technical preoccupation is further aggravated by the failure to transfer priority of use of the industrial complex to realization of the theory of continuous anticipatory economic volition from its preoccupation with the traditional and intermittent curative volition. Economic and eventually civil rupture ensues and the open warfare cycle is seemingly to be repeated.

As the science potential accelerates to greater magnitude, the severity of rupture would seem to promise like progression. But history has produced a fundamental surprise at this point, an entirely new orientation commensurable with our rotation of the frame of reference from a static to a velocity norm.

Historically viewed, wars were carried to a relatively remote front. When the front was driven home to one side, that side gave in. As wars have employed the industrial complex by mandate and as the industrial complex has come to be total to world resource, so has war become total. With the development of totality, war has come to be waged not as much on many fronts as on many spots. Differentiation of lands and sea has been lost in significance of one-sky. Blitzkrieg brought the war everywhere as multiple foci of sky-diving planes and land-crawling submarines. Total war involves ultimate controlling of missiles from anywhere on earth to anywhere on earth. Long distance is total and the concept of front has vanished.

War is dynamic and its two dynamic phases are offense and defense. As offense obtains omni-directional parity, supremacy lies in relative defense advantage. Relative defense advantage lies in the direction of relative mobility, in the ability to dodge widely and without loss of poise—not to dig in.

The historical surprise develops as the result of:

a. The contraction of interval between increasing emergencies until naught but emergency exists. (That is our condition today despite our none-too-confident whistling in the dark.)

b. Enforced occupation of hitherto hostile equatorial and polar environments.

c. The interim conquest of the environmental extremes in the military conquest of the air and the ocean depths.

d. Reorientation of the exploitation course of the industrial complex, with the ninety-two regenerative chemical elements isolated, and the original total industrial machine completed out of the inventory of the ninety-two regenerative chemical element resources, and with unlimited cosmic energy, piped and valved, ready to be loosed into economic circulation. It has been realized that, inasmuch as the technical advantage trends to the infinite production for increasing numbers by lesser numbers, the key to economic and subsequent political expansion is the consumer—the greater the number of consumers, the greater the expansion. The more numerous the consumers' needs and the more frequent their satisfaction, the greater the expansion. The economic volition trends to accelerate total world occupation by total world man in total dynamic enjoyment.

The biological competition (inherent in evolution) to accelerate standards of satisfaction hi-polarizes in total world struggle for management of the industrial complex. Conscious courting of world society as potential consumer by competitive world managements looms. Promises to world-man of advancement of his standards of living and growth by the competitive managements must be fulfilled.

e. Increasing world population by new birth and increasing longevity with growing actual or potential mobilization of the population and total potential communication and education has accelerated the individual pressures of society—as increased increment of energy accelerates the molecules of gases to exercise further pressure against circumventing systems. Historically, man's solution of increasing pressure has been linear. He has come to complete the network of total interlinkage of the pressurized centrals. Needing omni-directional dispersion for relief, he has been unable to deploy, other than in a veined or linear manner, as his increasing standards of mechanical advantage have been dependent upon piped, wired, tracked paths.

Dynamically speaking, his linear paths are all pipes—his car or his train is a section of pipe surrounding him, which section moves progressively to enclose him—to allow his existence in previously prohibitive environmental extremes. The linear frequencies of a sectional tube increase until the total linear dynamics approach the chain or escalator continuity of the tube. Radial and deploying veinage of the linear tubal expansion encounter geometrically diminishing economy. The dynamic population, increasingly energized from the cosmic resource, finding no relief in inter-center connections and being radially confined, trends to surge within the system with increasing velocity. The only relief for the surges, oscillating outwardly and inwardly, is that of centrally articulated skywardness, as the linear services of pipe and wire can only be economically extended at center. The upsurgings articulate in multiple-story and skyscraper structures until laws of diminishing return again set in. Pressures continue and fill all the static central interstices, designed for intermittent occupations of economic interaction in the fixed hoteling, thus keeping a shuttling population in constant occupation of the facilities. The centrally upward and outward pressures grow finally to articulate omni-directional outwardness by wireless, trackless and pipeless. Potential travel and communication become omni-directional. Next they become *frequency modulated.*

The surprise interaction of a, b, c, d and e is that scientific dwelling facility suitable for all times and climates, able to deploy the family to high standard living in a preferred location of natural privacy without sacrifice of potential participation in the total complex, is being advanced to first position of priority in the use of the industrial-scientific advantage not only by the military, by the political and by the industrial management, but by rank and file labor and (last, but not least) common man. In the ranks of common man, the clamoring for priority of the scientific dwelling facility and autonomous deployment and, thereby, historical emancipation of man becomes louder among the most recently maturing.

The physical key to rapid amplification of the industrial logisticability to provide additional deployed dwelling facilities for three billion people within decades, at hitherto undreamed degree of advanced technical standards, is the twofold key that unlocked the door to structuring the initial and total industrial complex. This key is the increasing physical abilities of man as *synergetic* (associative) and *energetic* (dissociative) controls.

Throughout the ages, man was limited in his structuring to the processing and manipulation only of the compressive functions and components of structure. Stone afforded twenty thousand pounds of compressive strength to the square inch. It was relatively imperishable. The best tensile abilities available in nature were provided by the vegetable fibers—as solid wood or separated fiber. Tensile strength of wood or fiber could not be counted upon for more than five thousand pounds to the square inch. Stone was almost imperishable. The wood and fiber were perishable. Stone and masonry could be counted upon to afford no more than fifty pounds tensile strength to the square inch. Man's structural ability seemingly favored compressive organizations on a four to one or better basis—width and weight were amplified to increase the stabilities. That his primary philosophic reference was inert and pressive was inevitable.

As structural systems are omni-directionally coherent, tensile factors were *unwittingly* taken advantage of to cohere man's compressive structures. Comprehensive tensile coherence provided by nature was atomic, the enormous amount of which induced into action was manifested by the weight of the structural masses. The invisible structure was $E=mc^2$.

With the coming of modern chemistry, man learned not only to extract but to alloy the metallic elements, in increasing quantity, to progressively reuse them, to progressively augment the sum-total of the metals in service by further extraction of the elements from their original invisible aggregate in the matrix of the earth and stone he had so ignorantly employed of yore.

With the availability of production metals for building, man's conscious employment of the tensile factor in his invented structures grew rapidly, both structurally and dynamically. The alloyed and worked iron, called steel, provided tensile ability initially at parity with allowed compressive abilities–twenty thousand pounds to the square inch. Since inauguration of metallic tensioning of structures, the tensile abilities have increased rapidly through chemical knowledge while compression ability has remained at its maximum of fifty thousand pounds. The last quarter century has seen tensile ability moved forward from fifty thousand pounds to the square inch to seventy to eighty to one hundred twenty to one hundred fifty to one hundred eighty-five to four hundred thousand and with no indication of a break in the increasing rate of ability.

The enormous increment of energy advantage in the industrial complex intellectual has been won directly by the intellectual activity which adduced the principle of tension and its improved rendering by complex industrial heat treatment alloying.

Throughout the universe, compression and tension are energetically juxtaposed. Their juxtaposition provides dimension–the basis of awareness of life itself. Compression is limited to dimensionally minuscule tasks in the universe, to the spherical convergencies of energy in elemental systems. The tight balls of energy–stars, planets, atoms–are ever-dynamically disposed and systematically positioned by energy as tension. Nonsimultaneous distances of the universe are methodically intercoursed by the incredibly compact ponderosities at incredible speeds and degrees of precision by functions of tension. Tension is comprehensive. Universe tensionally coheres nonsimultaneous events.

Man's structuring ability is by principle distinctly limited in the proportional ratios of width and length of compression members. Elongated compression tends to deflect and fail. The best compression abilities are in the planetary form of the sphere, whose neutral axis is dynamic through omni-directional symmetry. Ball bearings are man's best accomplishment in compressive structuring.

The tensile principle has no such ratioed limit of length to section. Tension members, no matter how elongated, tend to pull true. Tension is limited only to the initial cohesiveness of the chemical elements. As man's knowledge of chemical interaction improves the length of tensile members, relative to given section diameter or given stress, trends are to increasing amplification—to infinite length with no section. Incredible? No! Every use of gravity is a use of such sectionless tensioning. The electrical tension first employed by man to pull energy through the nonferrous conductors and later to close the wireless circuit was none other than such universally available sectionless tension.

In the phenomena tension man is in principle given access to unlimited performance. It seems fantastic, but there it is!

The essence of this essence of the historical surprise in general reorientations is the discovery that tension structure is not a linked, or chain, phenomenon. Tension members represent "milky way-like" arrangements of atoms, the atomic or inter-stellar spaces of which are relatively infinite. The tension members may no longer be thought of as chains, no stronger than their weakest link. Tension structures arranged by man depend upon his relative knowledge in purest principle—in purest initial volition of interpretation—of pure intellect. Universe is tensional integrity.

For nearly fifty years I have made sorties in the realm of mathematics. There has developed therefrom a rational system of mensuration comprehensive to physics and chemistry. It is a geometry originating in the assumption that dimension must be physical. It follows that, inasmuch as physical universe is entirely energetic, all dimension must be energetic. Vectors and tensors constitute all elementary dimension. Thus, original assumptions eliminate the necessity of subsequent assignment of physical qualities to abstract mathematical devices in the manner we have, of necessity, assigned progressively discovered attributes of physical universe to irrational relationships within the *a priori* ghostly Greek geometry.

The degree of new technical advantage provided by the discovered principles may be appreciated by the fact that one pound of structure can hereby accomplish space enclosure heretofore requiring one ton of structure (when complying with the scantiest of U.S. city codes), while at the same time arriving at predictably stable conditions under extreme stress of earthquake, typhoon, arctic cold and tropic heat in the presence of which the behavior of the contemporary city dwelling structure referred to is dubious. This two thousand to one ratio of comparative advantage is made regarding structures of approximately eight thousand square feet of ground coverage. The new structure has been named Geodesic Structure because of its employment of great circle geometry. Geodesics are "most economical relationships."

In 1949 the Air Force requested me to erect a small geodesic structure in the courtyard of the Pentagon Building in Washington. Army engineers on seeing it said, "Why, it is as good as a tent! No, it is better; it can stand stresses a tent cannot!" In 1954 the U.S. Marine Corps pronounced air deliverable geodesic structures "the first basic improvement in mobile environment controls in twenty-six hundred years." Space research's imminent solution of closed sanitary human metabolic circuitry-*livingry science!*

We have witnessed a half century's continuous shrinking of dwelling structures produced at increasing costs per pound and per cubic foot. During the same half century we have seen all the historical outdoor living controls—such as ice house, washing shed, root cellar, water supply and waste disposal—mechanized and brought indoors. To a gradually improving mechanics of solution of these facilities have been added an increasing host of controls and mechanical devices. Cold that required winter's harvesting and degrees of cold not to be "harvested" are arrived at in minutes and precisely maintained within increasingly economical weight/volume. Functions of the past which required months, weeks, days and hours have been reduced to minutes and seconds, while new degrees of precision of maintenance of desired conditions previously undreamed of are now routine. As an overall result, life expectancy at birth has been almost doubled in this remarkable yet short fifty-year era.

While we continuously lost advantage in degrees of *structural* satisfaction to be obtained per unit of investment (pounds, dollars, time and energy), we have continually gained in degrees of *performance* to be obtained per unit of investment in household mechanics. For fractions of a cent and ounces of material, we can get instantaneous reports from around the world where the same would have cost thousands of dollars and involved thousands of tons fifty years ago to obtain the same personal home facility.

In view of these trends and looking to their further extension in the next fifty years, I propose that we eliminate the shrinking and less economical house altogether and concentrate entirely on amplification of the mechanics. Let's go camping with paraphernalia competent to make us masters of our environment and time to a degree of which man has never dared to dream.

Briefly, I propose a super-camping structure consisting of a six hundred-pound, fifty-foot diameter hemisphere. It consists of a triangular network of aircraft tubing, laced together internally by aircraft cable. Its air frame structure rises into a rigid truss in seconds, as its steel sinews are hydraulically tensed, somewhat as a tinkertoy is drawn taut. A transparent plastic skin of double wall construction is inflated to withstand hail, or hurricane impact loads. An interior shuttering mechanism provides one hundred percent variable optic control opaque to transparent.

Accompanying the geodesic structure will be an autonomous dwelling package. Research regarding this was done in 1949 by forty advanced students in product design and architecture at the Institute of Design in Chicago. Given an hypothetical problem that: all cities of fifty thousand or more population were to be bombed within ten days, they were instructed to compile a household package of all equipment they might conceive of needing for luxurious living. Price was not to be considered; only the best merchandise in any field was to be "purchased." They shopped all the best sources—Marshall Field's, Macy's, Sears, and Wards—for furniture, electrical appliances, radios, cameras, sporting goods shops, garden club machinery, home machine and woodworking shop supplies. Every conceivable area of high standard of living was covered. A tabulation revealed that the whole package of modern mechanics for a family of six cost only eighteen thousand dollars and bulked one thousand six hundred cubic feet and weighed twelve thousand pounds!

Because this household machinery and paraphernalia had to be marketed piecemeal with unpredictable lags on shelves and in intermediary warehouses, its cost ran two dollars per pound for its net nine thousand pounds. The same grade of production goods when mass purchased and assembled by the automobile industry with appropriate wiring and plumbing, as are the radio and heater in the automobile, ran fifty cents per pound. Therefore, the total 1949 advanced standard of living package could also be mass produced, purchased, assembled and distributed under a comprehensive chattel mortgage at fifty cents per pound.

This may be immediately effected by integration of the electrical appliance and automobile manufacturing industries without inauguration of new components. It involves only modification of what is to be assembled along the production line. Each of the six surfaces of a 25'x8'x8' trailable container will move down the line separately. To them will be affixed all the household items of the super mechanical package. In logical use arrangement and spacing when the panels are hinged together and opened in an eight hundred and sixty-four-foot platform, the arrangement also allows the panels to be hinged into a closed box with intermeshing of the fixed parts. "A neat trick if you can do it, and we have!"

There were many other problems of water supply and sanitation, but all of these are now under control in an economical manner.

You may say, "What is new about a dome?" The answer is that while there is nothing new about a dome, the way that it is accomplished, in this case, represents, first, a new advantage taken of the most recent increases of tensile ability; second, of entirely new structural geometry; and third, of advancing mechanics.

Emulating the compound curvature trussing of the atom's dynamic structure, comprised of great circle forces, our geodesic structure, though not inventing the principles, employs them for the first time in a man-made structure. This was a patentable invention.

A barrel represents an advanced phase of the Roman arch or principle of stability accomplished by simple curvature. The parallel barrel staves constitute a ring held together in compression by encompassing tension bands. Thus compression, which tends to curve, is favored in that tendency until the curving line of compression closes itself to thrust against itself. The tension line, which tends to pull true, forms itself in a finite closure of short true chords—because tension members may be flexed while they are in tension without tendency to failure.

The tension ends are united to pull against one another. Thus we have closed circuits of tension arch-bundling compression in dynamic stability. Tension lines may also be flexed while under load, without tendency to failure, as a compound corollary of the principle to pull true and the ability to tolerate bending while tensed. Pressures exerted either outside or inside of the barrel result in outward thrust of the staves against the tension members. Thus, the latter absorb the working or random loads.

We can also demonstrate the great structural gain inherent in the principle of simple curvature over rectilinear structures when we take a limp sheet of paper and curve it into a tube. Previously, an amorphous diaphragm of little structural advantage, it affords dramatic structural ability in the form of a tube. When the paper is curved, the concave side forms an arch of infinitely minute parallel compression staves, fulcrums of pinched rows of atoms. The convex surface of the curved paper is stretched around the compression arch of parallel fulcrum lines—tensed atoms.

The paper may be reversed so that what has been the inside of the cylinder's surface becomes the outside surface. Thus it is seen that simple curvature structure is a principle and not a unique characteristic of the atoms constituting one surface or the other. The stability of simple curvature is enhanced by the length of the parallel lines. As the lines shorten to approach "points," the compression of the arch approaches the condition of a simply compressed ball point which then tends to curve in any direction. The curved compression in the barrel or cylinder was confined to articulate its tendency to curvature within one plane by the compression (strutted) positioning of every point of the line of curvature afforded by the parallelism of the staves, and their inertia.

Parallel lines can be torqued. So may the parallel lines of a cylinder be twisted as we see them in a rope. A rope and a cone are both forms of simple curvature.

When we press against a barrel, the stress is, as earlier noted, satisfied by the tension hoop. Each hoop represents the circle of a single plane. Thus it is seen that simple curvature stresses act in a single plane, ultimately articulating that stress in diametric opposition of a line within the plane. The stresses are then ultimately focused to the infinite poles of parallels, because the latter are unaided in interstabilization.

In a simple curvature tube of paper, all the circles of tension, including all the circles of compression, are parallel to one another and give one another no help. Therefore, a cylinder may be flattened—in which case each circle becomes a double line. In order to do this, we see that the tension circles exert all their pull in levering the many compression points within to compress exquisitely the two opposite or polar compression points. This is, then, the genesis of the ultimate two-way focusing compression tension line resulting from stressing simple curvature.

In our geodesic structures, the surface of a sphere is interlaced by an omni-three-way grid of great circles, which always uniquely intercept one another in such a manner that everywhere the surface areas described by the intersections are triangular. As triangles are nondistortable this intersecting, if substantially structured, represents a rigid trussing of the spherical surface. If, between each of the vertexes or intersections of the great circles occurring in the surface of the sphere, we construct chords or straight lines, these lines must fall below the surface between their surface terminals. The lines converging at any one vertex all leading away below the point on the surface must form a convex intersection or a pyramidal point. As we press against any convex vertex, where the other ends of the lines are elastically restrained, the vertex will subside and the lines will tend to form a flat plane.

As each of the chordal ends between vertexes of our geodesic structure is tensionally restrained by the comprehensive trussing of the sphere, it is seen that when pressure is exerted inwardly against any vertex it will thrust outwardly against each of the chords leading radially from it. It will be seen that, inasmuch as each vertex represents a pyramid of triangular planes, the bases of the planes opposite the vertex constitute a closed tensional ring. Because the linkage is of great circle chords and because sections of the great circle always represent the shortest distance between any two points on a sphere (and the chords of the great circle represent the shortest distance between the two points in space through the sphere), the ring of chords tensionally opposing the compression thrust of the pyramidal lines from any one vertex may not be elongated. The vertexes will not subside.

Thus it is seen that the geodesic structure employs the principle of compound curvature as the stress is radially distributed from a single point. All the vertexes surrounding any one vertex are secondarily actuated and each in turn thrusts outwardly to adjacent vertexes; rings of triangles of geodesic lines are successively activated from the original thrust against one vertex until six rings have been activated and the equator is reached. All thrusting outwardly against the equator symmetrically, their outward thrust is compoundingly restrained by the opposite hemisphere.

In the case of a geodesic structure representing a portion of a sphere, the functions of the balance of the sphere are rendered by the earth, which tends to complete the spherical structure by stress extension within the earth. Thus, in compound curvature structures of Nature, emulated in principle by our geodesic structure, working stresses are ultimately translated into omni-directional outward thrust from the stressed centers, and are ultimately satisfied throughout all the cohesiveness of all the enclosing tension. In contra-distinction to simple curvature, which is ultimately satisfied in polar focus upon two compression points, compound curvature invokes ultimate activation of comprehensive tension.

In a compound curvature sphere of paper all the surface represents an intertriangulation of great circles, wherefore each great circle helps the other. Each is a compression circle enclosed within a tension circle. If we try to flatten the sphere, its equator cannot move outwardly to accommodate the down thrust as did the girth of the paper cylinder. Therefore, no one circle can lever its compressive interior against polar points, and, disunited, fail. In the sphere, the pressure at one point must invoke an infinity of great circles to crush an infinity of points simultaneously in a progressively rolling radius as the sphere is pushed gradually inside out—but never flattened—and only rolls the wave to the equator, which holds. Even in its inside-outness the sphere maintains its comprehensive interaction of system, seeking to re-establish its shape. Thus do balls tend to bounce.

There are many ways of rendering geodesic structures, but all represent closed systems in which compression is comprehensively encompassed by tension. In principle, this emulates the structuring of universe.

Men have employed geodesic structures in the form of tetrahedrons, octahedrons, and icosahedrons. While useful in small structures, the relative sizes of spans or chords of these well-known continuities of great circle triangulation become so great in unsupported length when applied to structures appropriate to men's buildings that their virtues were unavailable for practical purposes.

The surprise factor in my introduction of geodesic structures is the surprise provided by Nature. We have discovered and not invented all-triangular interaction of twenty-five great circles and thirty-one great circles whose relative chordal lengths make them appropriate for structures up to unlimited diameter.

There are further occurrences in greater numbers of great circles embodying the all-triangular interaction. Because of the shortness of the chords, which make possible the application of compression members between vertexes of a practical length-width ratio, while the system of short compression members may be comprehensively cohered by ground-to-ground tension lines, it is now theoretically possible to conceive of structures of spans approximating the great suspension bridges. A dome one mile in diameter appropriately skinned in may, in the future, economically encompass the activity of a city. Such a city would require no weather walls for its individual buildings and yet could be entirely air conditioned.

There is special advantage of the hemisphere over other geometrical forms. For instance, the upper or enclosing surface of a hemisphere (geodesic) or of a half cylinder (quonsette) is always twice the area of its base (floor). The upper surface of a half cube structure (typical of one-story box house) is always three times its base (floor). The upper surface of a cube is always five times its base (floor). The above ratios indicate clearly the initial advantages of curved enclosure over rectilinear. The advantage is spelled out in the weight of material per unit of function and in surface cooling areas, etc. The peak-roofed box is at a greater disadvantage than the flat-roofed box. The dome sheds its snow and rain in a superior fashion to a peak or a cylinder.

While it is customary to identify office and manufacturing space in terms of square feet of floor area, the actual fact is that—because man and his goods are not two dimensional—the space is volumetrically employed. For this reason, the unique advantages displayed by the sphere (as dimension is amplified) in the rate of volumetric increase as of the third power over surface increase at the rate of the second power has direct bearing on use.

It may be argued that the hemisphere provides unusable heights of volume and, therefore, the floor area is a better means of appraising the value of the space, but this aspect is only true under special forms of use which emphasize the ground need.

Storagewise, the whole of the hemispherical volume can be employed. In the case of our geodesic housing where a fifty-foot hemisphere is employed, we find it appropriate to create a second deck. Geodesic domes eliminate interior columns.

Further uses are made of the hemispherical volume which take advantage of the unique geometry of the hemisphere; that is, atmospheric circulation takes advantage of the natural fountainwise flow of heated air (for air heated at the center tends to expand and rise as the heavier air is pulled down by gravity). As it rises it further expands; it cools and flows outward and downward to floor level, then recenters for reheating and recirculation.

This natural fountain motion of heated air may be observed as an isolated phenomena in the case of explosions and in great fires. Notably, the Bikini bomb may be remembered as demonstrating the upward-outward-downward and center-rolling doughnut-hemispherical shape. Inasmuch as this is the natural atmospheric circuit of energy as heat, it is seen that—if the hemisphere is designed of the right size to accommodate the natural dimensions of a given heat fountain—there is no tendency of heat to he lost nor additional energy expended to impel atmospheric flows through unnatural chambering in order to distribute "comfort" atmosphere. This pattern reverses and cools in summer.

The hemisphere has further advantages relative to the phenomenon energy-as-heat-in-the-form-of-radiation (in contra-distinction to energy-as-heat-as-articulation-by-molecular-acceleration in gases, which latter is commonly identified by the combined behaviors known as conduction and convection). Energy-as-radiation (heat or light or radio) is refracted by the atmosphere. The lumen reduction as the light meter recedes from the source of light is rapid. As the longer waves of light radiation are progressively deflected by air molecules, they tend to turn back on themselves. This atmospheric deflection effect on radiation may be witnessed by observation of a street lamp in a mist, in which it is seen that a unique sphere is illuminated, and that only a small fraction of the high frequency and shortest wave light penetrates to the distant eye.

The long infrared radiation is turned about most rapidly and forms a relatively small sphere around the heat-light source. We demonstrate our familiarity with heat radiations' spherical limits as we back into and walk away from the glowing fireplace. The spherical surfaces of *relative* heat "fronts" are well identified. Again, as in the case of convection fountain enclosure, it is seen that, if a structural hemisphere is of adequate size, heat losses by *radiation* (where the origin of heat is near the center of the hemisphere) may be scaled down to negligible, and that such heat radiation as does reach the surface may be turned around by reflection and thrown directly back toward the point of origin.

There is a third aspect of unique advantage in the matter of hemispherical volume, gained at the third power, against surface growth of the second power; to wit, that advantage accruing to "relative size." Relative size very naturally affects heat balance because extreme chilling by conduction occurs in direct relationship to the second power surface, while the heat is being impounded by the air mass growing at the third power. A large, heated sphere such as earth can maintain high internal heat without important challenge by the exterior cooling surface. A large internal combustion engine cylinder cools off slowly in comparison to a small combustion cylinder (large diesel vs. small motorcycle). In reverse, the principle of relative size effect may be noted in the relatively slow velocity at which a large cake of ice melts, as against the accelerating velocity at which a small cake of ice melts—icebergs and glaciers vs. snowflakes.

The principle of relative size effects may be observed where heat is no consideration; for instance, in the relative rate of dissolution of several small cakes of soap vs. one large cake of soap of equal total weight. The principle is exhibited by a steel needle floating on water vs. a solid steel rod sinking.

Because the amount of volume that can encompass a given center for a given amount of pounds of structure is larger in the case of the sphere vs. any other kind of geometrical form, and because our particular type of tube-and-cable "necklace" structure (which takes advantage of triangulation of geodesic lines) entitles us to the encompassment of relatively large volumes with relatively low logistic investment, optimum conditions obtain. Slackened necklace geodesic spheres, compactable as tight as hairnets, may be shot to the moon and tensibly self-motor opened.

There is a further advantage unique to this geometrical form not at first anticipated, and that is the exterior aeronautical advantage. The hemisphere provides the least resistant form (to the sum-total of omni-directional air motions about it) of any of the geometrical forms. (For this reason, hay mows do not tend to deform in the wind.) The wind tunnel discloses that interior heat losses of permeable wall structures are proportional to drag. This is to say that the exterior low pressures created by the passage of air about a structure are satisfied by interiorly generated energy expenditure to pass the high pressure gases through the permeable passages of walls of the structure. Geodesic domes optimally withstand nearby atomic bomb shock impacts.

Other experiments have disclosed these principles to be in operation. Cubical houses heated by return circuit hot water systems have been mistakenly supposed to be cool in the windward rooms in the wintertime because the wind was blowing on that side and was, therefore, supposedly chilling the radiators in the windward rooms. Experiments disclose that no heat rises from the boiler to the windward rooms because the total BTUs being generated are required to process the transfer of the heated atmosphere in the lee side of the building through the walls to satisfy the low pressure occurring in the lee exterior of the building and that the whole heat flow is to the lee side.

It can be seen that the four factors noted above—(a) heat convection fountain, (b) radiation refraction to spherical shape, (c) relative size, (d) aeronautical properties—combine to provide unique energy economies, but with no further expenditure in physical structure in the way of conduits, partitions or impellers thus displaying surprise advantage in new magnitudes of available low cost and low upkeep controlled environment.

Employing components now manufactured by American industry, one of our engineering research teams has now completed a tentative flow sheet of the sewage disposal and water supply system—the latter for six hundred gallons per day of chemically pure, sterilized, sweet water. This apparatus serves as an exchanger, taking heat from light and refrigeration systems to satisfy the pressure distillation processes. It heats the water for general cleansing purposes while shunting a fraction to refrigeration for chilling. This total energy-sanitation-refrigeration system weighs approximately one ton.

Autonomous living under a hurricane-proof hemispherical enclosure of fifty-foot diameter (eight hundred sixty-four square feet of platform plus nine hundred eighty-six square feet of interior garden), with all modern super-luxury appurtenances and sanitary controls, is now feasible. Weighing *in toto* fourteen thousand pounds, it may be mass produced at $ 7,000. Push button-erected, it may be occupied at one fifth the present cost of bare miniature-mansions sewered and paved together in "Siamese twinness." This can be realized only through true mass production.

12 Total Thinking

As I prepared Ideas and Integrities *for publication, I rediscovered Total Thinking which I had written at Black Mountain College, North Carolina, in 1949, prior to the electronic computer's present massive development and the latter's swiftly "fed-back" popularization of Professor Norbert Weiner's Cybernetics-born language of 1948. I had not read* Cybernetics[23] *when I wrote* Ideas and Integrities, *and I publish it now because its analytical epistemology unexpectedly provides a broad view of computer programming conceptions and experimental strategies which embrace potentially powerful forecasting capabilities.*

Man, in degrees beyond all other creatures known to him, consciously participates—albeit meagerly—in the selective mutations and accelerations of his own evolution. This is accomplished as a subordinate modification and a component function of his sum-total relative dynamic equilibrium as he speeds within the comprehensive and complex interactions of universe (which he alludes to locally as environment).

May 1949. The version published here appears verbatim from the original typescript in the Fuller Archive (Series 8 Box 8 Fol. 17 [49.08.01 Total Thinking]), with the sole exception of Fuller's handwritten addition at a later date of the very last sentence, "Bias precludes synergetic advantage."

---

23 Norbert Wiener, *Cybernetics: Or Control and Communication in the Animal and the Machine* (Cambridge, Mass., 1948).

As no energy may be lost of universe, and as all parts of universe act, theoretically, upon all other parts, man may accomplish modification of his particular evolution only by relative modification of the aspects of universe. The picture is of universe as a kaleidoscope of sum-total symmetry only, the relative aspects of which may be dynamically and infinitely reordered without exemption of, or addition to, the component totality. Every shift (in the energy balance accomplished by man at earth's crust) affects all universe. Though fantastic, this is the scientific truth. If man seems frequently frustrated in his attempts at evolutionary modifications, all his failures and successes may be truly evaluated in the scientific frame of total dynamic reference. It is an astronomical kaleidoscope—the little fellow is shaking—and from within. Even thinking about truth alters truth.

Modification may only be accomplished forwardly in time. The system is inherently irreversible. Here magnitude vanishes; only principles endure. The fantastic, being purely of superficial magnitude, vanishes in the face of principle. Man accomplishes the progressive modification of his evolution through the coupling and articulation of his subjectively and objectively imagined synthesis of the factors of experience. This modification of his own evolutionary relationships by man involves a continuity of the thought processes. Superficially challenged by the seeming discontinuity of death, man has become successful in his distinguishable degrees as evolution modifier by virtue of his ability to further the refinement of thought toward the evolution of truth, by communication of the truth refinements to the new life—the new life being spontaneously persistent, overlapping and only modifyingly nurtured by the synchronous continuity of old life.

The scientist as specialist in isolation of phenomenon from phenomena has now come—by progressive reduction of the superficially remote behavior complexities of the organic and inorganic worlds—to discover simplified common component-behavior phases of each world respectively. Here the energetic interactions of the resultant structures are uniform. Here the man-controlled original inorganic growth is in all ways congruent with the animate, organic, "de-grown" by man, or separated-out, toward primary functions of the original totality: universe.

This event within the lower reaches of the microcosmos has been accomplished by man despite all other outward, or further inward atomic complexities. At the 'tween stage of universe–'twixt micro- and macrocosmos–known as "everyday" and occurring in the narrow visible range of the total known spectrum, man has not been successful to date in constituting super-complexities-of-common-advantage from out of the host of potential components of the now-myriad of unique chemical (compounds) of relatively simplified order. Differentiation outdoes integration.

Man has been lacking in comprehensive disciplines and the developed ability to synthesize, essentially because of the bewildering arrays of complex behavior items of natural phenomena. Man shows synergetic re-genius inferior to Nature's regeneration.

Only by recourse to fundamental principles of the first order and to the whole family of such fundamental principles may man possibly comprehend (aware of the significance of his own species in the world of species, and of the significance of all his experience to all universe) to realize comprehensive advantage for his species, as a function of universe, by employment of the mathematical principles with which complex groups and super-complex groups may be handled comprehensively by man, as a responsible anticipatory designer of his own evolutionary mutations. The mental process may run as follows:

Consciously or unconsciously, life is systematically pulsive. The heart pulses without conscious authority. It ceases without recourse to man's assumed objective authority. It propagates.

Continuity of conscious life becomes personality and is a product of complex periodic interactions known as cycles, or periodic recurrences of a higher frequency order.

Primarily, the trending of men's lives and their spontaneous actions, as well as their premeditated undertakings in establishment and conservation of technical advantage seem, retrospectively, only to have been subjectively motivated and steered by the ricocheting succession of randomly willed impulsions and unpredictable repulsions of maximum and minimum experience, by the push-pulling alternations of scarcity and plenty, heat and cold, wetness and dryness, joy and sorrow, loving and hating, longing and fear, sum-totally operating on cyclic frequencies so transcendental to man's limited experience as almost to preclude attempts to analyze and predict the interprecessional recurrences.

Gradually apprehending the reciprocal and integrated nature of alternating experience, man has learned to measure and to plot relative degrees and magnitudes of Nature's behavior (including his own) and also, therefrom, to plot, not informative but provocative curves, so designated provocative because only possibly containing secondary keys which might unlock the doors to laws partially governing the non-self-requested experience of life.

The keys are only possible keys because the directional causes are not evidenced in the first order of plotted curves (only the latest maxima and minima of record are) without any indication whatsoever that the thus-far-experienced extremes constitute inherent limits of the variable. Limits would, if detected, constitute the possible turning points of trend.

Only after sufficient measurement gained by his intuitive probing in the direction of causes, with tools of assumption, may informed questions be asked by man, and calculated answers potentially be had. As with the waves of progressive advantage obtainable in the successive operations of the calculus, has man only now come in his evolution, as by the second and subsequent derivatives of his historical experience-equating, to the ability to identify in principle the systematic chemistry of his personal-process-continuity and his position on and the direction of the curves of his trending, and the rates of acceleration thereon.

Man first applied his newly won tools, of derived superior advantage of measurement-in-principle by realizing the predictable behavior of energy interactions, in shaping the designs of his accelerated velocity and magnitude extensions, his hurled, rolled, levered devices, his shots and ships. This priority of application was natural to man's having in boyhood thrown stones and sticks, hour after hour, into water, against rocks, through membranes and having later tried progressive acceleration in slingshots, archery and guns, and still later in propelled carriers in general.

The second derivative advantage accrued initially to the plotting of the data relative not only to the records of his running and jumping, but to his javelin-throwing sports, as well as accelerated mechanical novelties of impelled, flown, floated, wheeled, slid, levered and geared devices.

Turning to gain momentum, he could, unencumbered, jump over a six-foot bar; then, paradoxically, encumbering himself with a long pole, he could run with the same speed to vault over a twelve-foot bar. A regeneratively excited sense of perspective accrued to the relatively remote yet personally significant events of further extension—personal because the events were not only self-witnessed or experienced, but also were self-designed and self-executed—and proved on trial of the imagined conception to be accelerations to velocities and magnitudes greater than attainable by man's personal propulsion mechanics alone.

Thus, man accelerated extended communication to unexpected distances and with unexpected speed. Next he accelerated his personal conveyance, accelerating the evolution of his own extension from, for instance, the echoed voice of a poling raftsman to the forwardly informative radar manipulations of the stratojet piloting airman.

In order to apply the same degrees of skillfully interpolated advantage of knowledge in principle: of position, direction and relative acceleration, to man's immediate, everyday, and far less "exciting" environment-shaping, he must be able to write the cogent formula of comprehensive functions of the coordinate system of his own physical complex—of his life (personal, family and species) as reciprocally embraced by the complex of dynamic universe. This requires in essence: (a) the comprehensive-intuitive, that is, total subjective-objective thinking, (b) the assumption of the systematic or comprehensive special idea in view of its reciprocal implications, (c) the rigorous test, of physical trial, by precision tools and under the family of possible-and-probable variable conditions accelerated and amplified beyond working requirements.

Not having as yet applied scientific advantage to anticipatory design of the immediate environment continuities, the environment runs the man. Men may take at first none, and secondarily but little credit for their personal survival. Even in their mature years, primarily pitting themselves each against other men, but few of the species may claim conscious participation in the survival of the species and none for conscious contribution to the continuity of universe.

Ignorant of his own coming "blessed event," ignorant of the circumstances of his realization, ignorant of final causes and effects, ignorant of consequences and significance, and ignorant of absolute values, man is clearly *a priori* ignorant.

He is born helpless and nurtured by progenitors but meagerly understanding him, who in turn have experienced the identical involuntary helplessness and meager understanding. Ignorance is indeed *a priori.* (The most successful exploiters of the invention man, to date, are those who have bet on the supremacy of his ignorance and have, therefore, stressed the negative probabilities.)

In consequence of the above observations, it must be concluded that man's participation in the moderate success of his complex relationship to universe has of necessity been accomplished by a variety of indirectly-arrived-at advantages, only ignorantly induced, and conversely reciprocal to the original acts of ignorance. He backs into his future.

Ignorance hither-and-yons impulsively until brought up short at unpredictable periods by unpredictable push-pull limits. It is slowly becoming evidenced that, though man had been ignorant of the factors governing his successful survival as a species, the reciprocal positive functions governing the periodic alternations which net a successfully steered course may be adduced, only, however, by proper documentation and realistic inversion of the negative evaluations and predilections of ignorance.

Vanity and superstition constitute the plus and minus springs of ignorance, the expansive and contractive *raison d'être* of boast and fear. The boasts and fears of ignorance may be maintained spontaneously only when there is no obviously periodic contradiction in physical experience.

Abandoning vain boast, the competent but fog-shrouded navigator learned by experience to blow his horn to generate echoes from unseen headlands and thus to position himself and dissipate fears of danger. Ignorance is the inherently diminishing negative residue, the obscuring mist of the receding mental wilderness progressively dissipated by intellect, the inherent positive of universe that may by inference of the record turn every adversity to ultimate advantage.

Residual ignorance has employed the as-yet-primitive tools of mathematics in linear diametrics—in the "either yes or no" of two-dimensional oversimplification. Ignorance thinking in blackboard and paper planes labors protestingly over the geometry of reality. A complete reorganization of mathematics will probably occur within the next quarter century (or generation) with all the now so-called elementary phases relegated to non-sense and the ever most advanced intuitions shifted to elementary priority in the effective informing of the new life by the old.

Ignorance may only be dissipated as intellect traits by physical initiative in design realizations of anticipated periodic functions, designed to disclose coincidence with the periodic contradictions, forcefully experienced, and thus potentially further revealing in principle. Thus, the designed experiment is resolvable, eventually, into general behavior laws of the energetic universe, whose interactions in turn become subject to increasingly reliable predictions by man.

Education, in the sense of man's being *educente* (led out from) the monological fixations of ignorance, involves also being led into, *intro-ducente* (introduced to) the new awareness of the dynamic fluidity of the infinite persistence of complex-yet-systematic interaction of universal principles.

Education has now led us out and into a degree of meager awareness of universe, somewhat as though we had been given spectators' seats commanding an improved view of the game-of-games called "universe." It is, however, not as though we had been given better seats in the same old static stadium, within which the sports of extension of personal facility are tried, but more as though we have been given seats in a relay of refueled airplanes to command a view of a new kind of ocean race, a continuous around-and-around-the-world race of relay teams of deep sea craft. Both the frame of reference and the observed are in obvious continual motion and persist as individually composite dynamic continuities, though the separate men (invisible but implicit) and planes and boats and their component parts and sub-parts progressively shuttle or drop out and are eventually substituted for by inconsequentially increasing or decreasing numbers.

The whole dynamic assemblage of race and observer relays are invisible even to an observer at a thirty-thousand-foot altitude, let alone to an observer on Mars or on another planet of another star who could only observe the motion of earth relative to sun or the sun relative to galaxy, etc.

This schematically kinetic tapestry is the advanced concept of relativity—now, at last, popularly significant, because pivotal to the everywhere severe worldwide reorientation of all men's everyday affairs from a static to an *a priori* dynamic frame of reference.

The reorientation is severe because it is more than an uprooting. Realization of relativity spontaneously evokes a springing, to dive from a then vanishing springboard into an infinite dynamic sea where man must learn to swim tirelessly, naturally, before he sinks, but only because what he used to think was that he ought to "sink" rather than be attracted by dominant neighbors.

As man learns to eliminate his preposterous one- or two- or three-dimensional *a priori* references to a fixed level planar breadth and its inherent upwardness or downwardness of universe and substitutes therefor the now reliable sensation of an inwardness and outwardness relative to plural of centers, he will come naturally to his new sustaining awareness of the impossibility of his doing ought but sustain his equilibrious and navigable position. If there is no inherent "down" in universe, man cannot sink.

This is not a semantic abstraction. What did man mean when he said, "Up"? He meant two or more vertical and parallel lines perpendicular to the respective spots of a supposedly common plane whereon supposedly stood—fixedly in universe—both himself and his addressee, with whom he would, avowedly, communicate meaningfully.

But he is, in fact, employing non-sense. Unless one is standing on the other's shoulders, the direction of "up" for any two men on the curved face of earth is always geometrically different. They are respectively non-identical radii of their commonly predominant energetic center, the earth ball. It makes no difference what the local curvature of the earth may be; they each balance, "perpendicularly" independent, as radii of the "perfect" sphere.

By the time one man explains to the other by directional indication what he had meant by "up" of a moment ago, the direction "up" as registered in direction to the stars in universe—the other energy centers—has shifted angularly to absurd non-identity. In the clocktime course of a sentence, his succession of complex "ups" at earth's level has moved angularly thousands of miles;

and the beam of his continuous, up-pointing in the heavens, relative to sun and galaxy, has swept billions of miles. As he soon rockets toward the moon he will find his feet pointing gradually and comfortably toward the moon which he had just previously pointed to as "up."

If he persists in the up-and-down language, man may never communicate accurately with other men for they do not employ the same meanings, either from moment to moment, or in respect to their individual "ups" and "downs."

As man now flies about the earth, the absurdity of his up-and-down reference becomes apparent. In which of his many stop-overs is he upside-down? In Calcutta, Suez, Tokyo, Los Angeles or Rio? And in which is he downside-up? Englishmen used to be content to leave it to the Anzacs "down under" to work out for themselves their inherent handicap of having to negotiate all their lives upside-down in "space." And so also did the Americans to their Chinese "inferiors"–and vice versa.

Only when men learn to say in and out relative to designated common centers (for example, of earth) is the meaning constantly reliable. The sky is "outward" to all men, at all places, at all times, on any planet. While enjoying an infinity of individual "ins," we, anywhere in the universe, also enjoy one common nonsimultaneous, omni-directional aggregate called "out."

As the constantly reliable replaces the interrupted inaccuracy of the past moment, the yesterdays of inaccuracy dissolve in the presence of the finite dynamic constants of discovered energetic universe of now; the inherent continuity of understanding (of overlapping-periodic interruptions) becomes increasingly available.

Principles of physical universe may be treated of in words, which themselves were developed in principle out of dawning comprehension of implicit significance in the relative identities of complex bundles of principles. Relativity treats with concepts in principle; therefore, it can be treated in words as well as in mathematical phrasing. Relativity is inherently convergent, though convergent toward a plurality of centers of abstract truths. Degrees of accuracy are only degrees of refinement, and magnitude in no way affects the fundamental reliability, which refers, as directional or angular sense, toward centralized truths. Truth is a relationship. Articulated references of meaning are centrally embodied in commonly recognized, constantly reliable directions of inwardness and outwardness, in respect to the nominated centers of commonly experienced trend in principle.

The new reliable understanding of meaning, however, requires the revision not only of semantics but also of their complex aspect as thought habits employed to describe experience with accuracy, such as the substitution of the already-discussed in-and-out for up-and-down; or the substitution of "winds drafting to the southeast low pressure" instead of "blowing from the northwest (zephyrs)"; or the substitution of the word "realization" for the very inaccurate use of the verb "to create." Man creates naught. If he comprehends in principle, he rearranges locally in universe by realization of the interactions of principles.

So long as mathematicians can impose up and down semantics upon students while trafficking personally in the non-up-and-down advantages of their concise statements, they can impose upon the ignorance of man a monopoly of access to accurate processing of information and can fool even themselves by thought habits governing the becoming behavior of professional specialists, by disclaiming the necessity of, or responsibility for, comprehensive adjustment of the *a priori* thought to total reality of universal principles.

The everywhere-relative velocities and momentums of interactions, of energetic phenomena of universe, are central to the preoccupations and realizations of the comprehensive designer. The concept of relativity involves high frequency of re-established awareness, and progressively integrating consideration of the respective, and also integrated dynamic complexities of the moving, and transforming frame of reference and of the integrated dynamic complexities of the observed, as well as of the series of integrated sub-dynamic complexities, in respect to each of the major categories of the relatively moving frames of reference, of the observer and the observed. It also involves constant reference of all the reciprocating sub-sets to the comprehensive totality of nonsimultaneous universe, from which naught may be lost.

We have on the one hand the multiplicity-of-the-component-structures-and-moving-parts-of -the-airplane-carrying-the-observer, as an integrated whole, as he observes the set-of-all-the-boats called the race headed for the next marker—for instance, for Bermuda—maintaining their relative continuity with respect to each other externally, as the individual boats persist as a continuity of internal sets and sub-sets (to the power of any number) of synchronized interactions.

We have on the other hand the concepts of both the observer and the observed relative to their respective moving frames of environment reference and then both moving frames merging into one with the universe, but at two extremes of maxima and minima, that is, in the macrocosm and the microcosm. Both inwardly and outwardly and diametrically all eventuate in the same universe of fundamental principles governing energy as atom or galaxy aggregates of nonsimultaneous yet related events.

Returning to the concept of the moving observer in the airplane, we discover that, despite the numerically astronomical complexity of the total moving picture of his life at the moment, it is to be noted that he may gain immediate advantage over the total concept; because he can first resolve all phenomena into two prime subdivisions—he can treat each moving frame of reference, in the terms of the composite scene of their internal and external aspects respectively.

Internal to the observer's moving advantage, we have the concept of the supporting industry that produces the airplane and keeps it serviced for reflight and the sub-sets of atomic interactions and the sub-sub-sub-sets of all the atomic interactions comprising planet Earth and the even greater population of subsets of atomic interaction of the solar system, and the greater still population of the galaxy accumulation, and, finally, all atoms of the universe.

But as we come to explore for the fundamental principles of interpotentials and interactions called atoms, we find that, despite the astronomical number of aspects and events, only a few principles of behavior pervade the whole of universe as, for instance, ninety-two tendencies to self-impoundment of energy; a fundamental inwardness and outwardness relative only to the "system" center of observation; the corollary principles of inherent first tendencies to inward-outward pulsations and to precession, and the principles of inside-outing—convergence, divergence, spin and counterspin, torque and countertorque tension and pressure, the biological reciprocals of uni-verse (and diaphragming).

Relativity leads us toward fundamental classification of our experience and observation, in the terms of a few hierarchies of dynamic interactions and principle transformations of an all-energy, continuous-discontinuous, synchronous-dissynchronous universe tensionally cohered, precessional of local compressive spherical energetic collections—as (suns) stars or planets or moons or asteroids or meteorites; and the progression of withinward sub-sets of events of interactions at planet crust, etc., and inward to the ninety-two common principles of atomic convergence of energy in principle, and the pervasive sets of dynamic associations by contraction, expansion, spin, orbit, torque, push and pull and precession. This all brings us by progressive collections of thoughts into a fundamental twoness of dynamic reciprocities which, internally paired, ultimately become one with outwardly paired principles of reciprocity.

The becoming one of both the finity inward with the finity outward indicates a sensibility of experience preoccupying man as a superficial reality which only occurs at middling dimensions of universe and appears schematically as a magnetic field. Its flux patterns, like two tangent balls, include every size of particle, as their hour-glass-like tangentially linked inwardness, displays both inwardly and outwardly mingled sets of fountain and reverse fountain flows—concurrently at both ends—and through the middle. Periodically, the whole double-bulbed dynamic flux contracts axially, as the two bulbs of dynamic flow merge progressively, and then merge completely, and again separate axially. It is obvious that inasmuch as the whole system was always in flow that the new bulbs of flux are of necessity new and are therefore only identifiable in principle with the previous comprehensive duality of shapes. The system has inherent yet empty twoness.

The "reality" is real—or realized—in principle only, by events of relative interaction transpiring only in principle. The whole of the above pulsive-waveful-dynamic-duality is schematic, and is in principle clarifying only, for, though it progressively groups allenergy universe into an oscillating binary system, it must be understood that the whole scheme cancels out by virtue of a super paradox which finds that the infinity inward and the infinity outward of an infinite plurality of centers must be identical, and one with the infinity inward, of an infinite plurality of centers, and that: in comprehensive universe, dimension drops out and conceptual principle remains. Physical interferences of our sensibilities are alike true and real, or realizable, only in principle. Positive and negative cancel as the principle zero.

It is discovered in principle that probability probing of physical universe on a statistical basis is now becoming of necessity frustrated while, probing in empty conceptual principle could be instituted and accelerated for further advancement or fundamental information. Exploration in principle is re-rewarding.

It is necessary that the comprehensive designer explore in principle for verification of this significance of relativity, whereby it is discovered that in the consciously realizable comprehensive binary, truth may not be dealt with as isolated, but only as relative relationships of interaction governing in principle the interactions of specially nonsimultaneous sets of dynamic principles. The comprehensive realizer thus will come, with acceleration, to competence in rearranging forwardly anticipated events, measured in principle, and forwardly projected, in associated principles of reciprocal interaction and juxtaposition to the anticipated energetic magnitudes of variable stresses and flows. These interactions are known as structures and mechanics.

Thus it is discerned how the comprehensive realizer of relativity may become competent as an integrator of the until-then-threatening chaotic dissipation of common advantage of men in universe brought about by runaway, diametric preoccupations of specializations. The comprehensive realizer becomes a synergist.

These mathematical concepts of group phenomena may be acquired in principle by the willingness (subjectively initiated) of the individual to be governed by the integrity of "progressive conceptioning in principle" and to self disciplines of realization in principle—the objective synchronizations are implicit and unavoidable competence and comprehensive, realizable design will result. Let us pursue further the conceptioning in specifics of group principle.

It is not difficult to understand that the trends to synchronization by harmonic interval of one collection of events can seemingly and sum-totally create an aspect of such (superficial) incongruity in respect to the sum-total collected harmonic events of other phases of functional disposition, of the differentiable universe, as to predispose us to assume that there might never be synchronization of one major collection with another. We obviously incline to this predisposition by virtue of the persistence of the familiar in our own environmental close-up—thought, which causes the dynamic interpenetrations to appear as a static, rather than as a periodic-continuity environment reality.

This misapprehension of our own dynamic significance becomes in environmental close-ups a bundle of persistent periodicities developing into a spontaneous anticipation of repetition of harmonic intervals and their familiar synchronization. So marked is our proclivity for such anticipation that we set ourselves as though we were alarm clocks to waken at specific blocks of intervals of familiar periodicities of experience. We relate our own heartbeat to minutes of hours of days, and our meals—or chemical fueling—to the days of the postman's coming and going, and even to periodicities such as invented Father's Days and other soon-familiar invented conventions, of the persistent, complex periodic continuities of our days into years. The invented periodicities may become only monotonous.

Life in retrospect, however, may be informatively discovered to have been comprised of a progressive series of interruptions and penetrations of the successively latest *a priori* environment continuities—by unfamiliar frequencies or biodynamic groups of frequencies, always occurring as unfamiliar to the ignorantly accepted trend to mono-tony.

The new event always comes as an harmonic interruption of frequencies, or an interference with the increasing inventory of already assimilated synchronizations (up to the latest instant), which have only become obvious by virtue of the spontaneous synchronization of the sum-total of acquired experiences and progressively integrated interruptions.

It is necessary that the comprehensive realizer ascertain in principle how the mathematical proportioning of experience is persuasive to the erroneous concept that the sum-total bundle of already experienced frequencies constitutes so unified, or well synchronized an experience whole as to have seemingly always been "known." The comprehensive realizer will discover that his adequacy as rearranger of local universe, in principle, will, if competently effected, be acquired by men as an obvious accretion, and that the more competent his realizing-rearrangements of design, the less grateful the beneficiaries, which will be precisely the objective of the comprehensive-realizer.

A known personality, that is, a life—with which the comprehensive-realizer is concerned—is a unique bundle of accumulated experience to which the new experience must always be dissynchronous, but only at the moment of original interference, else the new interaction of the greater complex of truth would not have been recognizable and acquirable as new experience and tactical advantage.

The greatest over-all misapprehension regarding the complex-continuities is that which assigns a static or "at rest" analysis to the sum-total sensation of individual experience and consequently to the sum-total of all individuals' experience. Against the inertia of a seemingly static whole, each new harmonic incorporation of life therefore seemingly impinges as a dynamic perversity. This is why we frequently remark, "Man tends to back up into his future."

In addition to the simple arithmetical, algebraic and geometrical progressions of the first, second and third degrees of acceleration, mathematics discloses other series, and super series, of superficially unpredictable mathematical frequencies because they are composed of complementary and reciprocal numbers whose products alone, though never occurring simultaneously or in whole, are compositely congruent with complex progressions. But these complex components occur in discontinuous series, and are inherently self-inexplicable. The complementary functions must therefore impinge upon consciousness only as meaningless. As immediately contemplated upon first experience, they of necessity, alone, constitute seemingly absolute perversity of interference. Synergy—wholistic behavior unpredicted by parts.

It is, therefore, the unpredictable degree of the super and the super-super "n" degrees of complex associations of energy frequencies which seem most preposterous. We cannot view the great confluences of separately and remotely significant events forwardly resultant to now. Synergy is inherently surprising.

When, however, these complexities are viewed in reverse, from the advantage of even the most mathematically super-super interference, the whole regains the-acceptable-sublimity-of-aspect, such as a fleet of little ocean racers one hundred miles off Bermuda struggling with the waves of interference of the Atlantic turning the perversely interfering winds to advantage by virtue of the relative inertia of the relative waves of water, eventually to pass Bermuda, as the whole picture is observed from the airplane and its infinitude of subcomplexities.

Though both are designed with the same family of principles called "factors of ships," the comprehensive-realizer can see: that the superficial difference between the collections of frequencies which makes the Bermuda cruising boat seemingly different from the airplane—or indeed, man from elephant—may be in principle the same difference, as understandably exists between an early Wright airplane and the latest supersonic airplane, or, yet, between an early Chinese hot air balloon and a late helicopter.

The only difference between the Wright and the supersonic planes is the sum-total of recurrent-synchronized cyclic events, known as the "succession of (design) models,"—evoluted in complex out of the physical experience with each trial balance of the designed complex (effected by man) and as let loose, after staticload-tests-within-limited-controlled-conditions of variables, into the dynamic-load-tests within the unknown, uncontrolled, comprehensive (and *a priori*-design-complex) of the residual uncharted variables of universe. The uncharted residual (function of universe) balances the special-set function of derived functions—called from out the total principles of energetic universe by the designer as a newly realized mutation of species evolution accomplished by synergetic extension.

Though having no one common component part identification, the difference between the 1904 Wright brothers' biplane and the 1963 superjet, supersonic, stratosphere monoplane is only a group difference of a minor complex of almost sixty packed years of experience with the same body of principles called airship; which, in turn, only specialized in a few of the greater body of principles called ship; which specialized in a few of the greater body of principles called "earth"; which specialized in a few of the greater body of principles called motion; which specialized in a few of the greater body of principles called energy, which specialized as an original function for the comprehensive universe. The first derived coordinates of universe would seem to be functions of energy variant in respect to intellect.

We can see that the concept of original separation of universe into two inherent functions—and the further subdivision and expansion of one function into a unique plurality of subsets of functions—and subsequent acceleration of specialized experience with new design events of any one unique subset's evolution, as contrasted against another, can only accelerate superficial differences between any degrees of subsets.

It is obvious that, if the frequency of cyclic events differs in one geographical environment from another, the life within one environment may be accelerated to increasing degrees of experience over the life within another and, therefore, to sets of superficial difference of existence and trend. It can then be seen that what we might designate as natural education—by induced self discipline advantage—represents an accelerated testing of objective-subjective experience, and that acceleration is natural and that natural education may potentially evaporate the inadequacy predilections of original vanity and superstitions and that the original springs of action may become obsolete as the realizations of intellect and the hitherto preoccupations with seeming frustration and self-destruction may be supplanted, through the self-disciplining of the comprehensive designer to orderings of integrity of universe.

Where, geographically speaking, of *a priori* unique environment continuities, the inherent periodicity of the occurrence of interference is at a relatively low frequency, then the rate of dissipation of ignorance is proportionally low, and vice versa.

The relatively lowest inherent periodicity of interference of forceful variables—of experience in the dynamic environment (geography)—occurs on the dry land near sea level in the region of the equator. The periodic frequency of interference by physical variables increases outwardly from the earth's center into the colder climates of mountain and toward the earth poles. The periodicity and magnitude of forceful interferences increases even more upon the seas, and yet more as man penetrates outwardly from the unique energy fixations of earth into the cosmos of major categories—of general dynamic principles.

Sum-totally on earth the residual vanities and superstitions of the ego bulk up most obviously in the warm and mild climates, originally most favorable to the naked, ignorant man, and are most rapidly dispersed and replaced with intellectual ordering in the environments of highest frequency of unprecedented intensities of interference, penetrated now by man at will by virtue of his contriving of realizations in complex principles.

Each of the sum-total variety of biological forms represents in simple principle the complex bundling of unique internal experience continuities, and the latter's individual accumulations of external periodic experience, within the greater bundle of persistently unique environmental sequences—of variable geographic frequency bundle limitations. Humans have abstract "tree rings" of experience.

The circling bands of a cross-sectioned tree or the scalloped terraces of the shell fish are convergently secreted structures (interference of higher order) of cyclic bundling of experiences. Wave embodiments of cyclic experience appear everywhere in the accredited morphology of nature's omni-directional, convergent-divergent, synchronous-dissynchronous, infinite plurality of pulsating controls of interactive events in principle.

The cyclic wave accretions—unique to parent and parent's parent—make overlapping internal impressions of the periodic and cyclic interferences-structuring-by-accretion, prearranging thereby internal angles of the original turbining tendency of unfoldment, upon the gestating seed of periodic secretion of outside-in then inside-out pulsation-inversion, which we call regenerative birth. This is, of course, a union of the infinite inwardness with the infinite outwardness to fulfill the comprehensive duality principle of uni-verse. Human egos are multi-concentric frequency "halo" systems.

As with the complex of synchronized convergent principles called airplane, compounded of the succession of flight experiences with a succession of "improved" designs in-corpor-ating all previous experience in action-reaction juxtapositions (called structure and mechanics), a trend to further inclusion and refinement of accelerating-acceleration of improvement is inherent, but always the improvement is relative to the whole of already secreted true experiences, whether as yet detected or not, by the redesign-cycle mutators.

A new design's "sport" or subspecies may long be latent, a helicopter development postponed by preoccupation with the initial concepts of "airship." The relative, realized-complex trend accelerates itself in compounding degrees, whereby, eventually, the probability of numbers of immediately detected forward mutations to be refiningly anticipated exceeds in number the sum-total of the previously secreted, or experienced, impressions, innately preoccupying the species division.

An historical shift is now occurring in the scientific viewpoint, induced by this shift in balance of preponderant numbers of effective impressions, pre-and-post-natal, upon behavior probabilities of the various species to be affected preponderantly by the relative number of post-natal, periodic and cyclic accelerations.

Hazy awareness of the significance of this historically pivotal event is at the core of hastily taken political positions seeking to establish monopolistic validity of comprehensive viewpoint (where mono-logical explanation of the biologically functioning derivatives of universe may never be tolerable). Both sides are right about their specially selected cases; neither may increase their understanding by arbitrary limitations of experience and conception, regarding the next appropriate trial balance of potentials of the apprehended, and therefore anticipated, periodic inclusions of the subjective-objective "beating to windward" of the periodically shifting advantages of universe. The comprehensive realizers of all time have always realized the implicit truths of these relationships of uni-verse. Bias precludes synergetic advantage.

13 Prime Design

Energetic-synergetic geometry discloses Nature's own system of coordination. Possessing this knowledge and taking the design initiative, man can enjoy Nature's exquisite economy and effectiveness.

We are reminded that at the everyday level of reality men do not build houses with materials; they organize visible-module structures comprised of sub-visible module structures. The principles governing structure operate independently of man-tunable spectrum range. Associative chemistry is structure.

For all time man has subconsciously coordinated himself with universal evolution. He does not consciously push each of his millions of hairs out through his scalp at man-preferred rates or selected patterns and colors.

Man now enters the phase of meager yet conscious participation in the anticipatory design undertakings of Nature. This conscious participation itself is changing from an awkward, arbitrary, trial and error ignorance to an intuitively conceived, yet rigorously serviced, disciplined elegance.

Man has been flying blindly into his future on scientific instruments and formulas. The great news on the artist-scientist-intellectual frontier is that as the fog-and-black shadow of ignorance

May 1960. Originally published in the *Bennington College Bulletin*, with an editorial preface that reads, "Notes for a lecture by RBF to be given under the auspices of the Southern California Regional Alumnae Group at the Beverly Hill High School auditorium on May 27th." Fuller Archive Series 8 Box 17 Folder 5 (Prime Design 60.05.01). Fuller's daughter, Allegra Fuller Snyder, was a graduate of Bennington College.

and misconception recedes, there looms a sublimely comprehensible conceptual patterning, which characterizes all the mathematical principles heretofore only formulatively employed by the scientist, yet intuitively pursued by the artist as potentially modelable. Experimental science has validated the artist's intuitions but not his disciplines.

The frontiers of physical experimentation have found no basic "building blocks" structuring nature. There are no thing-particles. Only pattern transactions in pure principle have been discovered. Man has therefore been forced to abandon the misconception of a "smallest fundamental particle," upon which the age of materialism was axiomatically predicated.

Where do we go from here? We are dealing with a complex integrity of complementary patterning transformations. Realization is objective integrity. Science, in its disciplined preoccupation with myriad subjective differentiations, serviced by an inbreeding specialization, has unwittingly eluded comprehensive social responsibility for objective potentials or the consequences of its findings and acts.

Engineering and architecture, though objective and integrative, have no economic initiative. These men design professionally only when employed by a patron. The patron becomes the prime designer. The patron initiates that which is to be detailed within the patron-conceived limits of undertaking and responsibility.

Ivory towerism in the scientist and professional-securityism in the architect-engineer have left social initiative to political man, who in turn has passed the buck to the military. The hired military serviceman has done his best within his limits as prime design initiator. His design authority is limited, however, to the augmentation of his tools. His tools—weaponry; their physical objective—killingry, the negative of livingry.

The historic pattern of weaponry is epitomized in the TV Western. The bad man draws first; the good man starts late but finishes first. The bad man is finished. Now comes the surprise. The range has been so increased, and the dueling has become so sophisticated, that both sides can get their effective shots in, and nobody wins.

Today's warhead travels at fifteen thousand miles per hour. With five thousand miles to go, it takes twenty minutes to reach its target. Man's eyes, augmented by radar, penetrate around the world at a velocity of six hundred million miles per hour. As he spots the warhead's takeoff in his direction, he has more than nineteen minutes in which to get his own warhead under way. There is ample time for each side to obliterate the other. Both "good" and "bad" man lose. Even the world political leaders realize that the pursuit of weaponry has reached absurdity.

When Sputnik was launched, it made the airplane obsolete as the number one weapon. In the half century of the airplane's weapon supremacy, two and one half trillion capital dollars invested by the world nations,[24] converted the highest scientific and technical capabilities of man into the historically most advanced phase of integrated, generalized, mass production tooled industry.

No private individuals, nor the massed credit potential of any group of private individuals, could have underwritten so astronomical an acceleration in the comprehensive industrial technology as was underwritten by the negative mandate articulated by the military. So vast was the production facility thus developed that in this short fifty-year span, all that had been technically scarce, and therefore on highest priority, became plentitudinous.

All the future jet plane production requirements for the swiftly developing world transport system, and all the future military rocket production, together can utilize less than ten percent of the industrial mass-production facility created to implement the airplane as the premier weapon. Much excess capacity is generalized.

---

24 **$2.5 trillion in 1960, adjusted for inflation using the Consumer Price Index (CPI), is $18.22 trillion in 2009 dollars.** http://www.bls.gov/data/inflation_calculator.htm (accessed July 15, 2009).

History's amalgam of total experience, its derived knowledge and wisdom as altogether converted to highest industrial mass productability and omni-distribution, has boiled over. Wealth, as the organized physical ability to deal successfully with forward evolutionary events, has attained almost infinite magnitude.

The "organized physical ability" means entire automation of world industry. This eventuality was always inherent in the intellectual pacing of industry. Its complete attainment is suddenly imminent. Marx's worker, the automaton, the muscle and reflex machine, is replaced by automation. Man, losing all significance as physical producer, becomes utterly essential to the industrial equation only as the regenerative consumer. The industrial wealth potential of automated production capability may only be realized by an anticipatorily designed, systematically established and credit-accounted matching consumer capacity. The efficiency of the industrial equation is directly proportional to the numbers consuming.

The political economy, winning and holding the largest proportion of the world's consumer population, can operate at the highest efficiency, at the lowest cost, while attaining the fastest rate of realized wealth augmentation.

The world's political leadership will now undertake the exploitation of the abundance of the "bestest" to win for its respective political camps the heretofore unserviced world customers of the industrial equation. But they will discover also that total world resources invested at the performance per pound level of presently designed livingry will serve only forty percent of the world's population.

To serve one hundred percent will involve a world design revolution, not just design of end-products, but of the comprehensive industrial network equations including world-around livingry-service systems, at regenerative occupancy rentals, mutably installed in anticipatory facilitation of total world enjoyment of individually respected total man. This comprehensive design will include not only the network means of production, distribution, maintenance, search, research and continual improvement of service, but also the continual, methodical withdrawal of progressively obsolete facilities tonnage, its reprocessing and recirculation at ever higher performance ratios per pounds of physical resource investment—together with design of the economic implementation of greater numbers of consumers to match the increasing tooled-up production capabilities, and together with designed consumer traffic patterning controls permitting higher frequencies and velocities of electively enjoyed services devoid of individual interference incidents and restraints.

Such designing has brilliant prototype precedent in the telephone system's anticipatorily successful and inherently regenerative physical network instrumentation evolution. The contact instruments of the world-around livingry services must be anticipatorily networked and its consumer-contact instruments and facilities must be installed at consumer request (not sold) for a nominal service fee. The network services utilized by the consumer through his contact equipment will be billed only "after the month" and after the provision of the accruing regenerative advantage realizations by the consumer, whereby the wealth may be established to refund the services in the accounting system designed into the comprehensive undertaking. The prime design must also provide for the orderly transfer of the world consumer population from the obsoleting worker payrolls to the world educational system's advanced search, research and vital regeneration functioning. Einstein's norm of constantly transforming evolutionary patterning must designedly replace Newton's now invalidated static norm.

Prime designing augments wealth. Wealth permits increased freedom of personal time investment. Prime design may multiply the alternate physical facilities for desirable anatomical, mental and cultural development. Desirable time investment alternatives inherently decrease over-all baby-making time. That explains "the rich getting richer and the poor getting children." Prime designing commands the fundamental solution of the over-population threat. As with all fundamental problems of man on earth fundamental solutions are not to be had by political reforms of either the peacetime prohibitory law enforcement variety, or of the never convincing wartime annihilation variety. Fundamental solutions are not for sale. Mass subscriptions to support professional do-gooders are futile.

Fortunately population explosion is only the momentary social hysteria's cocktail conversation game. Real population crisis is fundamentally remote. There is room enough indoors in New York City for the whole 1963 world's population to enter, with room enough inside for all hands to dance the twist in average nightclub proximity. There is ample room in the New York streets for one half of the world's population to amble about in, leaving enough room inside buildings for the other half to lie down and sleep. This would be a good moment to call for all scientists, engineers, tool makers, machine fitters, mechanics and aircraft pilots present, all of whom amount to less than one percent of humanity, and to send them out from New York City all around the world to get total automation of world production and services going. After this the world's population could start enjoying the whole earth as students, archeologists, playwriters, players, poets, artists, dancers, skin divers, tourists, etc. There would be no further muscle and animal reflex jobs to be done and no need to earn a living, for the living would be generated as effortlessly as apples grow on trees. If you want to go to work you just tell yourself to go to work, you can shovel beach sand from here to there with the beach-playing children, or you can go to work in the library and find out, if you can, how this miracle came about and how to keep it going. You will have plenty of work to do.

The comprehensive prime design scientist-artist poet will have to do a great deal of work to comprehend his task and to discover the most efficient and effective order of priority of his progressive sets of anticipatory escalator undertakings.

Only the free-wheeling artist-explorer, non-academic, scientist-philosopher, mechanic, economist-poet who has never waited for patron-starting and accrediting of his coordinate capabilities holds the prime initiative today. If man is to continue as a successful pattern-complex function in universal evolution, it will be because the next decades will have witnessed the artist-scientist's spontaneous seizure of the prime design responsibility and his successful conversion of the total capability of tool-augmented man from killingry to advanced livingry—adequate for all humanity.

14 The Architect as World Planner

I have had the good fortune to be invited to more than one hundred universities and colleges around the earth.[25] I have, therefore, a certain experience which may be of value in respect to subjects which are apparently of inspiration to architectural students. I am convinced that they have a greater interest in comprehensive world patterns than had my generation, for instance.

I am sure it is my study of world-patterning which has gained for me student interest and support. The essence of world problems, as I see it, is as follows:

At the first moment in history when economic data was coming in from all around the earth, Thomas Malthus, integrating that data, discovered that the world's people were multiplying their numbers more rapidly than they were producing goods to supply themselves. Malthus' discovery coincided with the moment when Darwin was discovering his theory of evolution and adopting his hypothesis that the evolution was predicated upon survival of the fittest. As a consequence, Malthus' pattern seemed to indicate survival of the fittest to be a scientific fact.

July 1961. This essay derives from a transcript of a talk by Fuller to the 6th Biennial World Congress of the International Union of Architects (UIA) in London. A version of it was first published in *Architectural Digest*, August 1961. The original transcript also includes a section published in Fuller's *Education Automation* (Carbondale, Ill., 1962; Baden: Lars Müller Publishers, 2010).

---

25 Fuller's own staff-published "Basic Biography" was a kind of comprehensive 72-page curriculum vitae, which was regularly updated. The March 1983 edition indicates "1,035 invited visits at 544 educational institutions."

Up to this moment in history, whether world societies fared well or ill had seemed to be a matter of fate or a whimsical decision of the gods. Suddenly the Malthusian law of survival became an apparent scientific fact which confronted the statesmen and political leaders of nations. From that moment on it seemed clearly a matter of "you or me," and the leaders of great nations felt it was their obvious mandated responsibility to be sure that it was not their nation that went down. At this moment in history the "you or me" motivation founded on Malthus constitutes the mainspring of world political policy and action.

The solutions under the Malthusian "you or me" lead into two main political categories:

1. Ruthless but often polite decimation of the unsupportable fractions, or leaving the unsupportable fractions to their unhappy fate.
2. Socialism, the theory of austerity for all and sharing of the inadequacy with slow approach to certain untimely mutual demise.

In view of the seeming scientific inexorability of the Malthusian concept, it comes as a great surprise that in this century a new pattern has emerged which not only questions the fundamental validity of the Malthusian and Darwinian theory, but even seems to promise their invalidation in economic and social domains.

At the turn of the century the technology of the industrial revolution was beginning to integrate, developing patterns of higher leverage in the doing of man's work than had been anticipated. As of 1900, less than one percent of humanity was participating in the high advantages of the industrial equation.

(I developed a physical measure of what I mean by participating in the industrial equation when I was technical consultant to Fortune magazine in 1938. When the equivalent of the work that could be done by two hundred human slaves was available and being used in electrical and other energy units in the industrial network by a human family of five members, I rated this family an industrial "have" family Figure 10.)

Figure 10

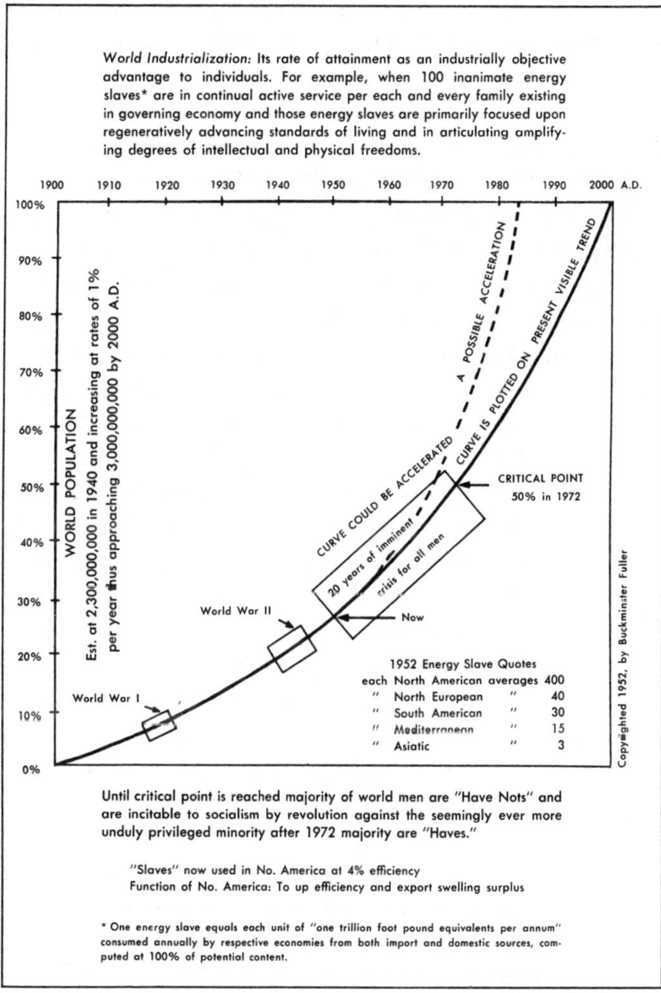

Have and Have-Nots chart by the author

Intertechnology gelling was occurring at such an important rate at the turn of the century that by 1914 and the beginning of World War I, the percentage of human family participating in the industrial network advantage had grown from less than one percent to six percent. It was unquestionably this swift integration of new levels of technology that emboldened the political world "outs" to challenge the political "ins" in World War I.

As World War II began, twenty percent of humanity was participating in the advantage of the industrial network. At the present moment approximately forty-four percent of humanity is participating in the higher advantages.

This emergence of the new pattern of man's advantage amplification rate may be news. (It is not surprising, because it is a discovery of my own and has not been widely published. The *New York Times* made mention of it in 1952.[26]) The curve of acceleration of those participating in industrialization indicates that the whole of the human family will be participating in the highest technical advantages before the end of the twentieth century, at a level of human satisfaction as yet not even dreamed of by any man.

To understand the surprising significance of this curve it must be understood that what I speak of as the industrial network embraces all the resources of the earth that enter into the establishment and maintenance of the industrial processes. As the percentage increased from one to forty-four, it meant that total organized world tonnage of metallic and metabolic resource utilization was supplying only one percent, then six percent, then forty-four percent. During this half century of industrialization, world's population has been increasing at a faster rate than additional resources have been discovered. That is, the ratio of world copper, mined or unmined, or of iron, mined or unmined, per capita, has been continually decreasing. Therefore this increase in numbers

26 Walter Dorwin Teague, "Gains of Industry Predicted for All: Engineer Tells Design Meeting World Should be Completely Industrialized by Year 2000," *New York Times*, June 26, 1952.

served has not been the result of the addition of more resources, but the consequence of the scientifically-designed multiplication of the performance per unit of invested resource. Transferring communication from wire to wireless is a typical means of doing more with less.

I am confident that architects will not claim that they were consciously engaged in coordinated improvement of this overall world performance pattern of resources use. This was not the declared policy of any nation. How then has it come about?

The answer is that it has been a by-product of the development of weaponry and the tools-to-make-tools investment to support that massive weaponry, with the fabulous capital investments for the weaponry predicated upon the Malthusian "you or me" concept. As each level of weaponry advance becomes obsoleted by a new level of attainment, the technology which arose to produce and support it at the obsoleting level then becomes available to world society for everyday technical-economic satisfactions.

The change in the world's standard of living, its utter change of man's ecological patterning from the 1900, local, on-foot sweep-out to the world-around sweep-out of 1961 has been, then, a second-hand by-product of the world's preoccupation with weaponry.

Two and a half trillion dollars[27] were invested by the nations of the earth in the subsidy of the airplane as a weapon in the first half century of the airplane. This amounts to sixty times the value of all the gold in the world. The two and a half trillion was a regenerative investing pattern employing the tooled wealth to create higher tooled capability and to inhibit more energy from world energy patterning by shunting that energy into man's industrial networks to apply it to the end of his larger levers. The accumulation is vast and has made gold utterly obsolete, as the wealth represented by industrial energy and tool capability and ever-improving know-how constitute the real wealth of the world.

27 See note 24, p. 325.

How did it happen that the native preoccupations of men in weaponry continually improved performance per unit of invested resource? It was because at that time the ability to carry the hitting power of the weaponry the greatest distance in the shortest time involved ships, and ships had limited displacement, due to Nature's pattern of floatability. Therefore, the design challenge was to produce the most powerful ship with the least weight invested in the ship, thus enabling it to carry the greatest load of weaponry and fuel to get it there fastest.

As we went from the ships of the sea to the ships of the air, the performance per pound of the equipment became of even higher importance than on the sea. Finally, with the breakthrough to rocketry, we see a transition of startling magnitude in speed, distance and energy load carried per weight of vehicle.

Architects know that neither they nor their patrons have ever been concerned with the weights of their buildings or with any ratings of performance per unit of weight investment. Neither the architects nor society know what buildings weigh. Society knows well, on the other hand, what the *Queen Mary*[28] and the Douglas DC-8[29] weigh; the public knows what their performance capabilities are. The world of housing, the world of architecture, has always been a world of dealing with the leftovers after the high-priority technologies had been applied to the weaponry.

The upping of the performance per pound of the world's resources for improving standards of living has never been a direct objective of the politicians or the military servants of the politicians. Gradually we have come to realize the startling quality of this emerging pattern of the improvement of the performance of the resources as applied secondarily to livingry of man.

This pattern indicates the inexorable realization of one hundred percent industrialization, and if left unattended, to be realized as a

---

28 See note 7, p. 77.

29 A DC-8 weighs 355,000 pounds at takeoff when completely full.

by-product of man's negative preoccupation, it means that it will be realized only through increasing successions of world emergencies of the kind which mankind now finds himself apparently helplessly enmeshed in.

Because the forward transformation of the resources from their going functions into other functions of higher performance represents a continual revolution in design, it is a pattern that could be anticipatorily mastered by man as designer, particularly mastered by a comprehension of the architect as the integrating designer in the era of great specialization.

If, however, architects and engineers, as has been their custom, wait for a patron to command their services before they engage in their designing practice, it is easy to see that neither the politician nor the industrialist nor any private patron will engage the architectural profession in this anticipatory design command of the resources investment and technical evolution, because the politico and the industrialist and the private patron are all as yet convinced of the inexorableness of the Malthusian "you or me" survival of the fittest.

I know the architectural profession is not only altruistic enough but is also prone to take the responsibility of comprehensive design anticipation and effectiveness. But research departments in their offices would be beyond the capacity of the architectural profession.

I have gradually realized through the years that there is a solution—to wit:

The architectural and engineering professions, governing the curricular policies of the university architectural schools, should tell the architectural faculties and students that they will foster and support comprehensive research and development within the architectural schools themselves where society has arranged for five-year sojourns of selected, high-capability, comprehensive-prone youth. The architectural professionals will from time to time rejoin the universities to participate in its research.

The architectural schools around the world should be asked by the International Union of Architects to initiate world design. (In April 1962, the executive committee of the I.U.A. officially adopted my proposal.)

15 World Planning

The entire world's industrial resources are now preoccupied in serving only forty-four percent of humanity with the advancing standards of living exclusively provided by the world's progressively enlarging and integrating industrial networks. Making the world's totally available resources serve one hundred percent of an exploding population may only be accomplished by a boldly accelerated design evolution which adequately increases the present over-all performance per units of invested resources. This is a task of radical technical innovation rather than political rationalization. It is a task which can only be accomplished by the world's architects, inventors and scientist-artists. The engineer has been deliberately trained by society to be an unquestionable authority: an engineer must not invent, for his authority is thus violated.

Since aircraft and space technology is already operating at high levels of performance per units of invested resources, the recent decade's realization that space can be enclosed for environment-controlling purposes with approximately one percent of the weight of resources at present employed by the conventional building arts for a given task, indicates that the conversion of the world resources from their present service of only forty-four percent to

1963. Prepared by Fuller for the 1963 Congress of the International Union of Architects (UIA) held in Cuba. As an American, Fuller was not permitted to go to Cuba and he presented this proposal to an international symposium held in Mexico City immediately after the Cuba meeting. The proposal is a project outline for Phase I of a "World Design Science Decade" and became the lead piece in *World Design Science Decade, 1965–1975: Document 1—Inventory of World Resources Human Trends and Needs* (Carbondale, Ill., 1963) by Fuller and John McHale.

service of one hundred percent of humanity is to be uniquely effected within the livingry arts in contradistinction to the weaponry arts. The latter alone up to this moment in history has been benefited directly by the highest science and technology. Any and all improvements in the home front's peace extending livingry advantage have been post-weaponry byproducts.

This brings the solution of the forward livingry design problems into direct focus as the responsibility of the architect (as the only technical profession concerned with "putting things together" in an era of the increased fractionation by intensive specialization). Since the practicing architect may operate only when funded by a client and there is no apparent client to retain the architect to solve this world problem, it may only be solved by the world architects taking the initiative, as have the medical scientists, in the development of a comprehensive anticipatory design science dedicating at least its next ten years to making the total world's resources serve one hundred percent of humanity at higher standards of living than hitherto experienced by any men through competent industrially producible design—rather than leaving the evolutionary advance to political reforms catalyzed by accelerating frequency of world political crises. Because the economics of the architectural profession, at present, precludes the devotion of adequate time and resources to the solution of this task by the graduate practicing architects, it is in evidence that the architectural profession may activate this comprehensive anticipatory design initiative through encouragement of its professional university schools of architecture to invest the extraordinary intellectual resources and available student time within the universities to the establishment of the design science and its application to world-planning. This could be inaugurated with a ten-year sequence of joined world architectural schools' annual programs organized for the progressive discovery and design solution of the comprehensive family of economic, technical and scientific factors governing such a world-planning program.

Several dramatically communicated solutions come immediately to mind, such as the use of the total facade of a skyscraper or a mountain cliff. The following is an example of a satisfactory solution: the design of a two-hundred-foot diameter Miniature Earth. This Minni-Earth could be fabricated of a light metal trussing. Its interior and exterior surfaces could be symmetrically dotted with ten million small variable intensity light bulbs and the lights controllably connected up with an electronic computer. The whole Minni-Earth array could be suspended by fine high-strength alloy wires from masts surrounding Minni-Earth and at some distance from it. If the sphere were suspended two hundred feet above the ground, the wires would become invisible and it would seem to hover above the earth as an independent asteroid At a two-hundred-foot distance away from the viewer, the light bulbs' sizes and distance apart would become indistinguishable, as do the size and distances between the points in a fine half tone print. Patterns introduced into the bulb matrix at various light intensities, through the computer, would create an omni-directional spherical picture analogous to that of a premium television tube, but a television tube whose picture could be seen all over its surface both from inside and outside not as a "framed" picture.

Information could be programmed into the computer, and "remembered" by the computer, regarding all the geographical features of the earth, or all those geographical features under a great variety of weather conditions. How exquisite the geographical data may be is appreciated when we realize that if we use the 35-millimeter contact prints of the photographs taken by the aerial surveyors at their lowest altitude of operation, in which individual houses, as homes of men, may be discerned by the naked eye, and paste them together edge-to-edge on a sphere large enough to accommodate them in their respective geographical positions, that sphere would be two hundred feet in diameter–the size of our hypothetical Minni-Earth. Man on earth, invisible to man even from the height of two thousand feet, would be able to see the whole earth and at true scale in respect to the works and habitat of man. He could pick out his own home. Thus Minni-Earth becomes a potent symbol of man visible in universe.

Man recognizes a very limited range of motions in the spectrum of motion. He cannot see the motions of atoms, molecules, cell growth, hair or toenail growth; he cannot see the motion of planets, stars and galaxies; he cannot see the motions of the hands of the clock. Most of the important trends and surprise events in the life of man are invisible, inexorable motion patterns creeping up surprisingly upon him. Historical patterns too slow for the human eye and mind to comprehend, such as changing geology, population growths and resource transpositions, may be comprehensively introduced into the computer's memory and acceleratingly pictured around the surface of the earth.

The total history of world population's progressive positionings, waxings and wanings, individual and popular migrations and redeployments could be presented and run off acceleratingly in minutes, disclosing powerful eastward, westward, northward and southward swirlings, thickenings and thinnings, with a center of gravity momentum of such trendings permitting the computer to surge ten or one hundred years ahead providing reasonable probability for the planner-designer's anticipatory advantage. So could all the patterns of man's removal from the earth's crust of the various minerals, their progressive forwardings and temporary lodgings in various design occupations—such as in buildings, ships, railway systems and factories and their progressive meltings-out and scrapped drifting into new design formulations in other tasks and other geographies.

Our hypothetical Minni-Earth, which the world architectural students may if they wish employ as their design facility, should be located as a major world city's focal design structure, analogous to the Eiffel Tower in Paris, as a continuing feature of World Olympic Games, to be reinstalled at each successive world site.

Or Minni-Earth might be suspended from masts mounted on the ring of rocks in midstream of New York City's East River, one quarter mile distant from the great east face of the United Nations building, to serve as a constant confronter of all nations' representatives of the integrating patterns, both expected and unexpected, occurring around the face of man's constantly shrinking "one-town world."

Designs should provide for computer housing remote from the sphere, and for ferries, bridges, tunnels or other approaching means to a position two hundred feet below the Minni-Earth's surface from which point mechanical means, such as elevators, will transport large numbers of people upward and into the sphere to a platform at the Minni-Earth's center from which, at night, individuals would be able to view stars in the heavens seen through the lacy openings of the Minni-Earth, giving them the same orientation that they would obtain if they could go to the center of the real earth and could look out with X-ray vision to see those very same stars seemingly fixed above specific geographical points of the earth. (A star seen in zenith over Budapest from the center of Minni-Earth could be checked by telephone with real Budapest as in zenith over that city at that very moment.) A press of a button would show the Minni-Earth central observer the position of all the satellites which men have now sent aloft and, though their circling of the earth is as slow as the circling of the hands of the clock and is therefore invisible, the touch of another button could accelerate their motions so that their total interactions and coursings for a period of years to come could be witnessed in a minute. (A bank of cloud lying apparently motionless in America's vast Grand Canyon was photographed over a long period of time by a cinecamera and the resultant picture accelerated into a one-minute sequence. To the surprise of the original viewers of the seemingly still scene a very regular pattern of waves such as those on the surface of a coffee cup in a railway dining car was seen to occur in the cloud surface between the Canyon walls.)

If the students choose to employ Minni-Earth as their facility, they will find the United Nations rich in economic, demographic and sociologic data. They will find the latest publications on the International Geophysical Year rich in data that may be dramatically displayed on Minni-Earth—for instance, an accelerated historical sequence of all the world's earthquakes would give startling indications of further recurrences. The world's electromagnetic field patterns, the varying astrophysical patterns would each provide spectacular Minni-Earth displays.

The students should consider their Minni-Earth as a twenty-four-hour visual phenomenon, in contradistinction to the conceiving of buildings as visible only in the daylight, a viewpoint which has recently been compromisingly altered by secondary lighting at night. The Minni-Earth should disclose the world news and events on a twenty-four-hour basis, its patterns being altered periodically for the disclosure of the longtime weather history integrated with the present forecasting.

The students will be greatly advantaged by the development of models of Minni-Earth at their own schools which could range from ten millimeters to thirty meters in diameter. Photographs of data arrays on their models would be appropriate for their final project forwarding to the U.I.A. Congress exhibition.

In the development of the research for and design solution of this world pattern inventorying facility, the usual procedure in respect to architectural problems may, with the approval of the schools' professors, be altered so that the students will co-ordinate their activities as a team, meeting daily to consider the whole progress of the undertaking, but deploying to perform their complementary missions in economic, technical, etc., data-procurement and information-gathering, processing and design realizations.

In the same way, within any one country, the schools might profitably divide up the many tasks in a manner appropriate to the special kinds of information most available in their respective localities or universities. If the students are willing, the advantages of team coordination might be instituted between countries. The expansion of the rate at which the team coordination advantage might enter into the ten successive years of the world-planning and design phases may develop its own logical pace, and students or universities electing to research and design the entire programs themselves would undoubtedly demonstrate unique advantages accruing to concentrated effort and would also serve as experimental controls for comparison with the results accruing to widely distributed coordinate team functioning.

The first year's design program of all individuals, university teams, continental or intercontinental teams should all include prominent citation of the second and *sequitur* years looming high priority design problems most evidently essential to the accelerated adaptation of man to his evolutionary trendings through comprehensive anticipatory design science.

The professors of universities or schools will establish the detailed programs themselves which will be proposed to their students. The time dedicated to the study of the project will be fixed by the program. It depends upon the organization of each school's teamwork.

The international program does not prescribe any particular drawing to provide; the choice is left to the professors. It is the same thing for the scale of these designs. The projects may be presented either in original drawing, or in any other way, under the condition that the sizes are kept (panels or shoots of 100 cm x 100 cm)—totaling two square meters rather than separate panels. The documents (drawings, photos, etc.) will be stuck on rigid panels (Isorel, light metal, or any other light material). The respective schools or students would be permitted to divide their total two square meters of surface into microfilm increments totaling that amount, and would consequently have to plan to install an automatic sequence-operating microfilm projector at the next U.I.A. Congress exhibition of the students' work.

In the advanced technology which this world-planning program is meant to employ in direct benefit to livingry, the parts production tolerances are held to sub-visible dimensions ranging from one-thousandth to one ten-millionth of an inch. Unlike present architectural practices, wherein prints of detailed drawings are translated by masons and carpenters into components with one-fourth inch errors tolerated, the advanced technology makes conceptually schematic drawings with schedules only of dimensions between theoretical points. The dimensioning is subsequently scheduled into the production work by instruments and indexing machines, controlling dimensions far below man's direct discernment. For the bold new design evolution to win the initiative in employment of the world's prime resources on behalf of livingry from its preoccupation in weaponry, will require the architectural students not only to employ the most advanced scientific designing techniques, but also to adopt a progressive, comprehensive education in mathematics, physics, chemistry, economics, sociology and general history.

The ten-year world-planning and design programming should at all times be considered in the light of its regenerative potentials. As with the calculus, we cannot ascertain the second derivative's challenging prospect until we have differentiated our way through the first phases. It may be assumed that the first year's work when finally presented at the U.I.A. Congress will not only be of interest to world architects and students but that the results of their work will, for the first time, catalyze world attention and recognition of the significance and potentials of their enterprise. The regenerative consequences will probably be of surprising magnitude.

16 The Long Distance Trending in Pre-Assembly

The advantages of producing and assembling precision mechanics under critically controlled conditions has long been obvious in respect to the production of instruments, machinery in general and, in the last half century, of large complex machines such as automobiles, trucks and giant aircraft. Large complex structures and mechanics have been produced under favorable local conditions as ships in shipyards. The true beginnings of what we know today as mass production, can be seen in the ancient shipyards of Venice. Here we discover not only the cradle for the ship mounted on seaward-inclined rails which will employ gravity in the eventual launching of the massive assembly, but also a complex of feeder railways, gantry cranes and other means for bringing large sub-assemblies from ships around the shipyard, within which shops under highly controlled atmospheres, the various uniquely differentiated fundamental components of the ultimate ship, are produced.

The earliest shipyards included rope warping buildings, iron foundries, great steel forges, chain-making shops, spar and frame-making shops, frame bending within special steam-box as typical environmental controls, sail lofts, design-pattern lofts, drafting and engineering shops, and machine shops. All of these fine component shops were fed from the hinterland and (in times of national emergency or moments of high national enterprise in

---

March 1962. First published in *Architectural and Engineering News.*

sending its ships to foreign lands) almost exclusively exhausted the total weaving, metal-working, woodworking, mining and other craft resources of the nation.

Only the ship itself, when she was a big one, was assembled out-of-doors. Big pieces were brought swiftly into place with cranes and soon the workmen were busy inside the ship where they could no longer be impeded by the rains, winds, snow, dust and other unfavorable conditions. Small ships were built entirely inside building sheds—that is, under essentially controlled conditions, shielding the worker and his work from excessive sunlight, rain, snows and dust clouds.

When the ship had been completed on the railway, her cradle was unblocked and she slid into the sea—that is, she was delivered into her ultimate service environment. All the stresses and loadings that had been highly concentrated by design into the ribs and further concentrated by the rib ends into the keel, and distributed from the keel by the snow-shoe-like cross-rails below the keel, resting on earth, upon reaching the water became almost uniformly distributed loads by virtue of hydraulic emersion and the even water displacement by the pneumatic structure which the shell containing air-space of the hull now constituted.

From this point on the ship was advantaged by the distributed loads and could carry enormous cargoes despite great buffeting by the sea and winds due to the total pneumatic hydraulic flexibility and load dispersion. Ships were then endangered only by the possibility of highly reconcentrated loadings, such as impact with a rock or another ship or other inert mass.

When the hull had been safely launched in the ancient shipyard, it was moved around to the outfitting dock—often a tide-dammed basin. Here the ship received its mast, spars, rigging, and all its secondary equipment. In many of the shipbuilding ports there was a scarcity of suitable mast timber. The fibers available to make the sails in most of the shipbuilding countries were relatively inferior in tensile and wearing properties, so also the rope fibers. When the ships had been rigged with the relatively inferior equipment of their national resource, they took on cargoes and proceeded in effect around the world, docking in country after country, trading their cargoes and taking on new and superior masts and spars, sails and ropes in the countries around the earth where these resources were notably at their finest. They took on excess cargoes of these superior components.

When the ship came into the home port, she was "gallant" beyond memory and dream. Thus, the ships became regenerative, bringing back the more able components for the building of more able ships, under the economically preferable controlled conditions of the home yard and its networked linkage to the organized home resources. The overland railway was an extension of the marine railway. The shipyard's donkey-engines were mounted on carriages. The load-distributing capability of the rails and crossties made possible the launching of the steam-engine-equipped "ship" back upward onto the land, to reach the inland resources.

The resource linking network plus mass production under controlled conditions in the shipyard and finally the moving of the total assembly complex from position to position around the world, to receive additional components, altogether became the fundamental prototype of modern industrial mass production. This was the scheme that Henry Ford employed. It involved the total control of natural resources from mine to in-service functioning.

Fundamental to this history is the fact that Nature had provided a means for floating large complex assemblies by the displacement principle. Because there was a fundamental limit of weight displacement for a given ship, the designers of the ship were confronted with the task of providing an assembly which could operate successfully under maximum hostility of Nature, in effect designing for the exploitation of the hurricanes, for seaquakes severer than land-quakes, for daily avalanches when mammoth seas curled over on the decks, for daily flood—in fact for all the conditions which threaten landed structures less frequently.

Because there was a limit of displacement, the designer had to develop high performance capability for specific structures and mechanical tasks. He ratioed the weight of resources invested to relative limits of capability. To make the sea venture worthwhile, minimum weight had to be invested in the sea-keeping capabilities, in order to invest a majority of displacement in wealth generating cargo.

With the development of the nonfloating airplane and the expenditure of part of the cargo as energy, to angularly drag the airfoil aloft to obtain its additional lifting power, the performance per pound requirements of the airplane became far more exacting than in the case of the sea ships. Because of shipbuilding's long tradition in producing higher performance per pound, out of world-around occurring resources, the shipbuilders' techniques were adopted by the aircraft industry. Aircraft were originally designed in the terms of "water-lines," and the mathematical "stations" of shipbuilding. Aircraft design was translated through the same "lofting" techniques. The heavier-than-air ship moved down the controlled environments production line, receiving its world-around-originating high capability components and was launched from the airstrip into its ultimate load-distributing medium, the air.

If we except tents, shacks and temporary hutments, we may state categorically that permanent buildings on the land were evolved in an entirely different logic. Buildings on the land were designed for permanence and therefore to withstand attacks of living enemies as well as attacks of weather and time. Permanent buildings developed essentially as fortresses and in order to be permanent even as storages, had to be fashioned of stone. Wooden ships could last long enough to make great wealth out of a few voyages. Ships had had the high priority technology, and the homes and shops in which the components of the ships were fashioned could be evolved from simple fortuitous building technique long since enjoyed without benefit of engineers or scientists in which materials not good enough for the ships would do for the shop buildings. Piling up of stone or wood or earth without thought of performance per pound, where inertia was a fortification virtue, resulted in the building arts being practiced without design reference to performance per pound ratios. All that men asked of their landed buildings was that they should last through siege and time—they did not design them for earthquakes or floods and when the latter came their buildings were devastated or unoccupiable.

Large buildings may not be centrally produced under highly preferred conditions without compromising their over-all organic conformation, if they have to be delivered over highways and railways, because of grade negotiating requirements of land transports, for they must penetrate mountains through tunnels and bridges. When the ship of the sea went up onto the land as the railway, its shaping was extruded into a "linkage of sausages" whose occupancy by human beings was characterized by jolt-and-joggle walking of its occupants through distinctly uncomfortable conditions. The American trailer, or its European counterpart caravan, is an extruded or elongated package of mechanics derived directly from the newest technology of the sea and air, but is frustratingly uncomfortable due to the bridge-negotiating function of its overland delivery. The only way in which large buildings or large building sub-assemblies can be delivered to occupation sites without organic confirmation compromise is through air delivery transcending bridges and tunnels.

There is another way in which buildings could be delivered overland, and that is if they were designed to be foldable, like an umbrella, without compromising the organic design. I have designed foldable buildings which are self-openable, which could be delivered overland or within the design requirement confirmation of rockets for delivery to the moon, or our own earth's mountain tops. All field assembly of structures brings about excruciating in-economies.

Radar enclosing plastic fiberglass D.E.W. Line radomes flown to their Arctic sites were assembled by Eskimos or others unfamiliar with such assembly, in an average of fourteen hours per radome. When assembled in New York City for an exhibition of the Museum of Modern Art, they required one month assembly time by so-called skilled labor, together with months of negotiation with the New York Building Department regarding their structural safety—despite their having successfully withstood Arctic storms of severities never occurring in New York City.

In 1954 the United States Marine Corps airlifted with a helicopter a thirty-foot-diameter geodesic dome having floor space meeting the minimum one-family U.S. dwelling requirements thus avoiding field assembly in-economies. The Marine Corps delivered this dome at a speed of sixty knots. Two years later the Marine Corps successfully flew fifty-five-foot three-helicopter hangers from aircraft carriers to the land at sixty knots. These hangars had two thousand square feet of floor space. In 1960 one-hundred-and-fourteen-foot diameter geodesic domes of ten thousand square feet of floor space, or approximately one fourth of an acre, were successfully delivered by air at sixty knots by one helicopter per dome. Plotting the curve of square foot floor sizes of geodesic domes, progressively air-deliverable at sixty knots in the last six years, discloses a curve of accelerating capability, indicating that by 1970 we will be successfully air-delivering stadium-covering domes of fifteen acres clear-span floor area by one airship at sixty knots.

Studies have been made of the delivery of large sub-assemblies of structural components for a two-mile diameter dome, which showed that a two-mile diameter dome could be assembled in six months by helicopter. The intelligence as well as direct statement by Russian engineers to this author, indicate that the Russians will, in the 1960s, begin to make air delivery and air drops of whole geodesic domed Arctic cities in one day.

A decade of geodesic structures which has seen almost two thousand domes,[30] mostly air-delivered into forty countries around the earth, has demonstrated that space may be enclosed and safely insulated against Nature's most hostile or unfavorable conditions, at approximately one percent of the weight of structure heretofore employed by the conventional building arts for a given volume. During this same period, the great automobile industry, which derived from the ship and airplane, building technology, have been giving larger and larger attention to the manufacture of the mechanics of living—refrigerators, washing machines, electric generators, heat exchangers, chemical process machinery, etc.

The present space age race finds billions of research dollars going into the problem of how to service the human metabolic process cycle under autonomously operating remote space requirements. This high priority science has for the first time in history been applied to a closed chemical circuit of ecologic sanitation and metabolic patterning of human life, not as curative but as anticipatory development of optimum environment conditions for protracted sustainment of high standard living of moon-rounding men. The combined effect of the space technology's autonomous living package and the automobile industry's engagement in livingry devices clearly indicate that the coming decade will see the mass production of autonomous living mechanics for use on earth with approximately exclusive air delivery of such mechanics to the air-delivered environment controls being distributed around the earth.

It is only when we realize that the changes about to take place around the earth in respect to the livingry arts, are emanating from the space technology and air-ship production and not from the old building arts, that we realize the changes ahead are as swift and abrupt as the change in our man-patterning on earth—from a

30 According to Fuller, by 1983 there were over 300,000 geodesic domes built throughout the world. Fuller's "Basic Biography," March 1983 (see note 25, p. 331).

century ago's on-foot and on-horseback to our present around-the-world, jet-flown physical sweepout and around-the-world witnessing events through television—all emanating from the weaponry industry originating scientific technology.

Unquestionably, the old building arts will persist in many ways and in special tasks for a long time. Realization by architects and engineers, scientists, lawyers and artists that one hundred percent of humanity could be serviced at higher standards of living than any men have yet known by the total industrial resources of the earth, rather than the forty percent that are now so advantaged if man applies the high performance per pound capabilities of the aircraft industry to that task, is not only inevitable of discovery but inevitable of swift realization. If man does not apply this excess high performance capability to his livingry, the economic machinery of world industrialization will break down.

There will be many economic and political crises in the immediate future out of which it is safe to predict will emerge a world society intent upon converting its history-long experience and "survival-of-the-fittest-only" pattern to one of comprehensive physical success of man on earth. There will always be problems ahead-problems are the essential catalysts of growthful life. The problems of tomorrow will not be predominantly physical but predominantly problems of intellectual integrity.

17 The Future

All mature people are now aware of the constantly accelerating rate of evolutionary transformation engulfing all humanity. The speed factor, however, is only of relatively minor significance in the complex overall process of transformation of man's universal experience and the consequent regenerative evolution of man's day-to-day unfolding thought patterns, their induced new initiatives and realistically followed-through preoccupations. Not the least of the new preoccupations is that of dealing with historically unprecedented magnitudes of multiplying wealth of productive capability.

In earlier yesterdays, the success of a nation meant personal economic success for only a few individuals. The immediate yesterdays' Western nations' joint prosperity, and particularly the economic success of crossbreeding world man on the American continent, has been historically phenomenal in the degree of its wide distribution of unprecedentedly high economic and technical advantage to the vast majority of its individuals.

The immediate yesterdays' most successful people are also those most humanly prone to stretch the after-image of the happenstance under which their success was realized beyond its economically

---

September 27, 1962. The original is an open letter from Fuller to "His friends amongst the university presidents, and deans and amongst heads of business and government establishments," which was to accompany advance copies of his *Education Automation* and *No More Secondhand God*, shortly thereafter to be released by Southern Illinois University Press. Deleted from the published version was the closing of the letter that addressed a comprehensive film documentation of Fuller "in development of these same thoughts" then being embarked upon by S.I.U.

valid limits. As a total consequence we now have world democracy potentially emergent at the historically highest level of economic and cultural effectiveness, yet momentarily becalmed in a doldrum stupor of mass-reproduced, world-around, split-second broadcast, news nonsense, serialized myths and obsolete local-focus hocus-pocus. Though Madison Avenue's advertisingly cherished, most desirable prototype of the U.S.A. citizen is purportedly the son of nine pioneering generations of an old and familiar local family and a permanent home-owning, geographically rooted fellow, today's typical Concord-Lexington, newspaper romanced minuteman resident is an M.I.T. professor, born in Budapest, high-schooled in Brooklyn, Ph.D.'ed at Stanford University, and off tomorrow for a post in Nigeria or a way station to the moon, and that new instant minuteman-American-crossbreed is indeed the prototype of tomorrow's scientist-world-citizen. With the exception of a swiftly dwindling minority of stay-putter residents, plus those who make a political business of staying put in order to exploit yesteryear's theoretically logical, and today's unrealistic persistence of a geographically based federal and state governmental representation of the democratic electorate. The widely ranging average U.S.A. family, as the federal census figures show, now leaves town *for good* every four years which is just about the time of the next election and will soon be leaving town permanently every three years. The average U.S. citizen's ecological acceleration is such that he will soon be disenfranchised for lack of adequate tenure of any fixed residence and that will make a "fine howdy-do"; out of it will finally emerge a dynamic, electronically articulate, constant world-democracy referendum whose computer-integrated voice and evolutionary wisdom will be stunning to all of yesterday's ignorant inertia and brilliantly competent in synchronized growth. Momentarily, democracy is walking, even running, in its sleep while minority-dictated political and economic world organizations push-pull it hither and yon. In concert with millions of other individuals, I am intent upon breaking out from our cocoon of impotence.

I am convinced that the breakout may only be effected by an intellectual reorientation and not by political revolution or world warring. *Ergo,* the following reconnaissance:

A half century ago the fundamental differences between Isaac Newton's universal norm of "at rest" and Albert Einstein's universal norm of "constant change" were only of academic interest. Today the economic significance of the replacement of "at rest" by "constant change" as the everyday normal condition upsets almost all of the traditionally practical stratagems of mankind. Yesterday the disruptive was abhorred; today it is welcomed not only by the intuitions of the young world, but also by the managers of mass production wheels. Yesterday's "square shooter" is today a boresome "square," which does not mean that our young world lacks or eschews integrity. It means that the young world's integrity is so trustworthy that it has been willing to jettison static security in favor of recognition of Einstein's dynamic norm. Yesterday's "rolling stones" who gathered no moss, meaning money, are today's big wheels receiving $250,000-a-year[31] salaries for keeping the changes in their corporate machines in constant evolutionary transformation at a rate anticipatorily synchronized with the generally accelerating total evolution of man's patterning in universe. Yesterday's moon shooters were lunatics. Today's lunatics have the highest academic standing and highest priority ratings in our regenerative investment economics.

Yesterday's symmetrical poesy and ecstatically violined liltings have become today's "corn," not because the young world has lost one wave length from its range of receptive tunability to the evolution regenerating universal energizations, but because the young world has found asymmetry as stimulating as symmetry; and in fact, that the spectrum range of human tunability is considerably greater than had hitherto been operatively accredited by man. The

31 **$250,000 in 1962, adjusted for inflation using the Consumer Price Index (CPI), is $1.79 million in 2009 dollars.** http://www.bls.gov/data/inflation_calculator.htm (accessed July 15, 2009).

young world has found the strange radiation doings vaguely identified by the word love to be equally present in the minor mode of music as in the major mode, and equally as effective in African drum-beats as in Viennese three-quarter time, and as equally effective in blue jeans as in black velvet and lace. The young world's emergent language as well as its thought is far more universal than yesterday's. Our young world realizes that Rudy Vallee's "If You Were the Only Girl in the World and I Were the Only Boy" is not only exclusive nonsense, but that realistically sustained happiness and welfare for anyone is utterly dependent upon the sustained happiness and welfare of the many.

The major significance of all the evolutionary symptoms of youth is that almost all of yesterday's fundamentally held and practical everyday causes and their resultantly adopted stratagems are obsolete; therefore, it is reasonable to suppose that, despite their venerated status, a large part, if not all, of our educational institutions and their disciplines are obsolete.

Better than ninety-nine percent of modern technology occurs in the realm of physical phenomena that is sub or ultra to the range of human visibility—for example, the dynamically operating functions of the transactions of information-processing within the black boxes of visibly wired static circuitry are entirely invisible. The invisible transactions oftentimes result in visual transformation of our environment. We can see the telephone wires, but not the conversations taking place therein. We can see the metal parts of airplanes or rockets gleaming in the sun, but there is nothing to tell us how relatively strong those metals are in comparison to other metals. Aluminum alloys as structural metals are commercially available which vary in strength so widely that some varieties are twice as strong, some four times as strong, and some eight times as strong as one class of aluminum. None of these varieties can be told from the other by the human senses, not even by scientists skilled in metallurgy, when unaided by instruments. The differences are invisible.

World society has throughout its millions of years on earth made its judgments upon visible, tangible, sensorially demonstrable criteria. We may safely say that the world is keeping its eye on the unimportant, visible one percent of the historical transformation, while missing the significance of the ninety-nine percent of overall, unseen changes. Forms are inherently visible and no longer can "forms follow functions," because the significant functions are invisible.

That era of essentially visible "modernism" is over. The architecture of superficial "functionalism" is meaningless and dead. What usually we speak of as our everyday world is a stage set with visible props which are easily manipulated by ignorant people to exploit the equal ignorance of others. The unreliable, uninformative and often deliberately misinformative scenery of that stage is soon to be radically altered due to the inexorable trendings in the sub- or ultra-visible alterations of man's relationship to universe.

The alterations are being made by scientists who are specialists, each preoccupied only with his special local evolutionary events. There are very few men today who are disciplined to comprehend the totally integrating significance of the ninety-nine percent invisible activity which is coalescing to reshape our future. There are approximately no warnings being given to society regarding the great changes ahead. There is only the ominous general apprehension that man may be about to annihilate himself. To the few who are disciplined to deal with the invisibly integrating trends it is conceptually probable that man will not destroy himself. Instead, it is increasingly readable in the trends that man is about to become almost one hundred percent successful as an occupant of universe.

As a consequence of fortunate circumstances, I found myself exploring in comprehensive anticipatory design science as a generalization of weapons systems design science to which I had been exposed at the United States Naval Academy almost a half century ago. Weapons systems and their subordinate arts of logistics, ballistics and navigation are founded both separately and jointly upon the sciences of incisive prognostication. I have invested the last third of a century of my time in that scientific inquiry and have had enough success in comprehensive trend analysis to make major predictions without fear of misleading those who listen to me.

As I am not a professional entertainer, I do not make predictions just to provide "conversation pieces." I will only make predictions to those who take the trouble either to read or to listen to the logic which leads to those predictions and thus may assess capably their validity.

If my education-automation's trend analysis and prognostication holds good, those university architectural departments that have the foresight to organize their capabilities in such a manner as to implement the general trends cited will find their departments going from the bottom rungs of the university's budget-priority ladder to the topmost rung. This transition will be as sudden and as swift as it is surprising.

The utterly revised education of the architect will be such as to adequately prepare successful students to operate on their own initiative and not as the economic slaves of technically illiterate clients; and on their own initiative to deal both comprehensively and in effective depth in mathematics, chemistry, physics, biology, geology, industrial tooling, network systems, economics, law, business administration, medicine, astronautics, computers, general systems theory, patents and the whole gamut of heretofore highly specialized subjects.

The revised architectural education will fit the graduating architect to take over in due course the functions of yesterday's patron despots and economic dictators and, on the architect's own initiative, to effectively integrate and develop the significance of all the information won by all the respective disciplines of the specialized sciences and humanities.

The successful architectural training of that period soon to come will be such as to ready the architectural graduates to convert all the subjectively harvested and integrated information into objectively operating, technical advantages for world society in completely tooled-up and well organized comprehensive, anticipatory livingry systems. Up to now killingry systems, or weaponry systems, alone have been advantaged by the totally integrated, highest physical and scientific capabilities of man and his economically organized world energy, materials and money resources.

Weaponry systems consist of vast complexes, such as battleships, cruisers, destroyers, submarines, aircraft carriers and the carried aircraft, guns, ammunition, and the supporting line of supply ships and the whole of the weapons and ammunition-manufacturing industry—all supremely commanded by one highest authority—the commercial or political masters of the moment, the prime architects of the successive chapters of history. In a manner similar to the past evolution in weaponry systems the new, architect-designed, world-around, livingry systems will be realized in progressive, economic-industrial-plan increments predicated upon pyramidal reinvestments of the forward years' regeneratively amplifying and progressive techno-economic advantages.

18 Continuous Man

The tentative encouragement in the direction of large geodesic domes for Europe and Asia experienced by recent observers, coincides with similar encouraging experiences which I have had. Many occurred during my most recent European travel. Largest encouragement is found, however, in my increasing communications. These accrue partially to my three around-the-world trips and to my 233 visits at 123 world universities[32] and news of geodesic dome developments. Most especially they accrue to my conceptual planting in the fertile minds of voluntary students. A "Dymaxion" educated generation has now developed a working conviction of the comprehensive validity of my viewpoint, which was to them at first only theoretical. Their own protracted and maturing post-graduate experience has witnessed multiplying realizations of Dymaxion concepts reduced to going economic practices all around the world.

In 1927 I published my conviction that two billion new era premium technology-dwelling devices would be needed within this century, requiring a whole new world-encompassing service industry. I predicted that it would take a quarter of a century to establish that new industry. In 1952, right on theoretical schedule, the Ford Motor Company was the first purchaser of my geodesic

January 1960. The original is a letter written by Fuller to a "Dear 'X,'—a leading U.S.A., industrialist."

32 See note 25, p. 331.

domes, which were the prototypes of the new era premium technology structures. By 1962, I was able to count over two thousand of my structures in forty countries.[33] The growth curve, slow in starting, is now rising in marked acceleration.

World-around employment of geodesic domes and autonomously packaged living mechanics now read clearly on my trend curves as the most powerful of immediately-future economic growths. That growth will be in acceleration for a half century. It then will level off at a steady rate of replacement evolution.

However, the present crux of domestic problems in respect to large geodesic domes is the high cost of installation. While welding operations on some types involve skilled labor at the site, most geodesic domes, including the Kaiser dome, do not require skilled labor at the site. In most geodesic dome cases, all the skill goes into the calculations, planning, and the development of unique tools, and the unique tools reproduce the unique end products, preferably within carefully controlled environmental conditions. If geodesic strategies of installation are properly designed, they do not even require importantly experienced scaffolding and rigger men at site. Best are the air-delivered domes.

The first U.S. Information Administration's nine-thousand-square-foot floor space, one hundred feet in diameter. International Trade Fair Geodesic Pavilion of aluminum tubing and outwardly stretched nylon-neoprene skin, was shipped in June 1956 by one airplane over the Atlantic to Kabul, Afghanistan, from Raleigh, North Carolina. It then was flown to New Delhi, to Burma, to Bangkok, to Tokyo, to Osaka, to Manila and then hack across the Pacific to South America. Since that time a number of similar international trade fair domes, each accompanied by one of our Geodesics, Inc. engineers, have been air-delivered, each entirely in one airplane, complete with scaffolding and erection tools—to Poznan, Poland; Milan, Italy; Salonika, Greece; Istanbul,

33 See note 30, p. 353.

Turkey; Tunis, Tunisia and a number of other European, African and Asian cities.

In approximately every instance, these domes were erected at their respective foreign trade-fair sites by completely unskilled native labor in less than forty-eight hours. They were color-coded for erection in any language; required no more than the ability to put nuts on bolts and match colors. The natives often thought they were building a cubical building and were amazed to find they had contrived a spherical structure.

Because the men erecting buildings have been historically associated by the public with the unique skills essential to old building, the public in each of the places where these domes have been erected have patted their own citizenry on the back for demonstrating the skill of erecting so unique and surprising a structure as the geodesic dome in so short a time. Pleased by the esteem, the native assemblers began to believe themselves geodesic experts. It followed logically that if they were responsible for the dome's fashioning that the dome must be a "native" art. Geodesic domes were declared in Afghanistan to be modern yurts of aluminum struts and nylon skins. Thus also it has happened in many of the countries, that the people, unaware of like events in other lands, have claimed the geodesic structures to be logical modern manifestations of their own unique native architecture. This was the result of my designing a generalized structure (which, to be called generalized, must be found true in every special case).

The United States Department of Commerce purchased the domes simply because of their low cost and last-minute availability to a headache foreign budget and had considered them to be only bad weather-excluding quick space controls. They were completely surprised to discover that the domes also had a unique social kudos factor. So greatly did the geodesic kudos factor multiply that it showed up in the foreign trade-fair experience as the prime local friends-winning factor.

When the Department of Commerce found we were to have our United States exhibit at Moscow, it decided that the geodesic dome would become the ace card in playing the Russian-United States cultural exchange game at Moscow in the summer of 1959. They asked me which dome I would recommend, and I said a hard shell dome as I wished to anticipate heavy snow loads in Russia and avoid the requirements of any field skills, such as welding and painting. Therefore, I recommended the Kaiser dome which was used and which evoked the direct statement by Khrushchev that "some American inventions are good," and that he would "like to have 'J. Buckingham Fuller' come to Russia and lecture to my engineers." [34]

I visited the Soviet Union in 1959, during which visit the Russians made it clear that they are going to go into geodesic domes in a big way. They told me they would probably erect an eight-hundred-foot geodesic clearspan dome over their Magneto Stadium in Moscow. They purchased the United States Kaiser dome after the exhibition for $350,000, probably for static-load testing in order to discover its structural theory, which is not in any of the engineering text books, else I could not have patented geodesic domes. This dome is now used for a sports palace in the winter and in the summer for housing international trade fairs. We also have used geodesic domes of aluminum tube, hub, and stretched nylon vinyl skin of ten-thousand-square-foot floor space, identical to the Kabul dome at a number of points in the United States, as for instance at the Golden Jubilee Fair at St. Louis six years ago. (The same dome was later re-erected and stands at present in Detroit's Northland Shopping Center.) In contrast to the forty-eight-hour foreign native installations of this type dome (which included the natives' ready assembly of the two aluminum, rolling-scaffold towers, included in the price of the dome with the tools), the St. Louis dome took a month and

34 Robert W. Marks, "The Breakthrough of Buckminster Fuller," *New York Times*, August 23, 1959.

a half to be erected by the Boilermakers Union at $5.50 an hour.[35] In St. Louis, the contractor had another union elevating the scaffold from time to time and pushing the towers around and handing up the parts while the boilermakers sat in chairs under sun shades atop the scaffolds in conversational pairs putting the nuts on the bolts. This occurred quite naturally, for in the United States we also erroneously assume that the building erector must be a skilled artisan.

I am far from an anti-labor man. I am a card-carrying journeyman-machinist in the International Association of Machinists, but it is clear to me that all the countries on both sides of the Iron Curtain are completely confused by the entirely unprecedented behavior requirements of the industrial equation, which, for instance, will shortly involve comprehensive, world-around automation, and will render man as a "worker" or automaton—a muscle and reflex machine—utterly obsolete. World peoples have confused this problem of disemployment by improving industrialization as one to be solved by the age-long political precedent of a class struggle.

Political class struggles relate to the all-history-long struggle for survival exclusively under the seemingly absolute fact of inherent failure of the majority of the human family, due to the entirely pre-industrial economic accounting of Malthus, which seemingly showed scientifically that world peoples were continually multiplying their numbers more rapidly than did their sustaining metabolic resources increase. It was thought politically that people could carry on either in socialism's austerity, a political scheme by which all peoples would die off slowly in commonly shared inadequacies, or by the mysterious political theory of "survival of the fittest class," which would progressively annihilate by warfaring, or leave to starvation, all the progressively unsupportable increments of self-multiplying peoples.

35 **$5.50 in 1960, adjusted for inflation using the Consumer Price Index (CPI), is $40.08 in 2009 dollars.** http://www.bls.gov/data/inflation_calculator.htm (accessed July 16, 2009).

I pointed out to the Russians, during their fair, in the summer of 1959, that the only difference between Russia in 1917 and 1959 was the same difference as that standing between the United States in 1775 and 1959, to wit, industrialization. If the 1917, preponderantly agricultural and craft Russia had since been modified only by socialism's political reforms, they would now have half as many grains of wheat per capita as they had in 1917 and fifty million instead of sixteen million people would have starved to death in the intervening years. If the agricultural and craft United States of 1775 had tried to solve the needs of an eighteen-fold multiplication of its population exclusively by social reform laws enacted by their democratically representative government, one hundred million people would have starved to death in the interval. Both Russia and the United States, together with the general European economies, have changed, due almost entirely to the twentieth century emergence of the nineteenth century's industrialization baby into a full grown giant—the "continuous man"—the name I have given to industrialization, the latter an awkward word. Continuous man swallowed hammer, sickle and shovel.

I have given the name "continuous man" to the slowly accumulating total world experience and total literate knowledge regarding all the discovered physical resources and generalized patterning principles—in contradistinction to the illiterate, discontinuous man, local in time and geography, whose nonrelayed experience-won knowledge limited his tool capabilities to devices which any one individual might invent entirely on his own initiative, starting nakedly in the wilderness. My definition of industry is a tool-regenerating complex in which none of the tools could be produced, operated, or used by one man—for example, the *Queen Mary,* Grand Coulee dam, the Pennsylvania Turnpike, etc.

All around the world are found unbelievably large heaps of artifacts of discontinuous man, each, in effect, starting all over again learning a little, incorporating the little in hand-crafted tools, dying without comprehension of aught but the local limitations and inadequacies of his infinitely surrounded and apparently exclusive local reality.

Though one third of our time is pre-allotted to the discontinuance of consciousness as sleep, the rotation of night as a shadow around the earth results in a rotating wave of shadow sleepers, while two thirds of all mankind are at all times continuously awake. My continuous man represents a world-around interlinked and continuously intercommunicating continuity of consciousness, which with the spoken word and the invention of mathematics and discovery of generalized principles operative in universe and discovery of the total resources of earth and the character of the total resources of universe, constitute a continuous extra-corporeal memory and a continuously enlightening experience, continuously translated into continuously improving extra-corporeal rearrangements of the total resource of unique pattern behaviors of physical universe within which only individual man is engulfed as an inherent island of physical discontinuity. The individual is linked, however, to continuous man by the extra-corporeal intellections recognized by individual intellect. Continuous extra-corporeal or industrial man is an extra-corporeal tool or pattern inducing continuity which renders industrialization identifiable as an extra-corporeal universal chromosome common to all men's post-natal evolutionary transforming beyond the patterning corporeally induced by the integral genes and chromosomes. The latter have so far failed to disclose any integral memory capable of inhibiting new pattern conceiving potentials; therefore industrialization may well be the second derivative, synergetic-surprise capability to remember and teleologically realize evolutionary pattern controlling.

Continuous man's intellectual capability multiplies geometrically as his experiences accumulate and their observed data are recorded and converted to the extra-corporeal chromosomic function of anticipatory patterning. Industrialization, or our continuous man, knows no national or political favorites. Continuous man's laws are of the universe and are only realizable through its comprehensively integratable and multipliable world and universe resources. The intellectual integrity of the industrial equation utterly reverses the history of inherent inadequacies of local agricultural and craftable resources.

As a result, the enormous energy-relaying patterns of universe are continually shunted by consciously continuous man in greater magnitude into the man-world patterning and applied to the ends of increasing numbers and lengths of levers. This tooling is in itself regenerative as man stands apart from and surveys and critically appraises and improves its working. There tooling rearranges universal energy flow patternings from which physical man can detach himself and enjoy new degrees of *a priori* energy environmental patterns control. In satisfaction of man's consciously apprehended needs and desires, his time is freed by the tooling to be invested in more perspective for realization of more tool invention. Tool capability becomes reinvested in improved tool birth and mass tool reproductability.

So enormous is the energy wealth of universe and so great is the memory and intellectual wisdom of continuous man in respect to his previous experiences, and so fundamentally has he inter-tooled his advantages, that it is completely clear that all men now may be successful in living in a progressively satisfactory enjoyment of total earth. This was unthinkable at the time of the Declaration of Independence. It was still unthinkable at the time of Marx and Lenin, though its pre-dawn and dawning must have bestirred the intuity of support of both the American and Russian revolutions, respectively. Lincoln initiated "right makes might."

Because individual men's concepts of adjustment to change are historically fixed upon earlier categories of social reforms, and because comprehensive economic commonweal seems to refer historically only to the category socialism, America has misinterpreted entirely the new realization potentials and credit-accounting requirements brought about by industrialization. It has interpreted the changing relationships only in the political economy terms of a class battle between worker and employer operating uniquely under obsolete, discontinuous man's either-you-or-me survival rules. World society everywhere has popularly misinterpreted the higher production per hour and its concomitant requirement of lesser production hours per function in the terms of social reform as seemingly won by the only and hard way—by organized labor from disgruntled employers in the U.S.A. and by lethal revolution in the U.S.S.R. Only techno-invention cuts work.

Though there is more than a dawning awareness of the real significance now emergent, the meagerness of that awareness is manifest both in labor's near-sighted drive only for shorter work week; and in management's drive to convert all techno savings to stockholder's dividends or to salary bonuses for management itself as "class war." The new frames of reference for realistic accounting must be (1) the lifetime economic security of all individuals and (2) their actively functioning peak physical coordination years. Instead of a four-day week of work with three days to spend on crowded highways getting to and from resorts, the additional fifty-two days per year could be added to the fifty-two Saturdays and provide fourteen continuous weeks away in battery-recharging sojourn and thirty-eight continuous weeks of forty-four hours each on the job. Further man-time gains of progressive automation would be realized in more continuous weeks away and lesser continuous weeks on the job, plus earlier and earlier full pay retirement.

With imminent completion of world-around industrial automation, man will have lost his significance as a worker altogether. Here we have need to recognize one of industrialization's most important principles—to wit, industrialization becomes increasingly efficient, *ergo* increasingly profitable in direct proportion to the total numbers of well-dollared consumers. (The more consumers the easier the amortization of the mass production setup's progressive stages.) Its corollary is that there are minimum numbers of consumers, without which industrialization cannot exist. For instance, the mortality in the 1920s of one hundred out of one hundred and twenty-five starting automobile producers taught that the mass buyer market could not be found or met in buying capability at yearly productions of less than one hundred thirty-five thousand cars. Mergers of bankrupt corporations' nonvanishing tool inventories and capabilities finally stabilized four residual major automobile producers' capabilities at well over the critical minimum for enjoyment of lowest mass production pricing, while all other makes had to earn premium prices to exist.

Man having lost his significance altogether as an automaton must now discover himself realistically as being essential to the success of industrialization only in the function of regenerative consumer. He must develop a world-around industrial economic accounting system which scientifically and comprehensively implements realization of this principle. Regenerative consumers continually become dissatisfied with each stage of technical improvement as experience teaches them where the inefficiencies lie. Universal evolution is continuous and only our continuous man synchronizes successfully with its patterning.

Even as we find ourselves forced to pay farmers not to use the productivity of their fields in order to avoid world market glutting and waste, in the same way we will soon find ourselves forced to pay people not to work. We may use a positive technique by employing them to go to school, as in the G. I. Bill, or by giving fellowships which employ them to go to graduate schools, or to pre-industrial research schools, or by pre-paying their continuance at school for indefinite periods, to become ever more competent in the general scientific searching for the principles operative in universe.

When we boast that we have sixty-nine million people employed in America as workers,[36] we ignorantly subscribe to the

---

36 One hundred forty million people are employed in the U.S. as of June 2009. "The Employment Situation: June 2009," Economic News Release, Bureau of Labor Statistics http://www.bls.gov/news.release/empsit.nr0.htm (accessed July 16, 2009).

fallacy of "survival of the fittest," seemingly securable only through yesterday's noble ruggedry, which pathetically clings to a hang-over morality economic requiring that people sacrifice themselves blindly in "sweat and tears" not only to justify their industrial consumer credit, but their right to live.

We don't seem to see that industrialization is inexorably displacing all incoherent systems as primary survival-amplifying mechanism. Instead of paying those boilermakers not to work and to go to research school in Florida, for fear that this is socialism, we are giving them $5.50 an hour[37] dole to sit up there and pretend to be capitalistic workers while putting nuts on bolts. Because these men can kid themselves into thinking that this is skilled work, they don't have to think of the $5.50 an hour as dole; therefore, they feel pretty good, and that is good. What is most destructive about it is the fact that the self-kidding also involves a comprehensive labor strategy of decelerated output in squandering its share of techno-industrial gains in battling equally ignorant management. This indirectly murders millions.

Another loss is that of a man's own self confidence and satisfaction in the knowledge that he is giving his best in commonwealth building—in fullest measure even as he enjoys doing so in his athletic battling. Much of the beatnik-into-delinquent stems from contempt of youth for the patent self-kidding of a social "class" struggle, which concept is no longer valid because economic scarcities causing aristocracy are swiftly vanishing. Many a U.S. worker citizen, participating in the installation of the American Exhibit dome in Moscow, looked with envious reminiscence upon the unstinted, unlimited hours of enthusiastic work dedication universally exhibited by the Russian laborers assigned to carry out the U.S.A. Exhibit's installation chores. The more work we gave them the more friendly they became.

37 See note 35, p. 367.

Deep within our subconscious reflexing which we speak of as intuition (which many seemingly fear to heed realistically) I experienced in 1959, in and about both the Russian National Exhibit in New York and the American National Exhibit in Moscow, a vivid awareness of the mutual superficiality of both the *communist* and *capitalist* game-playing by a world democratic man and woman richly alive in both the Americans and Russians which looked unself-consciously with deep, underlying, mutual, yet consciously suppressed, confidence to common emancipation from eco-political restraints soon to be inexorably removed by the inherently comprehensive ramifications of commonly recognized industrializations' accelerating acceleration of its self-reaugmenting capabilities. Each country naïvely thought itself to be the exclusive inventor and proprietor of industrialization—as children look at the outset upon their respective parents as being the only real, loving, living fathers and mothers and upon all other children's parents as formalized, game-playing impostors. But in 1959, in Russia and in America and everywhere else that I traveled around the world, *industrialization* as a generalized, impersonal, non-political realization of pure, mathematical, complex functions was everywhere dominant in emergently looming pure principle. Both Russia and American national expositions commonly celebrated the twentieth century's miraculous expansion of industrialization. Our *continuous man* was astride of all continents. Continuous man was performing so magnificently as the invisible family head and real breadwinner that the world's industrial people of both pseudo-*nations* could play their economically innocuous caps and commies comic games all day and all night without any historically deleterious effects—because poppa—the continuous man was so fabulously and realistically rich that a little overheating of air here and there just didn't matter. "I bet you don't dare—to play class warfare" phooey!

Amusingly, the same self-kidding in respect to work patterns holds true for most of the striped-pants officers in the increasing number of branch bank houses in the United States today. They have no true banker authority whatever in the pre-industrial and pre-1929 sense—that is, that the banker was a man of vast wealth who loaned his personal funds to industry and government. Today's vice-president "bankers" can compete for one another's bank depositors so that they can have more vice-presidents in their respective banks, but in the end they can function as bankers only when they loan not their own monies, but their depositors' monies. And this loaning can be arranged, not at the bankers' discretion in articulation of his economic acumen, but only when Federal regulations are closely observed. So much equity has to be pledged that if the loan is not paid, the bank realizes a profit by government fiat. In the end the government, which is the people, guarantees the whole banking transaction to itself—the people. Every time it shifts the same people's credit integers in and out of Federal and industrial accounts, it charges up enough interest to fund many other categories of seriously invented jobs. All of these services and in-and-out charges require large numbers of government bureaucrats to police them. In a complex game of intricate self-kidding and synthetic bias, which we call "capitalism," we, as our government through government "orders" to industry, as hidden subsidy have, since 1933's total unemployment and bank moratorium, put sixty-nine million people on the consumer rolls by pure but hidden socialist strategy.

We have subsidized our entire economy through bankable initiation of all prime capital undertakings of the accruing new capabilities potential, as exclusively articulated by our military servants under the negative political mandate of future defense which is always politically expedient to all parties. We pour in at the top end of the economic irrigation machine ninety billion dollars for internal and external government expenditures. We allow an average of ten percent subsidized profit on the external industrial corporation prime-contractor expenditures which is distributable in pseudo "earned" dividends to give purchasing power to another large population category called stockholders, a form of aristocratic doleship. Finally we take out our ninety billion in taxes at the bottom of the irrigation system and send it around again.

Each time this initiated credit is circulated, however, it allows industrial metabolics to grow far greater and more precise capabilities out of its intellectually multiplied continuous man comprehension, which objective intellectual capability augmentation is the invisibly and uniquely multiplying synergetic increment exclusively responsible for the swiftly amplifying regeneration of the industrial world's common wealth.

The Russians use the same political expediency to warrant initiation of their evolutionary participation in the comprehensive acceleration of industrial evolution. Russia, too, is going quickly toward automation. The meaning of Marx's workers will soon have to be looked up in the Russian dictionaries, its function will be so obsolete. And Russia, too, goes on with its own self-kidding by pretending that socialism and Marxism are exclusively responsible for its newly won success, whereas their success is the direct result of Stalin's dictatorial contracture with the Western world's industries to provide Russia with the prime components of industrialization's regenerative tooling.

I am not at all a reformer or at all against anything. I am not against either America's or Russia's legendary pretenses. I am all for the human dignity pageants and individual self-satisfaction of participation in the commonwealth building of continuous man.

I am, however, convinced that our world-around problems will become more excruciating until world man and his leaders, both industrial and political, are educated to realize that what we are going to have to do to make the world work is to get all of humanity onto the consumer-implementing payroll in progressively greater magnitude in direct proportion to the swiftly evoluting, increased capability of world-integrated productivity. I hope I have identified the comprehensive rationality by which we may be guided into the comprehensive separating-out of the function of consumer funding from its now lethally parasitic imposition upon and almost invisible insinuations within each and every important technical invention gain and its collateral functions.

The increase of consumer buying capability is historically essential, but it is economic suicide to superimpose costs where they do not belong and thus falsify fundamental economic data.

For instance, my comprehensive anticipatory design science has effectively realized the anticipatory concentration of all design skills into the industrial laboratory, where most favorably controlled field conditions surround the prototyping gestations. From the exquisitely controlled prototyping gestations emerge the scientifically tooled capabilities of automated mass production, which sends products ready-to-operate reliably under generally uncontrolled conditions, whose perversities are rendered innocuous by the anticipatory scientific capabilities fully designed into total industrial undertaking.

Built into the products are the immediately realizable capabilities of men to deal adequately and satisfactorily with the theretofore hostile conditions of Nature. The umbrella must, however, be openable by the user. If we have to have an umbrella opener's labor organization to open our umbrellas for us, just in order to get more consumers on the credit ledgers, we will all soon be wet. If we have to have a shirt button-upper's labor union to button our shirts in order to distribute consumer buying power, we will all soon lose all our shirts. If we have to have boilermakers open up and button up our buildings under noncontrolled rain and sun conditions, we are soon going to have to do without buildings.

Class warfare may force invention of invisible architecture. This would be a way in which men could go anywhere about the Tropics, the Arctic, the sea bottoms, and the air and airless sky without getting too hot, too cold, too wet, too dry, or too uncomfortably or too injuriously anything. Quite a trick but it's in the works. It was suggested almost a half century ago by an as yet little-known, but truly great new-era architect, Knud Lonberg-Holm, a Viking-American who has spent his life searching, researching and teaching industrial research departments how to anticipatorily realize the integratable myriad of evoluting industrially producible building products which have been progressively tooled into production over the last one third of a century. Thereafter, these building products were commercially catalogued, also under his guidance of general architectural and engineering office catalogue files which have become generally available for the last three decades' architects' general design-use which made possible what has become visibly recognizable as modern architecture—no one of whose shiny, nonrusting, neatly fitting and functioning parts were fashioned by craftsmen. Lonberg-Holm is the twentieth-century counterpart of the anonymous architects of the Gothic and Renaissance eras.

Returning from that long overdue digression of recognition—we see ourselves backing further into our future by adopting laws prohibiting any individuals from driving their own automobiles unless the other front seat is occupied by a member of the motorman's, truckdriver's, and conductor's union. This could mean forty million more jobs and enormous buying power. But we would all prefer to pay the professional "drivers" to stay out of our cars, though of course the cost of operation would be prohibitive either way. And that kind of nonsense goes on in the "building" arts, approximately without knowledge of the public and in utter frustration of the peaceful advance of democracy's fundamental wealth while fifty-six percent of humanity is in need.[38]

Why does the public not know of the ineconomy in the building arts? Because the costs are underwritten, deferred and hidden by the government's socialized subsidy of the uneconomic prototypes through mortgaged guaranteeing, and thirty-year amortization of the astronomical costs of homes, whose costs might otherwise be felt personally by the public.

38 See note 11, p. 107.

We are dealing with a comprehensive industrial accounting problem that has been misconceived of as a political class system problem. We are dealing with a mistaken inferiority complex identity. The problem is now for the first time in history subject to complete solution by comprehensive anticipatory design science in a way utterly painless to men and utterly non-reminiscent, *ergo,* nonarticulative of antipathetically conditioned reflexes.

All around there exist important reflex inertias which must be avoided by competent design rather than treated curatively with educational and political reforms. Political reform must be anticipatorily eliminated to die off altogether through the self-atrophy of obsolescence.

It is for all the foregoing reasons of complete detour of geographically concentrated negative inertias, reflexes, codes and mores that I myself started in 1927 to undertake the then seemingly preposterous air-deliverability of entirely tool-skill designed and tool-skill fabricated large buildings to remote parts of earth to be spontaneously installable and openable by entirely unskilled peoples within the extraordinarily critical time limits of predictably favorable conditions in the otherwise hostile frontiers. In 1927 I designed a ten-deck, air-deliverable apartment house for the Arctic. In 1960, my company, Synergetics, Inc., delivered two one-hundred-and-fourteen-foot-in-diameter "quarter-acre" floor-space geodesic domes to the Ford Motor Company, who by one helicopter each fly them to sites fully erected—where they are used as Ford tractor exhibition pavilions. The Ford Company has succeeded in eliminating a myriad of debilitating practices.

Much of the D.E.W. Line radome installation was accomplished by Eskimos. All of the geodesic radomes' installations averaged fourteen hours at their Arctic sites. The predictable limit of favorable hours was twenty. The same domes erected for testing on Long Island and Cambridge took a week each. The same dome in New York's Museum of Modern Art garden took three weeks using "skilled" union labor.

Luckily, in 1927 I had cast my lot with proving the economic feasibility of comprehensive anticipatory design science, as applied to the building arts, by priority of experiment in the Arctic and in remote foreign countries. I detoured so-called civilization.

When Sputnik suddenly displaced the man-flown airplane as the world's number one weapon of furthest, swiftest, greatest hitting power, the total world nations' capital investment in subsidy of the establishment and development of the comprehensive aeronautical realm of industry stood at $2,500,000,000,000,[39] approximately, in contradistinction to the $580,000,000,000 life insurance bet against themselves by America's seven percent of the world population which $580 billion capital bet by its life insurance buyers now constitutes the *only free enterprise venture capital,* unwittingly underwritten by mutual savings investors, and is in ludicrous contrast to the meager $40,000,000,000 worth of the world's total gold employed as prime capital by yesterday's "bankers." Most of the gold is owned by governments, primarily the U.S.A.

The British aircraft industry, in frank realization of their secondary position in any subsidized amelioration of the aeronautical industry's dilemma, has made a critical reconnaissance of their economic plight and states that the all-nations' total forward rocketry undertakings, compounded with all-nations' forward jet transport in accelerating freight and passenger accommodation, can employ but ten percent of the world's present total aeronautical industry's fundamental production and evolutionary support capability. In passing, it is to be noted that three fourths of San Diego, California's, million are engaged in the aeronautical industry. Swift allocations by Western governments of additional rocketry undertakings and collateral studies will have to stem the grave unemployment in San Diego due to this unique preponderance of absolute aeronautical industrialization and its promised letdown. Building unneeded air power is expensive make-do.

---

39 See note 24, p. 325.

Our American legendary success in seeming avoidance of socialism, deceptively occasioned by our extraordinary and complicated ecopolitical game-playing, in the economic roles and costumes of pre-industrial history, plus our powerful government lobbying capability in the sustenance of the legendary ecopolitical theatricals, altogether prevent the clear-cut statement that what hit America at the time of Sputnik was not a mild recession from yesterday's success patterns, controllable by soft and hard credit modulations, but was simply the sudden kicking out of the master's house of his fifty-year subsidized air industry mistress, and consequent lay-off of her vast retinue of first-, second-, and third-hand accomplices.

Every action must have its reaction; every priority must have its counterpart—anti-priority. While the aeronautical industry enjoyed its fifty-year supreme economic priority, as it went from utter scarcity to a surprising state of full-blown abundance of production capability, the uttermost economic anti-priority went to the housing and building arts which have for ages past occupied the cellars of economic advantage. In wartime it has always been considered utterly immoral to invest any of our technical and resource capability in furthering the home nestmaking, while sending our boys to the front. The entire housing arts represent, no matter how superficially glamorous, the all-time make-do with the leftovers of economically desirable resources—dirt and trees.

Obviously, the world aeronautical industry capability has now boiled over at the top, and we are about to witness the application of continuous man and all his wisdom and experienced memory to his historically deferred anti-priority problem for which I have invented the word livingry in contradistinction to weaponry. The prime focus of man's most highly developed capability is being transferred historically from destructive weaponry to constructive livingry.

I think we will see a world trend to establishment of rental service industry of livingry in enormous magnification of the telephone service precedent. Such a livingry service will then transfer the function of design evolution entirely into the laboratory. The design evolution will include all the functions of installation, maintenance, removal and reinstallation. The progressive problems hitherto relegated to social reforms by over-locally preoccupied exploitations will be progressively inhibited by competent anticipatory design science within the service instrumentations.

We will stop having the customers diagnose themselves, telling the professional doctors what it is they need, which is the as-yet-illogically-persistent case in the ignorant craft preoccupations of the building world.

When I compound what I learned reflexively from the Russian engineers' and architects' questioning of me, with my thirty-year study of Russian planning (in the light of my own very different economic strategy), my intuition tells me that the Russians, unembarrassed by lobbies to defend the enormous, relatively ignorant systems of solution of anti-priority building and building material problems, are right now in the process of converting their high aeronautical tool-up's advance industrial capability and large production capacity directly to livingry, to be first installed in remote places such as their vast Arctic frontiers. I think the Russians will be delivering the livingry equipment and environment-controlled structures of a city of ten thousand in a one-day air drop within the next five years.

Because of this historical reorientation of highest priority capability from weaponry to livingry, I am sure that Khrushchev is going to agree to much disarmament. I think you can safely say that this major shift of weaponry to livingry production is at the back of all his present strategy. Its interpretation in the United States and Europe as exclusively for propaganda is erroneous. It has favorable incidental by-products as propaganda favoring Russia's comprehensive attitudes. Khrushchev is glad to have his adversaries think of his desire for disarmament as constituting only propaganda, for this will give him just so much of an advance start in capturing consumers for his conversion of weaponry to livingry.

Khrushchev's present strategy started with his 1958 boast that by 1970 Russians would be enjoying a higher standard of living than that known by any other people at any other time in history. He certainly must have had in mind an entirely different economic strategy than that of just catching up to American standards, tastes and cultural proclivities, which do not always suit Russian and Oriental aspirations in any neat way.

Russian effectiveness in courting the favor of the majority of humanity, which is as yet scratching along unsuccessfully, will be enormously advantaged by Russia's converting its aircraft production capability to production of air-deliverable livingry. President Eisenhower's December 1959 statement on departure for his trip to India was that sixty percent of humanity is lethally ill-housed, ill-fed and ill-clothed. This corroborated my 1952 *New York Times* published figure of forty percent of the world's population having attained industrial have-ness status. My curve of world industrialization passes through the fifty percent point in 1970, which could only be realized by Russia's ten percent of the world's population being shifted over to the industrial have-ness column, which it was not in 1952.[40]

The next decade will see the industrial equation as employed on our side of the Iron Curtain forced to compete in livingry at a more advanced state of scientific capability than has yet been applied even to weaponry or rocketry.

These points are all indispensable and integral factors of the synergetic behavior of total world industry—synergetic because it is utterly unpredicted by behavior of any of its components.

To provide this leadership we will have to include helicopter delivery of whole structures which belong to the service company operating on service industry right-of-way franchises privately

40 In the 1952 article, reference is made to Fuller's assessment that 26% of humanity enjoyed a high standard of living, and his prediction that the number would increase to 50% by the year 1970. By 1960, assuming an exponential trend, the figure would be approaching 40%. See Figure 10, p. 333: Fuller's "Have and Have-Nots chart." See also note 26, p. 334 and note 11, p. 107.

negotiated with various governments of the world. Such service will altogether circumvent local ways and means contractual inertias. In contrast to U.S.A.'s big-industry strategy we will have to avoid the pitfall of exploiting the relatively low foreign wage scales vitiating foreign industrial consumers potential buying capabilities. We will have to act as swiftly as possible to adopt the highest of American wage scales in the relatively few industrial functions of an automated service industry's controlled condition products, thus increasing as swiftly as is permitted by the law of industrialization the establishment of increased numbers of advanced livingry consumers on an around-the-world basis.

We will also have to incorporate the extendably-autonomous, energy-exchanging, metabolical-mechanisms (that is, food conditioning and sanitary facilities) packages within our air-delivered environment-control structures. I am now working with a major industrial corporation on the development of such a package, which will be to the geodesic dome what the electronic relay core is to its environment-controlling tube.

These autonomous packages will be as jet power plants are to jet air frames, and their supply will emanate from the past suppliers of these respective categories in the aeronautical manufacturing industry.

These autonomous facilities and helicopter transport will make possible the initiation of utterly new civil centers requiring neither sewage, water nor power mains. This independence of mains will permit overnight air dropping of complete towns at new sites, together with earth-moving equipment and general employment of the typical logistical technology of advanced U.S. Marine Corps air bases.

We will also have to design our comprehensive economic strategy in the establishment of a world-around service industry of livingry, in view of the fact that a world-around livingry service can and should be organized outside the United States. Because there are no anti-trust laws governing the high seas which surround three fourths of the earth's surface, comprehensive capital facility can be subscribed to by all of major U.S. industry, probably of sufficient magnitude to cope with the safe launching of what will soon be the largest chapter of industrialization of all history.

Though anti-trust laws within the United States would not have permitted in 1917 the comprehensive underwriting of the new upcoming world aeronautical services industry, it is improbable that if the anti-trust laws had not existed, the integrated capital capability of the United States would, at that time, have had the vision to undertake and sustain the evolutionary development of the trillion dollar aeronautical undertaking. Certainly the forty billion dollars worth of gold capital would have been utterly inadequate. The economic strategy thoughts of those days linked wealth exclusively to a gold monetary capital. It also held changes to be abnormal and abhorrent to the enjoyment of already established industrial capabilities.

Science paces technology, technology paces industry, industry paces social economics, social economics paces political expediency and popular educational conceptioning. At the outset of the twentieth century the concept of change as normal to universal evolution displaced Newton's classical concept of the static as normal, quoting from Newton's first law of motion, "A body persists in a state of rest (or in a line of motion) except as affected by other bodies." Einstein saw that all bodies were always being affected by other bodies; *ergo,* motion was normal. Newton's "state of rest" became the special condition of a "chip on the shoulder," where two bodies happened to be in congruent motion.

It took the same half century that developed the aeronautical industry, and that very aeronautical industry itself and its militarily required accelerating evolution of transformation, to bring home Einstein's relativity to social economics.

The German Luftwaffe of World War II taught the Allied air strategists by accelerating design change that change was normal. The American mass production industry of Detroit, to which change orders were anathema, which had tried to freeze up mass production tooling of both bomber and fighter planes and which was relying strictly on mass production to offset any gains by the other fellow of superior design, had not counted on the fact that American democracy's representatives would not tolerate the mass slaughter of their most capable youth in the inadequate frozen mass production Flying Fortresses and Curtiss-Wright fighters.

The initiative in the production of airplanes and their design had to be shifted west of the Mississippi allowing the Detroit metal smashers to continue their contracts. Their obsolete planes were flown from the end of the production line to Kansas fields for graveyard storage.

The aeronautical manufacturing centers of Kansas, Texas and California then took over. Between the first and the hundredth B-29, over one million engineering design change orders in production tooling were written. Detroit would have fired five thousand men if one of those change orders were written. West of the Mississippi the aeronautical phase of world industry for the first time realized Einstein's conceptioning. They did not think of Einstein, but they were proving Einstein right. To the grand strategists of aeronautical production and to the legal fraternity that began to write the new contracts, there dawned the irrevocable awareness that change is normal.

Then the World War II premiership of the aeronautical industry in the comprehensive defense economics imposed change as normal upon the whole frontier of world economics. With this new great lesson learned, it will be essential that our world-around livingry service assumes in its now rejoined integrated capital capability that change is normal.

As the Bell Laboratories find it necessary to inaugurate new instrumentation throughout its network, the changes are scientifically fed into the continually realigning and regeneratively evoluting service. Change is normal to them. They anticipate it scientifically.

It is the factor of change as normal that is going to require that the world-around livingry industry be managed on a rental basis so that the consumers need not find themselves harnessed with progressively obsoleting "owned" equipment. Such a rental service can then improve at an evolutionary rate scientifically synchronized with the comprehensive capability advance. The service return when prior purchase is nonimposed will be so enormous as to represent very high annual profit as ratioed to comprehensive capital underwriting.

You must remember that the comprehensive capital underwriting is today not gold but tooled-up capability—tooled capability capacity over and above that necessary to the maintenance of already established standards. Investible industrial capital is surplus capability capacity, as modified by most recently accreditable scientific laboratory gains in mechanical efficiency potential. During World War II, corporations with large amounts of money frequently found that money was no longer the key to the industrial equation. What was needed over and above money was a U.S. government high priority certificate. Priorities meant access to the industrial capacity capability, and if a company had the right industrial capacity capability, it did not need money. It got the order and that was as financeable as a wild duck is eatable. Anybody will provide the salt and pepper which is the accounting function of money, all done in a big way with entirely abstract "credit of capability." This was the acid test which forever divorced the concept of capital from its historical wedlock with gold or any other metallic or raw realty base.

Our accounting system is based unrealistically on the nonfunctioning metallic, or intrinsic, dollar as the measure of wealth. Realistic accounting would be predicated upon the metals extracted from the ground and processed into tools, and the tools organized in a comprehensive industrial network. And the industrial network of tools is hooked up to the world's energetic metabolic system shunted into valvable articulation of the tooling. This is the real wealth of organized technical advantage capability which was employed by Germany after World War I when all monies were taken away from it. This organized industrial capability wealth was the wealth that was employed by Russia when it had no metallic money. This was the wealth that was employed by fascist Italy in the late 1920s and 1930s. The '30s saw all nations of the world go off the gold standard because of its complete inadequacy to implement the new magnitudes of the wealth transactions generated by the new realistic industrial capability wealth.

Industrialization ran into hundreds of billions of dollars whereas the total gold supply of the world amounted to approximately forty billion. In the late 1920s, when all the world nations were going over to the new industrial capability wealth and America was the creditor nation of the world, all the gold ended up in the United States and was stored in the Kentucky mountains at Fort Knox. World War II products and ignorance of wealth accounting saw the United States insisting on going back into gold payments. World War II industrial capabilities of Europe and the Orient saw the United States balancing its annual trading by shipping gold back into the world accounting system. Now as the foreign nations begin to take the world trading advantage away from the United States through lower wage scales and resulting lower pricing, the short-sighted accounting throwback will see the United States losing its position in world economics at a rapid rate. Major American industry is able to move out of the United States into its many acquired proprietorships of foreign manufacturing establishments, whose automobile production, for instance, has successfully invaded the American manner. This move of American industry out of the United States to enjoy the lower wage scales of the foreign countries and the superior technical and product exploitation is analogous to the wholesale abandonment of New England by the cotton manufacturing industry, when it moved into the South in order to institute its partial automation. Our approach to the new one-town world economic accounting is completely fogged with our mistaken concept that the rest of the world is trying to leech us of our economic advantage, and our ostrich theory that "minding our own business and letting the rest of the world tag along" will make for continuous prosperity is utterly fallacious. Our continuing emphasis on weaponry and de-emphasis of livingry or exploitation of our economic advantage by aping a Tudor, Georgian, or Victorian social mores are manifestations of our need for focusing the best minds of young America on the major patterns now emergent. We must provide the most powerful tools that can be devised for man's planning of his own future, as implemented to the fullest extent permitted by Nature and Nature's second derivative—continuous man's cumulative undertakings accomplished in world industrial network capability. It would be the greatest blunder of all time if at the moment man acquired the tools for his success he underplanned himself into great pain or failure because of myopic and political anarchies.

I have become disciplined through my comprehensive anticipatory design science explorations in the extraction of the minimum-maximum family of factors governing the successful design of comprehensive industrial enterprise initiations. I first generalized the laws governing comprehensive naval and aeronautical logistics and ballistics controls. I have been able to interpolate the mathematical formulations governing the target delivery of the greatest energetic hitting power the greatest distance in the shortest time from this problem of weaponry systems to the problem of livingry systems in such a manner that I am confident that we are now possessed of the scientific capability of delivering the most livingry to the comprehensive consumer target around the world in a satisfactorily operating manner in the shortest possible time.

19 The Designers and the Politicians

There is a new idea aloft in our era, one in which we do not think of our great world dilemmas in terms of politics. For years we have been telling the politicians to solve our problems, and yet the crises continually multiply and accelerate in both magnitude and speed of recurrence.

As automation eliminates physical drudgery, we will spend more time in the future in intellectual activity. The great industry of tomorrow will be the university, and everyone will be going to school. World society is going to concentrate on regenerating its capabilities and its wisdom of their employment.

When we talk about wealth today, we are not talking about money or gold. We went off the gold standard between world wars. There are still some gold exchange laws and international trade in which gold is involved, but they are ways of balancing books and not fundamental. After World War I, Germany discovered it would not, if it paid all its reparations, have the wealth necessary to rise again, so the agreement was simply abrogated by the establishment of a new government. The Germans had the blast furnaces, the iron, the coal and the know-how to make steel, so they began to make steel. They began to demonstrate what we really mean by wealth, which is to organize physical capability and to organize energy. Energy flows around the universe and is then shunted and canalled into valvability upon the ends of the levers

1962. Written specifically for *Ideas and Integrities*.

which we make out of the physical energies interactive in patterns which we call "matter."

Industrial wealth consists of three main constituents: energy, as matter which is energy as gravitation and the radiant energies. The radiant energies are focusable, and therefore canalizable, and we can get them valved out onto the ends of the levers. We then take the radiation energy we call power and apply it to the convergent energy we call matter, organized as machinery.

Physicists like Einstein and Max Planck saw that energy left one's system only by joining another system. They discovered, by experimentation, that no energy could be created and no energy could be lost. The physicists thus developed the concept, called the law of conservation of energy, that energy could neither be created nor lost. That's a finite package of energy, the finite physical universe, which is the Einsteinian world.

If no energy can be created and no energy lost, and we put together energy as matter and energy as radiation to make machinery run by power other than our backs and muscles, then the constituent of what we call wealth is actually indestructible. When I was brought up, we used to have the idea that wealth was something that was continually running downhill and wearing out. But the revival of the German economy without money taught us something new.

There is a third constituent of wealth, which is *intellectual.* Every time I make an experiment, taking some radiant energy and applying it to reforming metals and making a better piece of machinery, I have learned more. This constituent of wealth is therefore inherently and regeneratively self-augmenting. Even if a physical part wears out, the intellectual constituent improves. This concept of wealth is changing our whole system of life.

Conservation will no longer mean withholding from use, but insistence upon widest, practical, active usefulness. The physicist's law of Conservation of Energy means that the physical universe cannot wear out or run down or become exhausted by use.

The law of Conservation of Intellect tells us that human use of intellect always improves human capability. The new scientific era conservative is inherently committed to multiplying reinvestment of capability which is complex and provides the only experimental test of synergy. The conservative realizes that the more that wealth is usefully reemployed, for more people, the more wealth is amplified. Socialism was one of yesterday's ways of dealing with inadequate wealth. Socialism is now as obsolete as the stone hammer. So also is undeveloped static property, or gold capitalism. Gold coins wear out; land erodes. That is why capitalism is obsolete. Industry and biology are metabolic; they grow.

Up to and including World War I, there had been great masters of the earth, masters of commerce (you could call them pirates) who had built powerful ships and gone out and taken the other fellow; and they were running the world. They looked at the world as a great, comprehensive undertaking, where enormous wealth could be earned, and they planned a hundred years ahead.

With World War I the old masters went out of business because they were physically coordinated men who judged things in terms of their own eyes, ears, taste and touch. They didn't trust others. But with the new technology, ninety-nine percent of what was going on was utterly invisible, which is why we have scientists to deal with the invisible world. When the old masters went out, they were not coordinated in the invisible world, but in a sensorial world. Also, their gold was utterly inadequate for the magnitude of the new industrial productivity.

The world did not know of the departure of the old masters until the crash of 1929. The depth of the depression was 1932, when we completed the isolation of the ninety-second chemical element. Chemistry's pantry shelves were now full.

We were ready for a great new venture. If we only had known what we were doing–we were dealing in invisibles–we would have realized that our society was not in a mess at all. The economic disaster was simply a disaster in terms of the economics and accounting of the old masters, who had become obsolete.

When the old masters went, some of the citizens found that their economies were in great trouble. This led to the assumption of power by dictators because people didn't know what to do about their problems. It was the beginning of a society where people thought the politicians could solve the problems of the world, but the politicians have truly no idea of what to do about them.

In the hierarchy of events that reshape the face of the world as far as man's participation goes, man, ecologically, has been sweeping out larger and larger areas. Ecology, as I have explained, is the science of the various patterns of life, the different species of life, the flora and the fauna. There is a unique ecological pattern for each kind of life. Man is the only living species which has altered its ecological patterning in the history of life on earth. He has progressed from a local sweep-out of perhaps a twenty-four-mile radius in the early ages of man, or perhaps a walk to the visible horizon and back to his home.

Until World War I an American man walked an average of thirteen hundred miles per year, and rode three hundred and fifty miles by some other vehicular means. As we came out of World War I, Americans were sweeping out an average of sixteen hundred miles a year by mechanical means and still walking thirteen hundred; but for the first time man had become primarily a riding device instead of a walking device. Instead of sitting in a static chair, he sat in an automobile chair.

In 1941 we were averaging six thousand, five hundred miles a year, despite the fact that the housewife was covering ten thousand miles, the salesman thirty thousand and the airline hostess one hundred thousand (invalids and so forth brought down the average). At the present time our sweep-out averages twelve thousand miles a year.

So man has, from the beginning, been participating in larger and larger patterns on the earth. This is the hierarchy of events.

With the right kind of training the individual thinker as a scientist leads science and gives it new steps forward. Science paces technology, but it is hard for science to convince technology. Technology paces industry, but there is a long lag in the process. Industry paces economics. It changes the tools, a great ecological change. And in that manner we come finally to everyday life.

The politician is someone who deals in man's problems of adjustment. To ask a politician to lead us is to ask the tail of a dog to lead the dog.

While I was speaking at Harvard recently, a number of Harvard students went to Washington in company with students from many other universities. They saw their congressmen and pleaded with them to abandon war and nuclear bombs. They said their congressmen were wonderful and let the students talk a lot. But the representatives said, "Don't make us more miserable, we're already dealing in trouble, and you want us to be a little more negative about trouble."

Just being negative doesn't do any good. I tell students to stop using their feet and start using their heads. Our tails and our feet can't lead us. This realization is beginning to move students, and we will hear a great deal more about it. We will soon have to design the over-all industrial network for making the world work for all humanity.

In 1835 Thomas Malthus, a well-to-do man with some influence and access to government data, was able to see certain figures being collected by English economic representatives all over the world. It was the first time any one man was faced with the facts about population and production. And what Malthus saw was startling. It was apparent that people around the world were multiplying more rapidly than they could produce and support themselves.

A generation later Charles Darwin developed his concept of the interpatterning of all biological species and his theory of the evolution of the species, and its corollary, the survival of the fittest.

Up to this time in history, men had believed that their fate rested on the whim of God or gods. Armed with the information that there would not be enough production to go around, and that mankind was being subjected to a survival of the fittest, certain statesmen conceived the idea of national defense a century ago. When the old masters were gone, the politicians, finding potential in their economies, decided it was their mandate not to let their economies run down. So they tossed the problem to their military colleagues, ordering them to invest total scientific and technical capability in defense. This was the beginning of the great arms race.

It is important to realize that there are people in this world other than politicians trying to do something. I would guess that one hundred years from now, historians will note that in the period of 1927 to 1967, man was so preoccupied and so relatively illiterate that he thought it all right to leave the problems of the world to the politicians. This idea will look preposterous in the perspective of history.

We are shooting to get to the moon. What soldiers want is to get the first commanding platform in space. That's what the militarists are after. To be able to send a man to the moon, you first have to be able to give him his own private little earth, and he's been living on an enormous earth with great energy-exchanging patterns he knows very little about. He knows a little about the air he breathes or the gas plants give off. He doesn't know why men's temperatures are ninety-eight and six tenths degrees Fahrenheit when in good health. He doesn't really know about his extraordinary energy balance.

Our processes are so secret that nobody really knows anything about plumbing. Everything fundamental about our sewage system was invented in India by 2500 B.C. No one has made significant improvements since that time. No architect ever looks back of the purple tiles, no scientist ever studies plumbing. We never hire scientists to look at our homes. Scientists, however, work with weaponry, and its by-products go back into our homes, but it is completely inadvertent. What would happen if the scientists helped us to use everything he and we've learned to make the world a success for man?

This is what is going to happen with our explorations into space, because we can no longer be wasteful. We will have extraordinary energy cycles developed in our behalf by the scientists. We're going to have to give our spaceman enough food—he needs a ton a year, and he'll have to process that. We are going to have to find out how to use that valuable chemistry we have been turning over to Nature's landscape to process for us. While we look the other way the spaceman won't be able to get rid of it. If he spits there is no gravity to take it away. It stays right there in front of him in space. We are not going to send the spaceman out into space to find out what to do with his chemistry to make him survive. If our scientists on earth haven't figured it all out very satisfactorily in every respect, psychologically and aesthetically, as well as chemically, before we send that spaceboy "out," he'll never come back "in" again—alive.

For the first time in history we are employing scientists to work on a little house. It hasn't been thought of, architecturally, as a house, but it's the most important house that's ever been worked on. In America we are spending three billion dollars a year and in Russia they are spending six billion dollars a year on this autonomous dwelling device—for man.

The little black box that will take care of our sanitation will be more effective than anything that's been used before. Men will control their environment and be very healthy. I believe that the telephone company will start expanding those little country telephone booths into replicas of space houses. Out of the prototype for the space age will come the scientific knowledge for the actual production of this autonomous dwelling device.

In a few years you may be able to walk into a telephone company booth one morning and ask them to put up a dwelling device on a certain mountain that afternoon. When you're through with it, you will call the company and ask them to remove it. The company will have your environment control waiting for you wherever you want it at low cost for dream high standards.

There is a new dedication on the part of the young in this world. Students are corresponding with each other all over the globe. This young world is about to take over, to help us design ourselves to make man a success on earth. If this is successfully done, the Malthusian and Darwinian frustrations will be completely irrelevant. There will be enough to go around, and the politicians will have no mandate to build weapons. To get rid of weapons we must design our way to positive effectiveness, and not just be negative about politicians and what they are doing.

Index

Appendix

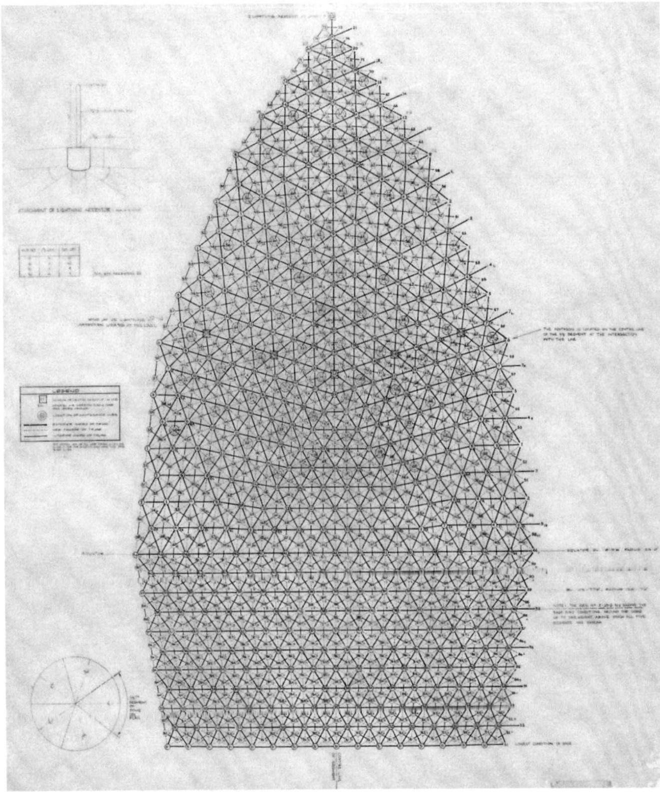

Cover image:
Buckminster Fuller/Fuller and Sadao, Inc./Geometrics, Inc., Associated Architects
Developed Exterior Elevation of One-fifth Segment of Dome for Montreal Expo 67, 1966
Ink on Mylar, 111.8 x 86.4 cm
(Collection of Fuller and Sadao PC)

392.

depositors' "monies". And this loaning can be arranged not at the bankers' discretion in articulation of his economic acumen but only when Federal regulations are closely observed and so much equity has been pledged that if the loan is not paid, the bank realizes a profit by government fiat. In the end the Government, which is the people, guarantees the whole banking transaction to itself--the people. Every time it shifts the same people's credit integers in and out of Federal and industrial accounts it charges up enough interest to fund many other categories of services and their "workers". All of these services and in-and-out charges require large numbers of government bureau "workers" to police them. In a complex game of intricate self-kidding and synthetic bias which we call "capitalistism" we have since 1933's total unemployment and bank moratorium put million people bank on the "consumer rolls".

We have subsidized our entire economy through bankable initiation of all prime capital undertakings of the accruing new capabilities potential as exclusively articulated by our military servants under the negative mandate of future defense which is always politically expedient to all parties. We pour in at the top end of the economic irrigation machine billion dollars for internal and external government expenditures. We allow an average of 10 per cent subsidized profit on the external industrial corporation prime-contractor expenditures which is distributable in psuedo "earned" dividends to give purchasing power to another large population category called "stockholders", a form of aristocratic doleship and finally we take our billion in taxes at the bottom of the irrigation system and send it around again.

Each time this initiated credit is circulated however it allows industrial metabolics to grow far greater and more precise capabilities out of its intellectually multiplied continuous man comprehension which objective intellectual capability augmentation is the invisibly and uniquely multiplying synergetic increment exclusively

In a complex and synthetic we, as our gov "orders" to in since 1933's moratorium, pu the consumer r strategy.

Bucky's and Robert Marks' notations on page 392 of the final manuscript of *Ideas and Integrities*—this for chapter 18, "Continuous Man," p. 375. Bucky's notation is clearly the crossed-out box with the text editing inside in his own hand; and as he would often do, he tapes on a new, retyped piece of text to the side margin of the page.
(R. Buckminster Fuller Archive, Special Collections, Stanford University)

ricate self-kidding
we call "capitalism,"
rough government
hidden subsidy have,
loyment and bank
ne million people on
re but hidden socialist

I FIGURE

FORE WORD

It is only fair to this soliloquy that those who read it in the inevitably changed mood of the world months hence from here, - Sunday afternoon November 7th, 1942, - take note that as I now sit down to my typewriter the radio program has just been interrupted with the announcement that "strong and modernly equipped American forces have landed on the Atlantic and Mediterranean coasts of North Africa."

Someday, probably not remote, we may have scientific measurement of the power regenerated in the individual by the telepathetic stream of emotions popularly propagated by such announcement as this. But certainly it is with a sense of unwilling personal remoteness from the excitement of the swiftly unfolding events that cerebral "I" withdraws to concentrate upon answering the earnest question put to me by a trade magazine publisher, - half in apprehension, half in business necessity, - "What do you figure to be the characteristics of postwar housing, speaking both generally and specifically?"

The suppositional setting of this day-after-sometime activity was not furnished. Many months, many years hence, - never? Housing, - that is an entirely irrelevant subject anyway; - or is it?

Could housing, for instance, have anything to do with whether it will be months or years to war's end? What nonsense - haven't they shut down on priorities for that housing stuff until the show is over? Has housing in fact anything whatever to do with war?

Within the Fuller Archive manuscript file for Bucky's essay "I Figure," which later became chapter 5 of *Ideas and Integrities*, there is a typed copy, bound with card stock and nylon cord, of the manuscript sent to the prospective 1942 publishers—ostensibly *Pencil Points* magazine (see his background notes on the chapter, p. 111). Following a page with Bucky's carefully inked signature is this first page of the manuscript.
(R. Buckminster Fuller Archive, Special Collections, Stanford University)

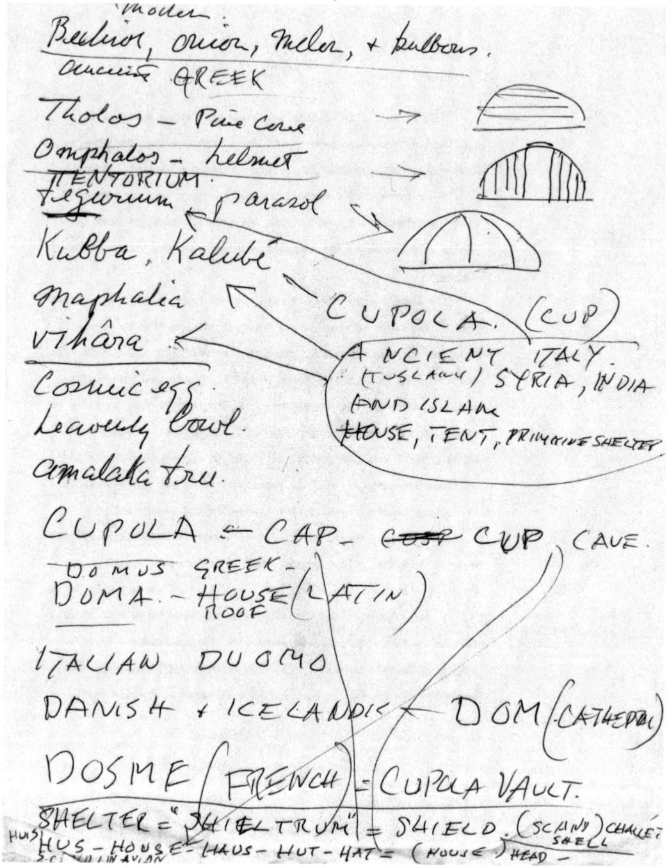

Bucky's notes on the historical and linguistic roots of "domes" in cultures around the world for chapter 8, "Domes—Their Long History and Recent Developments." See, for example, p. 209. (R. Buckminster Fuller Archive, Special Collections, Stanford University)

Resources

The Buckminster Fuller Institute
www.bfi.org
Founded in 1983, The Buckminster Fuller Institute serves a global network of design science innovators working at the leading edge of the design revolution Fuller inspired—including the Buckminster Fuller Challenge, an annual $ 100,000 prize to support the development and implementation of solutions to humanity's most pressing problems.
181 N. 11th St., Suite 402/Brooklyn, NY 11211/718 290-9280

The R. Buckminster Fuller Archive
www-sul.stanford.edu/depts/spc/fuller/index.html
Called in 1976 by archivists from the Smithsonian Institute, "the most extensive personal archive in existence," the collection contains over 1,300 linear feet of papers and manuscripts, 2,000 hours of video and audio recordings, and thousands of models and other artifacts.
Dept. of Special Collections/The Stanford University Libraries/Stanford, CA 94305

The Estate of R. Buckminster Fuller
www.buckminsterfuller.net
Fostering the preservation, publication, and dissemination of Buckminster Fuller's legacy.
P.O. Box 3248/Santa Barbara, CA 93130/Fax: 805 456-2912

The Earth Policy Institute
www.earthpolicy.org
The Earth Policy Institute, dedicated to building a sustainable future as well as providing a plan of how to get from here to there, publishes the remarkable book *Plan B 3.0: Mobilizing to Save Civilization* by founder and President Lester R. Brown (free online access).
1350 Connecticut Ave. NW, Suite 403/Washington, DC 20036/Fax: 202 496-9325

The ONE Campaign
www.one.org
The *campaign to make poverty history* is over 2.4 million people committed to raising public awareness about the issues of global poverty, hunger, disease, and efforts to fight such problems in the world's poorest countries.

Rocky Mountain Institute
www.rmi.org
An independent, entrepreneurial, nonprofit organization fostering the efficient and restorative use of resources to make the world secure, just, prosperous, and life-sustaining, co-founded by scientist Amory Lovins, and featuring publications such as their groundbreaking *Winning the Oil Endgame: Innovation for Profits, Jobs, and Security* (free online access).
2317 Snowmass Creek Road/Snowmass, CO 81654/970 927-3851

The We Campaign
www.wecansolveit.org
A project of The Alliance for Climate Protection—a nonprofit, nonpartisan effort founded by Nobel laureate and former Vice President Al Gore that aims to halt global warming through educating people in the U.S. and around the world that the climate crisis is both urgent and solvable.

Bibliography

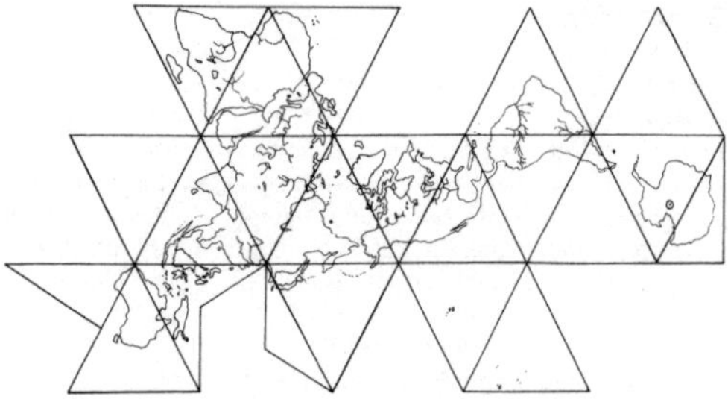

Fuller Projection World Map, 1938, 1954

Books by R. Buckminster Fuller
4-D Timelock, 1928
Nine Chains to the Moon, 1938
Education Automation, 1962
Untitled Epic Poem on the History of Industrialization, 1962
Ideas and Integrities, 1963
No More Secondhand God, 1963
World Design Science Decade,[1] 1963–1967
Operating Manual for Spaceship Earth, 1969
Utopia or Oblivion: The Prospects for Humanity, 1969
Buckminster Fuller to the Children of the Earth, 1972
Intuition, 1972
Earth, Inc., 1973
Synergetics: Explorations in the Geometry of Thinking,[2] 1975
Tetrascroll, 1975
And It Came to Pass—Not to Stay, 1976
On Education,[3] 1979
Synergetics 2: Further Explorations in the Geometry of Thinking,[2] 1979
Critical Path,[4] 1981
Grunch of Giants, 1983
Inventions: The Patented Works of R. Buckminster Fuller, 1983
Cosmography: A Posthumous Scenario for the Future of Humanity,[4] 1992

Published by Lars Müller Publishers
Ideas and Integrities: A Spontaneous Autobiographical Disclosure, new edition 2010
Education Automation: Comprehensive Learning for Emergent Humanity, new edition 2010
And It Came to Pass—Not to Stay, new edition 2008
Operating Manual for Spaceship Earth, new edition 2008
Utopia or Oblivion: The Prospects for Humanity, new edition 2008
Fuller Houses: R. Buckminster Fuller's Dymaxion Dwellings and other Domestic Adventures, Federico Neder, 2008
Your Private Sky: The Art of Design Science, Volume 1, 1999, edited by Joachim Krause and Claude Lichtenstein
Your Private Sky: Discourse; The Art of Design Science, Volume 2, 2000, edited by Joachim Krause and Claude Lichtenstein

1 With John McHale
2 In Collaboration with E. J. Applewhite
3 Robert D. Kahn and Peter H. Wagschal, editors
4 Kiyoshi Kuromiya, Adjuvant

Acknowledgments

From the bottom of my heart, I wish to thank all the devoted and inspired individuals who assisted me in preparing these new editions of Buckminster Fuller's books:

I could not have undertaken this project without the unswerving support of my beloved wife, Cheryl. She was my partner, primary advisor, and tireless editor in reviewing the new materials I wrote. She always encouraged me to seize this moment to bring focus to the grave challenges—and opportunities—facing our planet.

And as in any project I undertake at this point in my life, John Ferry is at my side—as he has been for over 25 years. He backed me up with finding photos, selecting images, assembling materials, researching background facts, and resolving any other loose ends, not to mention the management of our numerous other projects. This year, I deeply missed the direct assistance of Dr. Janet Brown, who passed on in April. After many years, we were able to work together again last year, when she joined me in the multi-month process of re-reading the books, updating facts and figures, and finally in being an expert editor, as we launched this series with Lars Müller Publishers.

I want to also thank Roberto Trujillo, Head of Stanford University's Department of Special Collections, and Mattie Taormina, Head of Public Services and Manuscripts Processing Librarian, for their support of my research at the R. Buckminster Fuller Archive. And I wish to thank Polly Armstrong, Public Services Manager, who facilitated my research and expedited my needs for scans of images from the Archive. Living nearby, it is always an unexpected treat to be able to spend some days in their beautiful reading room to joyfully connect with Bucky through his own working papers.

I particularly would like to express my appreciation for Lars Müller. Lars and I have been enjoying talking about this project for almost ten years, ever since he designed the two beautiful volumes of *Your Private Sky: The Art of Design Science*. Lars is a great artist of book design, and his encouragement all along the way inspired me to pursue the vision of presenting these books to a new generation in a fashion fitting their remarkable prescience. I want to also acknowledge his fine design and production team at Lars Müller Publishers in Switzerland: Ellen Mey and Martina Mullis; supplemented by the proofreading and editorial work of Jonathan Fox in Spain. I cannot imagine a more competent team to undertake such a task—not to mention their patience. It was a great honor and pleasure to work with each of them.

And finally I want to express my gratitude to my dear "Fuller" family. My sister, Alexandra May, a passionate champion of design revolution, who urged us to go for a design that would reach a vital new audience. My mother, Allegra Fuller Snyder, who cheered me on in this project, and gave of her aesthetic wisdom and deep sensitivity for Bucky's way of being. My father, the late Robert Snyder, who joined the fold and gave so much to this work as a pioneering documentarian of Bucky. My aunt Alexandra Fuller, who died five years before Allegra was born. And dear dear Bucky and Anne, who gave so much for us.

J. S.

R. Buckminster Fuller
Ideas and Integrities: A Spontaneous Autobiographical Disclosure

First edition 1963, edited by Robert W. Marks

New edition 2010, edited by Jaime Snyder

Except for very rare typographical or grammatical
corrections, Buckminster Fuller's words
have not been changed from the first edition.

Design: Integral Lars Müller
Copyediting and proofreading: Jonathan Fox
Printing: Beltz Grafische Betriebe, Germany
Printed on Munken Print White, 80 gm^2

Printed in Germany

Lars Müller Publishers
Zurich/Switzerland
www.lars-mueller-publishers.com

ISBN: 978-3-03778-198-2

Distributed in North America by ARTBOOK | D.A.P.
www.artbook.com

Printed in Germany